Briefcase on Contract Law

Third Edition

Simon Salzedo, BA (Oxon), ACA, DipLaw

Peter Brunner, BA, LLB (Cantab)

Third edition first published in Great Britain 1999 by Cavendish Publishing Limited, The Glass House, Wharton Street, London WC1X 9PX, United Kingdom

Telephone: +44 (0) 20 7278 8000   Facsimile: +44 (0) 20 7278 8080

E-mail: info@cavendishpublishing.com

Visit our Home Page on http://www.cavendishpublishing.com

British Library Cataloguing in Publication Data

Salzedo, Simon
Contract Law – 3rd edition (Cavendish Briefcase series)
1 Contracts – England   2 Contracts – Wales
I Title   II Brunner, Peter
346.4'2'02

ISBN 1 85941 541 5

Printed and bound in Great Britain

Preface

The principles of English contract law are mainly to be found in the reported decisions of the courts. Students on most contract law courses are required to know the details of several hundreds of those decisions. This book summarises those cases which most students need to know. The facts and decisions are presented concisely but with all the vital details needed for a full understanding. Extensive use is made of quotations to give a real flavour of the judgments themselves.

We hope that the arrangement of cases by the principles they illustrate will make this book as close as possible to the notes of cases which the student actually needs. We believe that this makes the book a great deal more user friendly than, for example, an alphabetical presentation.

Where a case is relevant to more than one heading in the book, it is only summarised in one place, but a reference is made to the section to which a particular argument in the judgment is relevant. The case is then cross-referred to that section. The questions given at the end of some cases do not usually have quick answers. Their purpose is to point out issues which are not decided by the cases as well as those which are. They are intended to suggest some avenues for further thought and reading, not to test understanding of this book.

Of course, no summary can give the same depth of understanding of contract law as a full reading of all the cases. But this book should provide a note of the cases which the student has personally digested as well as a way of filling gaps in reading which are often inevitable in a busy student's life.

This book is intended to be especially helpful to students when they come to revise for examinations or for lectures or tutorials on particular topics.

The two year period between the second and third edition of *Briefcase on Contract Law* has been a relatively quiet one for judgments of fundamental importance to contract law. However, five new cases have been added. The judgment of the Court of Appeal in *Attorney General v Blake* perhaps stands out as a decision (strictly, *obiter dicta*) which may prove to be of lasting importance because, for the first time, an English court has suggested general criteria by which restitutionary, as opposed to compensatory, damages may be awarded for breach of contract.

We have attempted to take into account decisions reported up to 1 October 1999.

Peter Brunner
Simon Salzedo
October 1999

Contents

Abbreviations

Ass	Assizes
CA	Court of Appeal
CCh	Court of Chancery
CCP	Court of Common Pleas
CE	Court of Exchequer
Ch	Chancery Division of the High Court
CKB	Court of the King's Bench
CLJ	Court of the Lords Justices
CP	Common Pleas Division of the High Court
CQB	Court of the Queen's Bench
EC	Court of Exchequer Chamber
FD	Family Division of the High Court
HCA	High Court of Australia
HL	House of Lords
KB	King's Bench Division of the High Court
KBDC	King's Bench Divisional Court
P	Probate Division of the High Court
PC	Privy Council
QB	Queen's Bench Division of the High Court
QBDC	Queen's Bench Divisional Court
RC	Rolls Court

Table of Cases

Table of Statutes

Table of Statutory Instruments

1   Offer and Acceptance

1.1   Offer

1.1.1   An invitation to treat is not a contractual offer

Spencer v Harding (1870) CCP

The defendant's circular advertised that 'we are instructed to offer to the wholesale trade for sale by tender the stock in trade of Messrs G Eilbeck & Co ... which will be sold at a discount in one lot'. The plaintiff made the highest bid, but the defendant did not accept it.

Held the circular was (*per* Willes J) 'a mere attempt to ascertain whether an offer can be obtained within such a margin as the sellers are willing to adopt'. It did not amount to a contractual offer to accept the highest bid. Therefore, the defendant had no obligation to accept the plaintiff's bid.

Harris v Nickerson (1873) CQB

The defendant advertised *bona fide* that an auction of brewing materials, plant and office furniture was to take place on 12, 13 and 14 August 1872 at Bury St Edmunds. The plaintiff came from London on 12 August with a commission to purchase the office furniture. On 14 August, the defendant gave notice that the office furniture would not be put up for sale. The plaintiff claimed two days loss of time, the third class railway fare and two days board and lodging.

Held the advertisement was not a contractual offer, but (*per* Archibald J) 'a mere declaration of intention', so the plaintiff had no claim against the defendant.

Rooke v Dawson (1895) Ch

The defendants were trustees of a scholarship fund. The trust deed provided for an award to a student from Mill Hill School who had gone to study at either University College London or New College London and who had done best in an examination set by the trustees. The defendants advertised and held the examination, which was entered by the plaintiff and one other candidate. The plaintiff obtained the highest marks, but the defendants declined to award the scholarship to either candidate.

Held the advertisement was (*per* Chitty J) 'nothing more than a proclamation that an examination for a scholarship will be held, and there is no announcement that the scholarship will be awarded to the scholar who obtains the highest number of marks'. The court refused to import the terms of the trust deed into the advertisement and so, following *Spencer v Harding* (above), there was no contract between the parties to this case.

Grainger & Son v Gough (1896) HL

The appellants were wine merchants and agents for Louis Roederer, the French wine and Champagne merchant. The appellants circulated a price list for Roederer's wine, took orders and passed them on to Roederer who sent the wine from France. The appellants received a commission from Roederer on all wine sold in this way. The respondent tax inspector sought to tax the appellants as if they were carrying on a trade in Roederer's wine in the UK.

Held there was no trade in the UK because the customers' contracts were made with Roederer in France and not with the appellants in England. *Per* Lord Herschell LC, the 'price list does not amount to an offer to supply an unlimited quantity of the wine described at the price named'. Offers were made by customers placing orders and they were accepted by Roederer who retained a right to refuse any order.

Pharmaceutical Society of Great Britain v Boots Cash Chemists (Southern) Ltd (1953) CA

The defendants owned a self-service shop where customers took goods from the shelves and presented them at a cash desk before leaving. Among the goods were certain drugs that were required by the Pharmacy and Poisons Act 1933 to be sold only by or under the supervision of a pharmacist. The defendants' pharmacist remained in view of the cash desk and he supervised transactions involving the relevant drugs in so far as they took place at the cash desk. The plaintiffs asked whether the sale was supervised as required by the Act, the question being whether the contract of sale was concluded at the cash desk or at an earlier stage.

Held the sale did take place at the cash desk so it was supervised as required. In a supermarket the customer makes an offer by indicating the goods he requires and the shopkeeper or cashier accepts.

Note

Other analyses of offer and acceptance could give the same result in this case, so the Court of Appeal's detailed analysis may be *obiter dicta*.

Q   How would you analyse offer and acceptance in a self-service shop like the one in this case?

Fisher v Bell (1961) QBDC

The defendant's shop window display included a flick knife with the label 'Ejector knife 4s'. Under the Restriction of Offensive Weapons Act 1959, it was an offence to 'offer for sale' such a knife.

Held the phrase 'offer for sale' in this statute must be given its meaning in general contract law. In contract law, to display goods in shop window is not to make an offer for sale. A window display is merely an invitation to treat.

Partridge v Crittenden (1968) QBDC

The defendant, Mr Partridge, placed a classified advertisement in the periodical, 'Cage and Aviary Birds', advertising bramblefinches at 25 shillings each. Under the Protection of Birds Act 1954, it was an offence to 'offer for sale' live birds of various species including bramblefinches. The defendant appealed against his conviction by Chester magistrates for that offence.

Held the advertisement was not an offer for sale for the following reasons. (I) *Per* Ashworth and Blain JJ, *Fisher v Bell* (1.1.1) must be followed. (II) *Per* Lord Parker CJ an advertisement or circular could not be supposed to be intended to bind its author to sell an unlimited number of some product to anyone answering the advertisement.

Q What is the difference between an advertisement which is a binding offer to all the world as in *Carlill v Carbolic Smoke Ball Co* (see 1.4.1) and one which is a non-binding invitation to treat as in this case?

Gibson v Manchester City Council (1979) HL

The defendant sent the plaintiff a letter including the words:

> The corporation may be prepared to sell the house to you at the purchase price of ... £2,180 ... If you would like to make a formal application to buy your council house, please complete the enclosed application form and return it to me as soon as possible.

The plaintiff returned the form with a letter seeking a lower price, which the defendant refused to grant. Then, the plaintiff asked the defendant to 'carry on with the purchase as per my application'. In the meantime, control of the defendant council had passed from the Conservatives to the Labour Party and the defendant now refused to sell the house to the plaintiff.

Held the defendant had not made an offer and so was not bound to sell to the plaintiff. In the Court of Appeal, Lord Denning MR had found, by looking at the 'correspondence as a whole', that there was an agreement for the sale of the house between the parties. However, in the House of Lords, Lord Diplock said:

I can see no reason in the instant case for departing from the conventional approach of looking at the ... documents ... and seeing whether on their true construction there is to be found in them a contractual offer by the council to sell the house to Mr Gibson and an acceptance of that offer by Mr Gibson.

Using the 'conventional approach', the House of Lords found that the defendant council had not made a contractual offer to the plaintiff, so there could not be a contract.

Note

For Lord Denning MR's 'whole correspondence' approach, which Lord Diplock appears to criticise in this case, see, also, *Butler Machine Tool Co v Ex-Cell-O Corporation* (1.2.1) and *Trentham Ltd v Archital Luxfer* (1.2.3).

1.1.2 Tenders

Spencer v Harding (1870) CCP

See 1.1.1.

Harvela Investments v Royal Trust Co of Canada (1985) HL

The first defendant, R, invited the plaintiff, H, and the second defendant, O, to submit sealed bids for certain shares and promised to accept the highest bid. H bid C$2,175,000 while O bid the higher of C$2,100,000 and 'C$101,000 in excess of any other offer ... expressed as a fixed monetary amount'. R believed itself bound to sell the shares to O for $2,276,000 and R's solicitors sent a telex to O and H saying 'In the circumstances, our clients are bound to accept and do hereby accept the offer received from [O] ...'. H sought a declaration that R was bound to transfer the shares to it and an order for specific performance.

Held (I) On its true construction, R's invitation to bid created a fixed bidding sale and it was not consistent with an intention to accept referential bids (those calculated by reference to other bids). Therefore, R was obliged to accept H's bid as the highest valid bid submitted. (II) The telex accepting O's bid was an attempt to fulfil existing obligations between R and O and so it was not an offer or acceptance of any new contract. It therefore did not give rise to any obligation to sell the shares to O.

Blackpool and Fylde Aero Club v Blackpool Borough Council (1990) CA

The defendant Council invited tenders for operating pleasure flights from the defendant's airport, which were to be submitted by 12 noon on 17 March. The plaintiff delivered a tender into the Town Hall letter box at 11.00 am on 17 March, but the defendant's staff only emptied the box on the next morning when the plaintiff's tender was date stamped with '18

March'. The defendant, believing that the plaintiff's tender had been submitted late, did not consider it and awarded the concession to another company.

Held for the plaintiff, there was an implied offer in the invitation to tender that timely tenders would be considered. The plaintiff had accepted the offer by submitting a timely tender.

Q   Since there is no obligation to accept any tender (see *Spencer v Harding*, 1.1.1), how can the plaintiff's loss be measured?

1.1.3   Auctions

Payne v Cave (1789) CKB

The defendant bid at an auction for the plaintiff's goods but withdrew his bid before the hammer fell.

Held each bid is an offer, so a bid can be withdrawn before it is accepted 'by knocking down the hammer'. Therefore, the defendant was not bound to buy the lot in this case.

Note ———

This rule is now codified in s 57(2) of the Sale of Goods Act 1979 (below).

Warlow v Harrison (1859) EC

The defendant, an auctioneer, advertised an auction of three horses 'without reserve'. The plaintiff bid for one of the horses but there was a higher bid from the vendor of that horse. The plaintiff therefore bid no further but claimed the horse from the vendor, offering him the amount of the plaintiff's last bid, which the vendor refused.

Held the plaintiff was entitled to damages on the basis of a breach of his contractual right to buy the horse at the amount of his last bid because (*per* Martin B) 'the auctioneer who puts the property up for sale upon such a condition pledges himself that the sale shall be without reserve; or, in other words, contracts that it shall be so; and ... this contract is made with the *bona fide* bidder'. If the vendor's bid was accepted, this would amount to a reserve price.

Note ———

This rule is now codified and expanded in s 57(4) of the Sale of Goods Act 1979 (below).

Q   How did the auctioneer's statement that the sale would be without reserve become a contract? Can you identify offer and acceptance in this case?

Harris v Nickerson (1873) CQB

See 1.1.1.

Sale of Goods Act 1979

Section 57   Auction sales

(1)   Where goods are put up for sale by auction in lots, each lot is *prima facie* deemed to be the subject of a separate contract of sale.

(2)   A sale by auction is complete when the auctioneer announces its completion by the fall of the hammer, or in other customary manner; and until the announcement is made any bidder may retract his bid.

(3)   A sale by auction may be notified to be subject to a reserve or upset price, and a right to bid may also be reserved expressly by or on behalf of the seller.

(4)   Where a sale by auction is not notified to be subject to a right to bid by or on behalf of the seller, it is not lawful for the seller to bid himself or to employ any person to bid at the sale, or for the auctioneer knowingly to take any bid from the seller or any such person.

(5)   A sale contravening sub-s (4) above may be treated as fraudulent by the buyer.

(6)   Where, in respect of a sale by auction, a right to bid is expressly reserved (but not otherwise), the seller or any one person on his behalf may bid at an auction.

1.1.4   Answering a question is not an offer

Harvey and Another v Facey and Others (1893) PC

Three telegrams passed between the parties all on the same day. First the appellants telegraphed to the respondents 'Will you sell us Bumper Hall Pen? Telegraph lowest cash price'. The respondents replied 'Lowest price for Bumper Hall Pen £900'. The appellants then telegraphed 'We agree to buy Bumper Hall Pen for the sum of £900 asked by you. Please send us your title deed in order that we may get early possession'. The respondents did not complete the sale and the appellants sought an order for specific performance.

Held there was no contract. *Per* Lord Morris:

The first telegram asks two questions ... [the respondents] replied to the second question only and gives his lowest price ... The reply telegram from the appellants cannot be treated as an acceptance of an offer to sell to them; it is an offer that required to be accepted by [the respondents].

The telegrams did not satisfy the formalities for a sale of land which would now be required by statute.

Q Might this decision have been different if the subject matter of the telegrams had been a commodity other than land?

1.2 Acceptance

1.2.1 A counter offer is a rejection

Hyde v Wrench (1840) RC

The defendant offered to sell a farm to the plaintiff for £1,000. The plaintiff offered to pay £950 which the defendant rejected. The plaintiff then purported to accept the original offer to sell for £1,000. The defendant refused and the plaintiff sought specific performance of the sale at £1,000.

Held by making a counter offer, the plaintiff had rejected the original offer and the rejection of an offer cancels its binding effect. Therefore, there was no contract between the parties.

Tinn v Hoffman & Co (1873)

The defendant wrote to the plaintiff on 24 November 1871: 'We ... offer you 800 tons [of] ... pig iron ... at 69s per ton ... delivery 200 tons per month, March, April, May and June 1872 ... Waiting your reply by return.' The plaintiff failed to reply by return but replied on 27 November: 'The price you ask is high. If I made the quantity 1,200 tons delivery 200 tons per month for the first six months of next year, I suppose you would make the price lower? Your reply by return will oblige.' The defendant wrote on 28 November: 'We are willing to make you an offer of further 400 tons ... pig iron, 200 tons in January, 200 tons in February, at the same price we quoted you by ours of the 24th inst ... Kindly let us have your reply by return of post as to whether you accept our offers of together 1,200 tons.' On the same day, when he had not received this last letter, the plaintiff wrote: 'You can enter me 800 tons on the terms and conditions named in your favour of the 24th inst, but I trust you will enter the other 400, making in all 1,200 tons, referred to in my last, at 68s per ton.' The defendant gave the plaintiff one more chance to buy at 69s per ton but the plaintiff replied later than was required and the defendant then refused to sell him any iron since the market price for iron had risen in the meantime.

Held (I) there was no binding contract. (i) The offer of 24 November was rejected, either because the plaintiff's letter of 27 November was a rejection, or because the plaintiff failed to reply by return. (ii) The defendant's letter of 28 November made a new offer of 1,200 tons and did not revive the old offer of 800 tons. Therefore, it was not open to the plaintiff to accept only 800 tons. (II) (*Obiter*) Brett, Keating and Blackburn JJ commented that, even if the plaintiff's letter of 28 November had been in the same terms as the defendant's letter of the same day, there would still be no contract because, *per* Blackburn J, 'The promise or offer being made on each side in ignorance of the offer on the other side neither of them can be construed as an acceptance of the other'.

Q Would the 'whole correspondence' approach (see *Butler Machine Tool Co Ltd v Ex-Cell-O Corporation (England) Ltd*, below) give a different answer (a) to this case, or (b) to the hypothetical case of cross-offers?

Butler Machine Tool Co Ltd v Ex-Cell-O Corporation (England) Ltd (1977) CA

On 23 May 1969, the plaintiff seller made an offer to sell a Butler Double Column Plane-Miller machine to the defendant buyer. The offer incorporated the seller's standard terms which were printed on its reverse side. One of these read: 'All orders are accepted only upon and subject to the terms set out in our quotation and the following conditions. These terms and conditions shall prevail over any terms and conditions in the buyer's order.'

The buyer then placed an order that included the buyer's own standard terms and a slip that said: 'Please sign and return to Ex-Cell-O. We accept your order on the terms and conditions stated thereon.' The seller signed and returned the slip on 5 June with a covering letter saying: 'We have pleasure in acknowledging receipt of your official order ... This being delivered in accordance with our revised quotation of 23 May ... We return herewith duly completed your acknowledgement of order form.' As Lord Denning MR asked: 'No doubt a contract was then concluded. But on what terms?'.

Later, the machine was made by the seller and delivered to the buyer. The seller's terms included a clause allowing a price increase. The buyer's terms did not allow a change in price, so the buyer refused to pay the higher price demanded by the seller.

Held the buyer's terms prevailed so the lower price was paid. The following reasons were given. (I) Lord Denning MR said:

> ... in many of these cases, our traditional analysis of offer, counter offer, rejection, acceptance and so forth is out of date ... The better way is to look at all the documents passing between the parties and glean from them, or from the conduct of the parties, whether they have reached agreement on all material points.

He held that 'as a matter of construction ... the acknowledgment of 5 June 1969 is the decisive document'. (II) Lawton and Bridge LJJ found that the buyer's order was a counter offer and so, following *Hyde v Wrench* (1.2.1), it cancelled the seller's earlier offer. (III) All three of their Lordships agreed that the reference in the seller's letter of 5 June to the seller's quotation of 23 May should be construed as referring to the price and identity of the machine, but not to the terms and conditions attached to the quotation of 23 May.

Note ───

For criticism of Lord Denning MR's 'whole correspondence' approach, see *Gibson v Manchester City Council* (1.1.1).

Q   (a) Had the parties 'reached agreement on all material points'?
(b) How important is it to the result that the parties had already acted upon the contract when the dispute arose (see, also, *Trentham Ltd v Archital Luxfer*, 1.2.3)?

Norfolk County Council v Dencora Properties (1995) CA

The plaintiff council leased some offices from the defendant company. Under the 20 year lease, the tenant had a right to determine the lease after 10 years but only by giving two years' notice to the landlord. The first 10 years would end on 25 March 1995; therefore, the council was required to give notice by 25 March 1993 if it wished to break the lease after 10 years rather than 20. In late 1992, the council asked the landlord to vary the terms of the lease so as to give the council a more flexible option to determine it. The landlord responded thus:

In order to assist, we are prepared to postpone the notice period to break the lease to 1995 or 1996, but not both. The two year notice must remain.

The council then wrote to the landlord:

It is difficult therefore to forecast with any precision, but doing the best I can, it would seem that to be required to vacate in March 1997 cuts it too fine, and to vacate in March 1998 may be too long.

I appreciate your assistance to date and agree to the two year notice, but ask if this could be given at any time but not earlier than March 1995. We could then gauge with some accuracy when the police should vacate Dencora House ...

The council's suggestion was rejected by the landlord and the council then tried to accept the landlord's offer for a break in the lease in 1998 by serving notice in 1996. However, the landlord said that its earlier offer was no longer open.

Held the council's letter quoted above was a rejection of the landlord's offer accompanied by a counter offer, as in *Hyde v Wrench* (1.2.1). The interrogatory form used by the council ('but ask if this could be given ...') did not bring the council's letter into the category of a mere query like that in *Stevenson, Jacques & Co v McLean* (1.2.2). Accordingly, there had been no agreement to vary the terms of the lease.

1.2.2   A query is not a counter offer

Stevenson, Jaques & Co v McLean (1880)

The following events happened in this order. (1) The defendant seller offered to sell to the plaintiff buyer a quantity of iron for '40s, nett cash, open till Monday'. (2) At 9.42 on Monday morning, the buyer telegraphed to the seller 'please wire whether you would accept forty for delivery over two months, or if not, the longest limit you would give'. (3) The seller received the buyer's telegram, but did not reply. (4) The seller sold the iron to a third party. (5) At 1.25 pm, the seller dispatched a telegram to the buyer saying that he had sold the iron. (6) At 1.34 pm, the buyer dispatched a telegram to the seller saying 'have secured your price for payment next Monday – write you fully by post'. (Payment on the following Monday was the accepted practice in that market.) (7) The seller's telegram in (5) arrived at 1.46 pm.

Held the buyer's telegram in (2) was a mere query and not a counter offer, distinguishing *Hyde v Wrench* (1.2.1). Therefore, the original offer remained open to acceptance by the buyer until the seller's revocation was communicated which only happened at (7). Thus, the buyer's acceptance at (6) was effective and the seller was bound to sell to him.

Q   How clear is the distinction between a query and a counter offer?

1.2.3   Acceptance may be by conduct

Brogden and Others v Metropolitan Railway Company (1877) HL

B, the defendants, had been supplying coal to the plaintiffs, M, since the beginning of 1870. On 18 November 1871, B suggested a price increase and a new contract. At a meeting on 19 December 1871, M handed to B a draft contract with blank spaces for details like the date and the name of the arbitrator. B filled in the gaps, made some other small changes and signed the draft contract. On 21 December, B's agent returned the contract to M with a letter that concluded 'If you have anything further to communicate letters addressed to "Tondu" will find me'. This reached M at whose office it was placed in a drawer, used for storing contracts, where it remained until a dispute arose on 7 November 1872. During 1872, B supplied coal to

M from the date of commencement of the draft contract, 1 January 1872, at the new price as specified in the draft contract, often up to but never exceeding 350 tons per week, which was the maximum authorised by the draft contract.

Of the various letters which passed between B and M during the year, Lord Cairns LC commented:

> ... having read with great care the whole of this correspondence, there appears to me clearly to be pervading the whole of it the expression of a feeling on one side and on the other that those who were ordering the coals were ordering them, and those who were supplying the coals were supplying them, under some course of dealing which created on the one side a right to give the order, and on the other side an obligation to comply with the order.

However, M argued that, in the absence of acceptance by M of B's offer, there was no contract.

Held (I) There was a binding contract upon the terms of the uncompleted draft held in M's drawer. *Per* Lord Cairns LC:

> ... there having been clearly a consensus between these parties, arrived at and expressed by the document signed by [B], subject only to approbation, on the part of the company, of the additional term ... with regard to an arbitrator, that approbation was clearly given when the company commenced a course of dealing which is referable in my mind only to the contract, and when that course of dealing was accepted and acted upon by [B] in the supply of coals.

Per Lord Hatherley, 'the agreement was complete when the first coals ... were invoiced at the differing price, and when that differing price was accepted and paid'. (II) Neither M's silence in response to B's agent's letter of 21 December 1871 nor any merely mental or private acceptance by M would have completed the contract. *Per* Lord Blackburn, 'when you come to the general proposition ... that a simple acceptance in your own mind, without any intimation to the other party, and expressed by a mere private act, such as putting a letter into a drawer, completes a contract, I must say I differ from that'.

Q (a) When exactly was the contract completed? (b) Does this case give any support to the view that a contract does not always require offer and acceptance as expressed by Lord Denning MR in *Butler Machine Tool Co Ltd v Ex-Cell-O Corporation (England) Ltd* (1.2.1) and by Steyn LJ in *Trentham Ltd v Archital Luxfer* (below)?

Carlill v Carbolic Smoke Ball Co (1893) CA

See 1.4.1.

Trentham Ltd v Archital Luxfer Ltd (1992) CA

The plaintiffs, T, were the main contractors in the building of some industrial units. The defendants, A, carried out some of the work on windows etc for T as sub-contractors. The terms of the agreement between A and T were negotiated in a complex process starting on 12 January 1984. Although a contract was concluded on 2 February 1984, negotiations about certain terms (including whether the contract incorporated T's standard terms or A's) continued into April 1984. The negotiations concerned several separate points and no finally agreed document was ever even drafted. Work by A had started in February and payments from T began in early March. When a dispute arose, A argued that there was no contract.

Held (by Steyn LJ with whom Ralph Gibson and Neill LJJ agreed) there was a contract. His Lordship's reasoning included the following: (I) Following *Brogden v Metropolitan Railway* (1.2.3) 'a contract can be concluded by conduct'. (II) 'The contemporary exchanges and the carrying out of what was agreed in those exchanges support the view that there was a course of dealing which on [T]'s side created a right to performance of the work by [A], and on [A]'s side it created a right to be paid on an agreed basis'.

[III] The coincidence of offer and acceptance will in the vast majority of cases represent the mechanism of contract formation. It is so in the case of a contract alleged to have been made by an exchange of correspondence. But, it is not necessarily so in the case of a contract alleged to have come into existence during and as a result of performance ... The judge analysed the matter in terms of offer and acceptance. I agree with his conclusion. But I am, in any event, satisfied that in this fully executed transaction a contract came into existence during performance even if it cannot be precisely analysed in terms of offer and acceptance.

[IV] It does not matter that a contract came into existence after part of the work had been carried out and paid for. The conclusion must be that when the contract came into existence it impliedly governed pre-contractual performance.

Q (a) See argument (III) above. Note that Steyn LJ did not express a firm view as to whether this contract could be analysed into offer and acceptance. Has this case revivified the 'whole correspondence' approach to contract formation (see *Butler Machine Tool Co Ltd v Ex-Cell-O Corporation (England) Ltd* at 1.2.1 and *Gibson v Manchester City Council Ltd* at 1.1.1)? (b) See argument (IV) above. Does the idea that earlier acts can be governed by a later contract create as many problems as it solves?

1.2.4 Acceptance must be communicated to the offeror

Felthouse v Bindley (1862) CCP

The plaintiff's nephew planned to dispose of his farming stock, including a certain horse, by an auction to be held at Tamworth and conducted by the defendant, an auctioneer. The plaintiff wanted to buy the horse and negotiated orally with his nephew. Following a misunderstanding about the price for the horse, the plaintiff uncle wrote to his nephew on 2 January 1862: 'As there may be a mistake about him, I will split the difference – £30 15s – I paying all the expenses from Tamworth. You can send him at your convenience, between now and the 25 of March. If I hear no more about him, I consider the horse mine at £30 15s.' The nephew did not reply and on 25 February the defendant sold the horse at auction for £33. On 26 February, the defendant wrote to the plaintiff apologising for his mistake and, on 27 February, the nephew wrote referring to the mistake over the horse 'I sold to you'. The plaintiff brought an action for conversion claiming that the horse was his when the defendant sold it on 25 February.

Held the plaintiff did not own the horse and had no valid claim. *Per* Willes J:

> ... it is ... clear that the uncle had no right to impose upon the nephew a sale of his horse for £30 15s unless he chose to comply with the condition of writing to repudiate the offer ... The horse in question being catalogued with the rest of the stock, the auctioneer (the defendant) was told that it was already sold. It is clear therefore that the nephew in his own mind intended his uncle to have the horse at the price which he (the uncle) had named – £30 15s: but he had not communicated such an intention to his uncle, or done anything to bind himself.

Q Can silence never amount to acceptance, or does this case merely show that an offeror cannot force an offeree to be bound by his own silence? In other words, would the uncle have been bound by a contract if the nephew had tried to enforce it?

Allied Marine Transport Ltd v Vale do Rio Doce Navegacao SA: *The Leonidas D* (1985) CA

The plaintiff owners chartered *The Leonidas D* to the defendant charterers in April 1975. In December 1975 and March 1976, disputes arose which led the charterers to claim some $110,000 from the owners. The dispute would be settled under the time charter (the contract between the parties) by arbitrators. The parties each appointed an arbitrator in April 1976, but the arbitrators failed to appoint a third arbitrator. The time charter was extended and operated until May 1977 without any further complaints or any mention of the original dispute on the part of the charterers. Indeed, the charterers did nothing more to pursue their claim until August 1981 when they gave notice of their intention to proceed with the arbitration. The owners now sought an injunction to prevent the charterers pursuing the arbitration, raising arguments based on the long delay.

Held the charterers could not be prevented from pursuing their claim. (I) There was no agreement to abandon the arbitration in the absence of any offer and acceptance. *Per* Robert Goff LJ, giving the judgment of the court:

> We have all been brought up to believe it axiomatic that acceptance of an offer cannot be inferred from silence, save in the most exceptional circumstances.

In the absence of such circumstances, there were too many possible explanations of the silence of both parties to allow the court, adopting an objective test of their behaviour, to infer either an offer or an acceptance of an agreement to abandon the arbitration. (II) (3.7.2) Similarly, the owners could not rely on promissory estoppel:

> It is well settled that that principle requires that one party should have made an unequivocal representation that he does not intend to enforce his strict legal rights against another; yet it is difficult to imagine how silence and inaction can be anything but equivocal.

In Re Selectmove Ltd (1993) CA

The company owed to the Inland Revenue over £20,000 of taxes under Pay As You Earn. At a meeting, the company offered to pay the arrears by monthly instalments of £1,000 each starting on 1 February 1992. The Collector of Taxes said that he would have to obtain approval from his superiors but that he would he would come back to the company if the offer was not acceptable. He did not do so and the company paid the first and second instalments on 3 March 1992. The company had made seven such payments when, in September 1992, the Revenue brought winding up proceedings based on the remaining arrears. The company sought to oppose winding up on the basis of its scheme of payment by instalments.

Held there were no substantial grounds upon which the company could oppose the winding up. (I) There was no acceptance of the offer to pay by instalments. (i) The silence of the Revenue did not preclude the possibility of acceptance. After referring to the *dicta* of Robert Goff LJ in *Allied Marine Transport Ltd v Vale do Rio Doce Navegacao SA* (1.2.4), Peter Gibson LJ, with whom Stuart-Smith and Balcombe LJJ agreed, said:

> When the offeree himself indicates that an offer is to be taken as accepted if he does not indicate to the contrary by an ascertainable time, he is undertaking to speak if he does not want an agreement to be concluded. I see no reason in principle why that should not be an exceptional circumstance such that the offer can be accepted by silence. But, it is unnecessary to express a concluded view on this point.

(ii) However, the Collector did not have authority to bind his superiors to accept the offer, so they were not bound until they accepted it themselves, which they never did. (II) (3.7.5) If there had been acceptance of the offer, there would not have been sufficient consideration for the Revenue's acceptance of instalments. The company argued that the decision in *Williams v Roffey Bros and Nicholls (Contractors) Ltd* (see 3.7.4) should apply to this case. *Per* Peter Gibson LJ:

> I see the force of the argument, but the difficulty that I feel with it is that if the principle of the *Williams* case is to be extended to an obligation to make payment, it would in effect leave the principle in *Foakes v Beer* [see 3.7.5] without any application. When a creditor and a debtor who are at arm's length reach agreement on the payment of the debt by instalments to accommodate the debtor, the creditor will no doubt always see a practical benefit to himself in so doing. In the absence of authority, there would be much to be said for the enforceability of such a contract. But, that was a matter expressly considered in *Foakes v Beer* yet held not to constitute good consideration in law. *Foakes v Beer* was not even referred to in the *Williams* case, and it is in my judgment impossible, consistently with the doctrine of precedent, for this court to extend the principle of the *Williams* case to any circumstances governed by the principle of *Foakes v Beer*.

(III) (3.8.2) The doctrine of promissory estoppel could not apply here because: (i) the promise to accept instalments was not made by the Revenue since the Collector of Taxes did not have or claim the authority to do so; and (ii) since the company made some of the payments late, it was not unfair or inequitable for the Revenue to enforce the debt.

Note ———

In contrast to these cases, see the *dicta* of Lord Steyn in *Vitol v Norelf* (13.2.2).

1.2.5 Acceptance may be communicated by posting

Adams v Lindsell (1818) CKB

On 2 September 1817, the defendants wrote to the plaintiffs with an offer to sell them '800 tons of wether fleeces' asking for an 'answer in course of post'. However, the defendants' letter was misdirected so that the plaintiffs only received it on 5 September. The plaintiffs replied that evening and the reply reached the defendants on 9 September. Assuming no misdirection, the defendants knew they would have received a reply on 7 September, so on 8 September they had sold the wool to someone else.

Held contracts by post would be impossible if acceptance became binding only on receipt by the offeror. Since the delay was the defendants' fault, 'it therefore must be taken as against them, that the plaintiffs' answer was received in course of post'.

> Note
>
> This case is the source of the 'postal rule', that where post is a reasonable way to accept an offer, the acceptance is effective on posting. Many commercial contracts expressly exclude the postal rule.

Q (a) Does the rule apply if the acceptance is misaddressed? (b) What if the delay in reaching the offeree had been very long? (c) If an offeree accepts by post, can he telephone and withdraw acceptance before his acceptance reaches the offeror?

The Household Fire and Carriage Accident Insurance Company Ltd v Grant (1879) CA

The defendant offered to buy some shares in the plaintiff company. The offer was accepted by an allotment letter which was posted to the defendant, but which never arrived. Some three years later, the company was liquidated and the liquidator sought the amounts not yet paid on the defendant's shares.

Held the defendant was a shareholder and was therefore liable to pay the sum claimed. The post was a reasonable mode of acceptance in this case so, applying the postal rule, there was a contract on the posting of the allotment letter. Bramwell LJ dissented, arguing that acceptance should only take effect on being communicated to the offeror.

Byrne & Co v Leon Van Tienhoven & Co (1880) CP

On 1 October 1879, the defendants (in Cardiff) wrote to the plaintiffs (in New York) offering to sell them 1,000 boxes of tin plates on certain terms. On 8 October, the defendants wrote again cancelling their offer. On 11 October, the plaintiffs received the offer and they accepted it by telegram on the same day, confirming by letter on 15 October. On 20 October, the defendants' withdrawal of the offer reached the plaintiffs.

Held there was a valid contract because a withdrawal of an offer must be communicated to the offeree to be effective. The postal rule does not apply to a withdrawal which is only communicated when the offeree receives it. This is because the postal rule is (*per* Lindley J):

> ... based upon the principle that the writer of the offer has expressly or impliedly assented to treat an answer to him by letter duly posted as a sufficient acceptance and notification to himself, or, in other words, he has made the post office his agent to receive the acceptance and notification of it.

Henthorn v Fraser (1892) CA

The plaintiff (who could not write) was at the defendants' office in Liverpool on 7 July 1891 when they handed him an offer to sell him certain houses. The plaintiff took the letter home to Birkenhead. On 8 July, between 12.00 and 1.00 pm the defendants posted to the plaintiff a withdrawal of their offer. At 3.50 pm, the plaintiff's solicitor posted the plaintiff's acceptance of the offer. The defendants' withdrawal arrived at 5.30 pm and the plaintiff's acceptance arrived at 8.30 pm.

Held there was a contract because acceptance was complete at the moment of its posting, even though the offer was not made by post. Lord Herschell and Kay LJ both rejected the idea that the postal rule was based on implied authority from the offeror to the offeree to treat the post office as the offeror's agent. *Per* Lord Herschell:

> I should prefer to state the rule thus: where the circumstances are such that it must have been within the contemplation of the parties that, according to the ordinary usages of mankind, the post might be used as a means of communicating the acceptance of an offer, the acceptance is complete as soon as it is posted.

Lindley LJ did not comment on this aspect, but concurred with the judgment of Lord Herschell.

Q   Is there any possible case where Lord Herschell's formulation of the basis of the postal rule would give a different result from Lindley J's formulation in *Byrne & Co v Leon Van Tienhoven & Co* (above)?

In Re London and Northern Bank ex p Jones (1899)

On 15 October 1898, the applicant applied for 1,000 shares in the company. On 26 October, he sent a registered letter withdrawing his application. The withdrawal arrived at 8.30 am on 27 October and was opened by the company secretary at 9.30 am. In the meantime, on 26 October, the board of the company had resolved to allot the shares to the applicant and had written accepting his offer. The allotment letters were collated during the night and were taken out to be posted at about 7.00 am on 27 October. At about 7.30 am, the letter was handed to a postman in a London street. The post mark showed that the letter left the post office at 11.00 am.

Held the company had failed to show that the acceptance of the applicant's offer was posted before it received his withdrawal at 8.30 or 9.30 am. *Per* Cozens-Hardy J:

> The *Postal Guide* ... expressly states that town postmen are not allowed to take charge of letters for the post ... I cannot, therefore, regard the postman as anything better than a boy messenger employed by [the company] to post the

letters and the mere fact of handing the letter to the postman ... was not a posting of the letter.

Manchester Diocesan Council for Education v Commercial and General Investments Ltd (1969) Ch

The plaintiff wished to sell the building of a school which was to close in August 1967. In 1964, the plaintiff asked for tenders, to be received by 27 August 1964. Condition 4 of the sale by tender was:

> The person whose tender is accepted shall be the purchaser and shall be informed of the acceptance of his tender by letter sent to him by post addressed to the address given in his tender.

The defendant made a tender in a letter that included the words:

> ... we agree that in the event of this offer being accepted in accordance with the above conditions ... we will ... complete the purchase in accordance with the said conditions.

The defendant made the highest tender and, during September 1964, there was some correspondence between the plaintiff's surveyor and the defendant's surveyor. On 15 September, the plaintiff's surveyor wrote to the defendant's surveyor:

> The sale has now been approved by the Manchester Diocesan Council for Education ... [The] diocesan registrar ... has been instructed to obtain the approval of the Secretary of State for Education. As soon as this is given he will be getting in touch with ... your client's solicitors.

The approval of the Secretary of State was obtained on 18 November. On 23 December, the plaintiff's solicitors wrote to the defendant's solicitors to confirm the contract. On 5 January, the defendant's solicitors replied that they could 'not confirm that there is a binding contract in this matter'. On 7 January 1965, the plaintiff's solicitors wrote to the defendant at the address given in the tender form and accepted the offer.

Held there was a contract. (I) The letter of 15 September 1964 was an acceptance even though it appeared not to comply with condition 4. Buckley J had two reasons for this decision. (i) A request by the defendant offeror for a certain method of acceptance would normally be construed as a request for that method or another which was as good. *Per* Buckley J: 'If an offeror intends that he shall be bound only if his offer is accepted in some particular manner, it must be for him to make this clear.' (ii) Condition 4 was introduced into the bargain by the plaintiff: 'It would consequently be a term strict compliance with which the plaintiff could waive, provided the defendant was not adversely affected.' (II) (1.3.2) In any case, the letter of 7 January 1965 was a valid acceptance in accordance with condition 4. The rule that an offer lapses if not accepted within a reasonable time is based on 'the question ... whether the offeree should be held to have refused the offer by his conduct'. Following the letter of 15 September 1964, it was clear that plaintiff had not refused the offer, so acceptance was still possible on 7 January.

Q Do you agree that the letter of 15 September was a valid acceptance in these circumstances?

1.2.6 Acceptance may be communicated by telex

Entores Limited v Miles Far East Corporation (1955) CA

A contract for the sale of 100 tons of copper cathodes was made by telex between the plaintiff in England and the defendants in Holland. The defendants appealed against the granting of leave to serve a writ out of the jurisdiction. *Per* Denning LJ:

> The offer was sent by telex from England ... and accepted by telex from Holland. The question for our determination is where was the contract made?

Held a telex contract is made where acceptance is received, in this case in England. There is a general rule that acceptance should be communicated to the offeror and the postal rule is an exception to this. It is the general rule that applies to instantaneous communications including face to face speech, the telephone and telex. This is because the sender of an acceptance in such circumstances generally knows whether or not the acceptance has been received by the offeror. *Per* Denning LJ (*obiter*): if a case arose where an acceptance was not received and the offeror was at fault in not informing the offeree of the problem, the offeror would be estopped from denying receipt and would be bound by the contract.

Brinkibon Limited v Stahag Stahl GmbH (1982) HL

A contract for the sale of steel bars was made by telex between the appellants in London and the respondents in Vienna. The appellants sought leave to serve a writ out of the jurisdiction. The question was (*per* Lord Wilberforce) 'whether an acceptance by telex sent from London but received in Vienna causes a contract to be made in London, or in Vienna'.

Held Entores Limited v Miles Far East Corporation (above) was correctly decided. This was (*per* Lord Wilberforce):

> ... the simple case of instantaneous communication between principals [so that] the contract (if any) was made when and where the acceptance was received. This was ... in Vienna.

However, their Lordships left open the possibility that the rule might not apply to a less straightforward telex case. *Per* Lord Wilberforce:

No universal rule can cover all such cases: they must be resolved by reference to the intentions of the parties, by sound business practice and in some cases by a judgment where the risks should lie.

1.3   Termination of offer

1.3.1   An offer may be withdrawn until it has been accepted

Payne v Cave (1789) CKB

See 1.1.3.

Routledge v Grant (1828) CCP

On 18 March 1825, the defendant offered in writing to buy a lease from the plaintiff on certain terms concluding 'a definitive answer to be given within six weeks from the 18 March 1825'. (The six weeks were up on 1 May.) The defendant withdrew his offer on 9 April and the plaintiff sought to accept it on 29 April.

Held there was no binding contract. *Per* Best CJ:

... if six weeks are given on one side to accept the offer, the other has six weeks to put an end to it ... Till both parties are agreed, either has a right to be off ... As the defendant repudiated the contract on the 9 of April, before the expiration of the six weeks, he had a right to say that the plaintiff should not enforce it afterwards.

Dickinson v Dodds (1876) CA

The defendant offered in writing to sell to the plaintiff certain land for £800 adding the post script 'this offer to be left over until Friday 9.00 am, 12 June 1874'. Both parties believed that the post script was binding on the defendant. On the morning of 11 June, the plaintiff decided to accept the offer. That afternoon the plaintiff heard from a third party that the defendant had been 'offering or agreeing' to sell the property to one Thomas Allan. In fact, the defendant had concluded a contract of sale with Allan on 11 June. That evening the plaintiff tried to contact the defendant and succeeded in informing the defendant of his acceptance of the offer at 7.00 am on 12 June.

Held there was no contract between the plaintiff and the defendant. (I) The defendant's promise to keep the offer open until 12 June was given for no consideration and so it was not binding. (II) Once an offeree knows that an offer has been withdrawn (*per* James LJ) or that the property has been sold (*per* Mellish LJ), it is too late for him to accept the offer.

Q (a) Is there a withdrawal when the offeror is intending to sell to another, or when he negotiates with another or only when there is an actual sale? (b) Would it make a difference if the offeree only suspects but does not know of the offeror's withdrawal?

Byrne & Co v Leon Van Tienhoven & Co (1880) CP

See 1.2.5.

1.3.2 An offer lapses after a reasonable time

Ramsgate Victoria Hotel v Montefiore (1866) CE

The plaintiff company was registered on 6 June 1864. On 8 June, the defendant offered to buy 50 shares. On 23 November, the directors allotted the shares and wrote to the defendant accepting his offer.

Held the defendant was not bound to buy the shares. 'The allotment must be made within a reasonable time, and ... the interval from June to November was not reasonable.'

Manchester Diocesan Council for Education v Commercial and General Investments Ltd (1969) Ch

See 1.2.5.

1.4 Offer and acceptance of unilateral contracts

1.4.1 An advertisement can be a contractual offer to all the world

Carlill v Carbolic Smoke Ball Co (1893) CA

The defendants advertised that they would pay £100 to anyone who contracted influenza having used their smokeball three times a day for two weeks and they declared that £1,000 was on deposit with the Alliance Bank 'showing our sincerity in the matter'. The plaintiff used the smokeball as directed and caught influenza, whereupon the defendants declined to pay the £100.

Held the plaintiff had a good claim to £100 from the defendants for the following reasons. (I) The advertisement was not a 'mere puff', or an invitation to treat, and it could be an offer to all the world. *Per* Bowen LJ: 'why should not an offer be made to all the world which is to ripen into a contract with anybody who comes forward and performs the condition?' (II) (1.2.3) An offeror may dispense with notice of acceptance or specify its mode. *Per* Lindley LJ:

... in a case of this kind ... the person who makes the offer shews by his language and from the nature of the transaction that he does not expect and does not require notice of the acceptance apart from notice of the performance.

(III) (3.2) The defendants requested that the plaintiff should use the ball and the plaintiff's using it was therefore sufficient as consideration for the defendants' promise. In general, the inconvenience of one party at the other's request is sufficient consideration.

Note ————————————————————————————————

Catching influenza was not requested by the defendants so it was a condition not consideration.

Q (a) When exactly did the plaintiff accept the offer? (b) How and up until when could the defendants have withdrawn their offer? (c) Did the plaintiff ever become bound by the contract (see *Errington v Errington and Woods*, 1.4.3)?

Bowerman v The Association of British Travel Agents Ltd (1995) CA

The plaintiffs booked a school skiing holiday with a travel agent who was a member of the defendant Association, ABTA. The travel company became insolvent and an alternative holiday was provided, funded by ABTA. However, ABTA refused to reimburse the travel insurance premium of £10 per person. This was the plaintiffs' claim for that sum of £10 each. The plaintiffs relied upon the notice which they had seen in the travel agent's office, headed 'Notice describing ABTA's scheme of protection against the financial failure of ABTA members'. Paragraph 5 of the notice provided as follows:

Where holidays or other travel arrangements have not yet commenced at the time of failure, ABTA arranges for you to be reimbursed the money you have paid in respect of your holiday arrangements. In some instances, ABTA may, however, be able to arrange for the existing arrangements to proceed as planned or offer similar or alternative arrangements.

Held the plaintiffs' claim succeeded. (I) Paragraph 5 of the notice was wide enough to cover the insurance payments. (II) The ABTA notice as a whole contained (*per* Waite LJ) a 'bewildering miscellany ... of information, promise, disclaimer and reassurance ...'. However, it 'would be understood by the ordinary member of the public as importing an intention to create legal relations with customers of ABTA members'. *Per* Hobhouse LJ, the notice was not 'simply telling the public about the scheme which ABTA has for its own members' but 'goes further than this and contains an offer which a member of the public can take up and hold ABTA to should the ABTA member with whom the member of the public is dealing fail financially'. *Per* Hobhouse LJ, the arguments of ABTA echoed those of the defendant in *Carlill v Carbolic Smoke Ball Co* (1.4.1) and failed for similar reasons. The consideration given by the customer to ABTA is entering into a contract with the ABTA member, which is a collateral contract analogous to the contract in *Shanklin Pier Ltd v Detel Products Ltd* (4.2.4).

1.4.2 Acceptance of offers to all the world

Williams v Carwardine (1833) CKB

The defendant put up posters offering £20 reward for information leading to the discovery of the murderer of William Carwardine. The plaintiff gave the information 'in consequence of her miserable and unhappy situation, and believing that she has not long to live ... to ease her conscience, and in the hopes of forgiveness hereafter'.

Held the plaintiff was entitled to the reward despite having given the information for other reasons than to be able to claim the reward. Her motives in claiming the reward were irrelevant to her right to do so. At least two of their Lordships (Denman CJ and Littledale J) gave significance to the fact that the plaintiff knew of the reward when she gave the information.

R v Clarke (1927) HCA

The government of Western Australia advertised a reward of £1,000 for information leading to the conviction of the murderer of two policemen. The petitioner saw the reward notices. Later, he was arrested for the murders. In order to clear himself, and without giving any thought to the reward, he gave the vital information which led to the convictions of two others for the murders.

Held because the petitioner did not give any thought to the reward until after he had given the information, he never accepted the government's offer so there was no contract. *Per* Higgins J:

> He did not mentally assent to the Crown's offer; there was no moment of time at which there was, till after the information was given, as between Clarke and the Crown, a consensus of mind.

The court considered *Williams v Carwardine* (above) and concluded that the plaintiff in that case must have had the reward before her mind when she gave the information even though the reward was not her primary motivation.

1.4.3 Withdrawal of offer of unilateral contract

Errington v Errington and Woods (1951) CA

In 1936, E bought a house in Newcastle for £750, paying £250 himself and taking out a mortgage for the remaining £500. The house was for E's son and daughter-in-law to live in, but E owned the house and E was the borrower on the mortgage. E handed the building society book to his daughter-in-law and told her not to part with the book and that the house would belong to the son and daughter-in-law when the mortgage was paid. The couple stayed in the house and paid the mortgage of 15s a week, though E paid the rates of 10s per week for them. In 1945, E died leaving all his property to his wife. Then, the son left the daughter-in-law and went to live with his mother, E's wife. E's wife, the plaintiff in this case, then sought possession of the house against the daughter-in-law who continued to live there with her sister, W.

Held the daughter-in-law was entitled to remain in the house. E's promise to transfer the house to the couple if they paid the mortgage amounted to a unilateral contract which continued to bind his successor, the plaintiff, after his death. *Per* Denning LJ:

> ... the father [E] expressly promised the couple that the property should belong to them as soon as the mortgage was paid, and impliedly promised that so long as they paid the instalments to the building society they should be allowed to remain in possession.

The father's promise:

> ... could not be revoked by him once the couple had entered on performance of the act, but it would cease to bind him if they left it incomplete and unperformed.

On the other hand, the couple were not bound to pay the mortgage instalments, even after they had started to do so. (The payments of rates by E were simply gifts, not made under a contract.)

Q (a) Was there a collateral contract that E would not prevent the couple from paying the mortgage? (b) How could it be determined whether the couple had left 'the act ... incomplete and unperformed'? (c) Is the idea of a contract which binds one party but not the other satisfactory?

Daulia Limited v Four Millbank Nominees Limited (1977) CA

The plaintiffs and the defendants agreed the terms upon which the plaintiffs were to buy certain properties in London from the defendants. The defendants orally promised that they would enter into a contract for the sale if the plaintiffs attended the defendants' offices before 10.00 am on 22 December 1976 and tendered to the defendants the plaintiffs' part of the contract for the sale and a banker's draft for the deposit. The plaintiffs duly attended with the contract and banker's draft, but the defendants refused to exchange contracts.

Held the defendants' promise to exchange contracts was an offer of a unilateral contract. The plaintiffs had fully performed the acts necessary for acceptance. *Obiter, per* Goff LJ:

... there must be an implied obligation on the part of the offeror not to prevent the condition becoming satisfied, which obligation it seems to me must arise as soon as the offeree starts to perform. Until then, the offeror can revoke the whole thing, but once the offeree has embarked on performance it is too late for the offeree to revoke his offer.

The unilateral contract would not be enforced, however, because it was a contract for the disposition of an interest in land which was not enforceable without writing under s 40(1) of the Law of Property Act 1925.

1.4.4   Obstruction of the offeree's performance by the offeror

Luxor (Eastbourne) Limited v Cooper (1940) HL

The defendants wanted to sell certain cinemas and the plaintiff was to find a buyer and negotiate the price (that is, to act as an estate agent). The defendants made clear that they required a certain price and then wrote to the plaintiff 'on completion of the sale of the ... cinemas ... a procuration fee of £10,000 is to be paid to [the plaintiff]'. The plaintiff found a buyer willing to pay the price required by the defendants, but the defendants refused to go through with the sale and so refused to pay the plaintiff's fee.

Held the defendants were not obliged to pay the fee. The express terms of the agreement required payment only on completion of a sale. The question was whether a term would be implied (see 5.5 for implied terms) into the agreement that the defendants would not unreasonably prevent the completion of the sale. Each contract must be looked at on its own merits. In this case, there was no necessity to imply such a term as an estate agent must expect to bear the risk of the vendor withdrawing in return for a substantial reward if the sale goes ahead.

Q   This case was not cited in *Errington v Errington and Woods* (1.4.3) or in *Daulia Limited v Four Millbank Nominees Limited* (above). Does this case restrict the application of, or reveal an exception to, the principles of those two cases?

1.5   Contracts between more than two parties

Clarke v The Earl of Dunraven and Mount: *The Satanita* (1896) HL

The Mudhook Yacht Club advertised a regatta to be held on the Clyde in July 1894. Entrants had to sign a letter to the secretary of the Club agreeing to be bound by the rules of the Yacht Club Association. Along with other yacht owners, the two parties, each having signed such a letter, entered their yachts, *The Satanita* and *The Valkyrie* in a race. During the race, *The Satanita* ran into and sank *The Valkyrie*. The question was whether the rules of the Yacht Club Association could be enforced with regard to the amount of compensation to be paid by the offending boat's owner to the owner of the damaged *Valkyrie*.

Held the rules could be enforced. *Per* Lord Herschell:

> I cannot entertain any doubt that there was a contractual relation between the parties to this litigation. The effect of their entering for the race, and undertaking to be bound by these rules to the knowledge of each other, is sufficient, I think, where those rules indicate a liability on the part of the one to the other, to create a contractual obligation to discharge that liability.

Note ───

For a contract between three parties, see *In Re Wyvern Developments Ltd* (3.4).

Q (a) Can you entertain any doubt whether the parties were in a contract together? If not, can you identify the parties to the contract, the consideration, the offer and the acceptance? (b) If this case arose today, would it be decided in negligence rather than in contract?

1.6 Relationships created by legal compulsion

Norweb plc v Dixon (1995) QBDC

Mr Dixon moved into a flat and requested Norweb to supply him with electricity there, which they did by installing a meter which required the insertion of electricity payment cards. A year later, Norweb told Mr Dixon that he owed them a debt of £677.86 in respect of electricity supplied to premises at 25 Lownorth Road. In fact, Mr Dixon had never lived at 25 Lownorth Road and was not responsible for the debts. Norweb then arranged for one of their inspectors to visit Mr Dixon to inspect his meter. Unknown to Mr Dixon, the inspector recalibrated his meter so that it would require greater payments for less electricity for the purpose of collecting the 'debt' of £677.86. As a result of the increased electricity payments and various letters sent by Norweb, Mr Dixon was extremely worried and on occasion went without food. When these events came to light, Norweb was charged with the offence of harassing another person with the object of coercing that person to pay money claimed as a debt due under a contract, contrary to s 40 of the Administration of Justice Act 1970. Having been convicted by the magistrates of this offence, Norweb appealed to the Divisional Court arguing that the sum of £677.86 was never claimed 'as a debt due under a contract' because arrangements for the supply of electricity did not amount to a contract.

Held there was no contract here and Norweb's appeal succeeded. In the absence of exceptional circumstances, Norweb was obliged to supply electricity on terms which were largely dictated by the Electricity Act 1989. *Per* Dyson J:

There are many examples of cases where the law to some extent restricts the freedom of parties to enter into a relationship, but where the relationship that results is a contract ... But, there are other cases in which a relationship created by legal compulsion is clearly not contractual. Thus, a person whose property is compulsorily acquired against his will does not make a contract with the acquiring authority, even though he receives compensation: see *Sovmots Investments Ltd v Secretary of State for the Environment* (1977). In *Pfizer Corporation v Ministry of Health* (1965), the House of Lords held that a patient to whom medicines are supplied under the National Health Service does not make a contract to buy them either from the chemist or the Minister of Health even if he pays a subscription charge. The transaction is *sui generis*, the creation of statute and not a sale pursuant to a contract ... The issue in this case is: which side of the line does the relationship between a tariff customer and a public electricity supplier fall? In my judgment, the legal compulsion both as to the creation of the relationship and the fixing of its terms is inconsistent with the existence of a contract.

2 Certainty and Intention to Create Legal Relations

2.1 Certainty

2.1.1 Sale of Goods Act 1979

Section 8 Ascertainment of price

(1) The price in a contract of sale may be fixed by the contract, or may be left to be fixed in a manner agreed by the contract, or may be determined by the course of dealing between the parties.

(2) Where the price is not determined as mentioned in sub-s (1) above, the buyer must pay a reasonable price.

(3) What is a reasonable price is a question of fact dependent on the circumstances of each particular case.

Section 9 Agreement to sell at valuation

(1) Where there is an agreement to sell goods on the terms that the price is to be fixed by the valuation of a third party, and he cannot or does not make the valuation, the agreement is avoided; but, if the goods or any part of them have been delivered to and appropriated by the buyer, he must pay a reasonable price for them.

(2) Where the third party is prevented from making the valuation by the fault of the seller or buyer, the party not at fault may maintain an action for damages against the party at fault.

2.1.2 The cases

Guthing v Lynn (1831) CKB

The plaintiff agreed to buy a horse from the defendant, the consideration for the horse being 60 guineas and that if the horse was lucky the plaintiff would either pay another £5 or buy another horse.

Held the luckiness of the horse and the agreement to buy another horse were both too vague for the court to enforce. The enforceable part of the consideration was only the payment of 60 guineas. *Per* Lord Tenterden CJ:

We must suppose the substantial part of the contract to be that declared upon, and consider the rest as amounting merely to one of those honorary engagements which seem very much to prevail among persons in this way of business.

May and Butcher Limited v R (1929) HL

Following the First World War, the government established the Disposals Board to dispose of surplus goods. The Board made several agreements with the plaintiffs for the sale of tentage (materials for constructing tents). The first agreement was made in April 1920 and the parties operated on the same terms which were renewed from time to time until a dispute arose over the agreement made at a renewal in January 1922. The agreement was that the plaintiffs would deposit £1,000 with the defendant Board and the Board would sell to the plaintiffs:

> ... the whole of the tentage which may become available in the United Kingdom for disposal up to and including 31 March 1923.

The clause in respect of the price for the tentage was:

> The price or prices to be paid ... shall be agreed upon from time to time between the Commission and the purchasers as the quantities of the said old tentage become available for disposal, and are offered to the purchasers by the Commission.

There was also an arbitration clause:

> It is understood that all disputes with reference to or arising out of this agreement will be submitted to arbitration in accordance with the provisions of the Arbitration Act 1889.

Held there was no enforceable contract due to uncertainty. (I) If a critical part of the contract is left undetermined, there is no contract. *Per* Viscount Dunedin 'price is one of the essentials of sale, and if it is left still to be agreed between the parties, then there is no contract'. (II) According to s 8 of the Sale of Goods Act 1893 (re-enacted in s 8 of the Sale of Goods Act 1979, see 2.1.1), if the price is not determined by being fixed in the contract, by being left to be fixed in a manner agreed in the contract or by the course of dealings between the parties, then the buyer must pay a reasonable price. Their Lordships held that this meant that a reasonable price would be implied when a contract was silent on price. However, in this case, the contract was not silent but made an agreement to agree the price later. (III) The arbitration clause did not provide a mechanism for agreeing the price because, *per* Lord Buckmaster:

> The clause refers 'disputes with reference to or arising out of this agreement' to arbitration, but until the price has been fixed, the agreement is not there.

Hillas and Co Ltd v Arcos Ltd (1932) HL

The plaintiff buyers were timber merchants; the defendant sellers were the English company through which the Government of the Soviet Union sold timber in England. On 21 May 1930, the parties made a written agreement which started with the words, 'We agree to buy 22,000 standards of softwood goods of fair specification over the season 1930 under the following conditions'. Various conditions followed that were numbered (1) to (11). Condition (9) was:

> Buyers shall also have the option of entering into a contract with the sellers for the purchase of 100,000 standards for delivery during 1931. Such contract to stipulate that, whatever the conditions are, buyers shall obtain the goods on conditions and at prices which show to them a reduction of 5% on the fob value of the official price list at any time ruling during 1931. Such option to be declared before the 1st January 1931.

The parties traded in accordance with the agreement through the 1930 season. However, on 20 November 1930, the sellers contracted to sell the whole of the 1931 output to a third party and on 22 December the buyers (knowing of that sale) wrote to the sellers purporting to exercise their option under condition (9).

Held the option was an enforceable contract. (I) It was not a mere unenforceable agreement to make an agreement for two main reasons. (i) Reading condition (9) as part of the wider agreement of 21 May, the words 'of softwood goods of fair specification' (which appear at the start of the agreement) must be implied in the clause after '100,000 standards'. The words 'of fair specification' meant a fair mix of kinds, qualities and sizes as they meant in the main agreement for the 1930 season which had been operated successfully by the parties. (ii) The reference in condition (9) to 'whatever the conditions are' did not refer to conditions left to be decided in the contract, but to conditions in the market for softwood. (II) *May and Butcher Limited v R* (2.1.2) did not lay down a general rule. Instead, these cases are a matter of the construction of individual agreements. *Per* Lord Wright, it was 'the duty of the Court to construe such documents fairly and broadly, without being too astute or subtle in finding defects'.

Foley v Classique Coaches Ltd (1934) CA

The plaintiff owned some land. On one part of the land, he had petrol pumps. He sold the other part of the land to the defendants for use in their coach operating business. The contract for the sale of the land was conditional upon an agreement made the same day by which the defendants promised to buy all the petrol for their business from the plaintiff. The agreement included an arbitration clause. For over three years, the parties acted on the agreement. Then, the defendants wanted to buy petrol elsewhere and they repudiated the agreement. The defendants argued that the agreement, which did not fix the price of the petrol, was too uncertain to be enforced.

Held the agreement was enforceable. There was an implied term that the petrol would be supplied at a reasonable price and be of reasonable quality and, if the parties could not agree on a reasonable price, it would be decided by arbitration. The parties thought they were making a binding contract as they had traded under it for three years, and it was linked to the contract for the sale of the land.

Scammell v Ouston (1940) HL

The plaintiffs negotiated to buy a new van from the defendants. They agreed a price and a part exchange value for the plaintiffs' old van. It was understood through the negotiations that the plaintiffs wanted to buy on hire purchase terms and the final note of the agreement sent by the plaintiffs to the defendants included the words 'This order is given on the understanding that the balance of purchase price can be had on hire purchase terms over a period of two years'. The defendants withdrew from the sale and argued that there had never been a contract.

Held there was no contract. (I) The agreement to adopt 'hire purchase terms' was too vague to be enforced. Hire purchase agreements could take many forms and there was no evidence that any particular terms were intended by the parties. (II) It was an agreement to agree which would not be enforced. (III) The parties never got beyond negotiations and never reached agreement at all.

Nicolene Ltd v Simmonds (1953) CA

The plaintiffs offered to buy 3,000 tons of steel reinforcing bars from the defendant. Details as to price and the sizes of the bars were agreed. The defendant's letter accepting the offer included the words:

> As you have made the order direct to me, I am unable to confirm on my usual printed form which would have the usual *force majeure* and war clauses, but I assume that we are in agreement that the usual conditions of acceptance apply.

The plaintiffs sued the defendant for breach of contract when the defendant failed to make delivery under the agreement, and the defendant argued that there was no concluded contract.

Held there was an enforceable contract. The words 'the usual conditions of acceptance apply' were meaningless but could be severed from the rest of the contract and ignored. The words were meaningless because the defendant did not have a printed form or any usual conditions. (He was referring to the form and conditions of a limited company with which he was associated.) *Per* Denning LJ:

A clause which is meaningless can often be ignored, whilst still leaving the contract good; whereas a clause which has yet to be agreed may mean that there is no contract at all, because the parties have not agreed on all the essential terms.

Edwards v Skyways Ltd (1964) QB

The plaintiff was employed as an airline pilot by the defendant company. The company wanted to make some pilots, including the plaintiff, redundant. The company negotiated with the British Air Line Pilots Association which represented the plaintiff and others. At a meeting, they agreed that each pilot who was dismissed would be offered:

> ... an *ex gratia* payment equivalent to the company's contribution to [that pilot's] pension fund.

The company said that the agreement was for an amount 'approximating to' the contributions. The plaintiff claimed the payment but the company revoked the agreement arguing that it was not legally enforceable.

Held the agreement was enforceable. (I) (2.2.2) There was an intention to create legal relations. (i) *Per* Megaw J:

> ... the subject matter of the agreement is business relations, not social or domestic matters ... In a case of this nature, the onus is on the party who asserts that no legal effect is intended, and the onus is a heavy one.

(ii) The words *ex gratia* in the agreement merely meant that the company did not admit to a pre-existing legal liability to make the payment, not that the agreement itself was without legal effect. (II) The agreement was not too uncertain to be enforced. *Per* Megaw J:

> At most, 'approximating to', if that were the contractual term, would on the evidence connote a rounding off of a few pounds downwards to a round figure.

Courtney and Fairbairn Ltd v Tolaini Brothers (Hotels) Ltd (1974) CA

The defendants, who were property developers, wanted to build a motel, a filling station and an hotel on a five acre site in Hertfordshire. The plaintiffs, who were building contractors, offered to introduce the defendants to a source of finance for the development in return for being given the building contracts for the projects. The plaintiffs wrote to the defendants asking for confirmation that if the introduction led to a financing arrangement:

> ... you will be prepared to instruct your quantity surveyor to negotiate fair and reasonable contract sums in respect of each of the three projects as they arise. (These would, incidentally be based upon agreed estimates of the net cost of work and general overheads with a margin for profit of 5%) which, I am sure you will agree, is indeed reasonable.

The plaintiffs requested agreement in writing to their terms, which the defendants provided. The financing was duly agreed between the defendants and the financier introduced by the plaintiffs, but the parties could not agree terms for the construction work and the defendants instructed another contractor.

Held there was no binding contract to give the construction work to the plaintiffs. There was a mere agreement to agree which the court would not enforce. The price was left for later agreement and, *per* Lord Denning MR:

> ... the price in a building contract is of fundamental importance. It is so essential a term that there is no contract unless the price is agreed or there is an agreed method of ascertaining it, not dependent on the negotiations of the two parties themselves ... A contract to negotiate, like a contract to enter into a contract, is not a contract known to the law.

His lordship also pointed out that:

> ... if they had left the price to be agreed by a third person such as an arbitrator, it would have been different.

Sudbrook Trading Estate Ltd v Eggleton and Others (1982) HL

The plaintiff lessees leased four industrial premises in Gloucester from the defendant lessors. The four lease agreements all included a stipulation similar to this one:

> ... that if the Lessees shall desire to purchase the reversion in fee simple in the premises hereby demised and ... shall give to the Lessor notice in writing to that effect the Lessees shall be the purchasers of such reversion as from the date of such notice at such price not being less than twelve thousand pounds as may be agreed upon by two Valuers one to be nominated by the Lessor and the other by the Lessees or in default of such agreement by an Umpire appointed by the said Valuers ...

The lessees duly gave notice of their desire to buy the reversions of three of the leases, but the lessors refused to nominate a valuer and argued that the agreement to do so was not binding.

Held the agreement was a binding contract (overruling an old line of authority which had bound the Court of Appeal to find for the lessors). The court would order an inquiry into a reasonable price, which the lessors would have to accept. (I) *Per* Lord Diplock the option clause was a unilateral contract which gave both parties obligations from the time that the lessees gave the required written notice. One such obligation was to appoint a valuer. (II) *Per* Lord Fraser 'the clause should be construed as meaning that the price was to be a fair price'. The machinery for setting the price was incidental to this purpose and thus not essential to the contract (though it would have been different for a contract which named a particular person as valuer). If the chosen method breaks down the court can 'substitute other machinery to carry out the main purpose of ascertaining the price in order that the agreement may be carried out'.

Walford and Others v Miles and Another (1992) HL

The defendants wanted to sell their photographic processing business and premises. They agreed the main terms of a sale to the plaintiffs who promised to provide a letter of comfort from their bankers that they would have finance available for the transaction in return for the defendants' promise not to negotiate with anyone else. It was also alleged that the defendants had promised to continue negotiating with the plaintiffs. However, the defendants withdrew from the sale to the plaintiffs and sold the business to another buyer.

Held the defendants had not breached any enforceable contract. (I) An agreement that the parties will negotiate (a 'lock in') is unenforceable because, *per* Lord Ackner, 'like an agreement to agree ... it lacks the necessary certainty'. (II) An agreement that one party will not negotiate with others (a 'lock out') could be binding. However, in this case, the agreement failed to specify how long it would last, which is an essential element, so it would not be enforced for uncertainty.

2.2 Intention to create legal relations

2.2.1 Presumption against the intention in domestic or social agreements

Balfour v Balfour (1919) CA

The plaintiff wife married the defendant husband in 1900. The husband worked in Ceylon and the parties lived there until 1915, when the husband had leave. When the husband had to return to Ceylon at the end of his leave, the wife was advised by her doctor to stay in England. Before the husband went back to Ceylon, the parties agreed that he would send the wife 30 shillings per month. Some months later, the husband suggested they should remain apart. The wife then sought to enforce the agreement for 30 shillings per month.

Held this was not an agreement the court could enforce. (I) Since the couple were living in amity at the time of the agreement, it would be presumed that they had not intended that the agreement should be legally enforceable. The wife had failed to rebut the presumption in this case. *Per* Atkin LJ:

> Agreements such as these are outside the realm of contracts altogether. The common law does not regulate the form of agreements between spouses. Their promises are not sealed with seals and sealing wax.

(II) *Per* Warrington and Duke LJJ, the wife had not bound herself to do anything, so she had not given any consideration.

Simpkins v Pays (1955) Ass

The plaintiff lived in the defendant's house, paying the defendant for board and lodging. Together with the defendant's granddaughter, Esme, the parties entered newspaper competitions together. One of the competitions was in the Sunday Empire News and involved making three forecasts of the correct order of merit of eight fashion items. For seven or eight weeks, the plaintiff, the defendant and Esme each contributed one forecast to a coupon which was submitted in the name of the defendant. Then their entry won the £750 prize and the plaintiff sued the defendant for a third share. The winning line had been composed by Esme.

Held the plaintiff was entitled to £250, and so was Esme. *Per* Sellers J:

> I accept the plaintiff's evidence that, when the matter first came to be considered, what was said, when they were going to do it in that way, was: 'We will go shares,' or words to that effect ... It may well be that there are many family associations where some sort of rough and ready statement is made which would not, in a proper estimate of the circumstances, establish a contract which was contemplated to have legal consequences, but I do not so find here. I think that in the present there was a mutuality of arrangement between the parties.

Parker and Another v Clark and Another (1959) Ass

The plaintiffs were Commander and Mrs Parker, the defendants Mr and Mrs Clark. Mrs Parker was Mrs Clark's niece. The Clarks were in their late seventies and the Parkers used to visit them often, sometimes to help the Clarks domestically. After one such visit which had lasted for two or three weeks, Mr Clark suggested that the Parkers should come and live with the Clarks. Commander Parker wrote to Mr Clark expressing interest in the suggestion but pointing out that the Parkers would have to sell their own house. Mr Clark wrote back saying that this problem could be overcome by the Clarks leaving their house in their wills to Mrs Parker, the Parkers' daughter, Pamela, and Mrs Parker's sister. He also set out in some detail the arrangements for household expenses and promised to buy a television and a new car. Commander Parker accepted the proposed arrangements and the Parkers sold their house. They lent most of the proceeds to Pamela so that she could buy a flat. They informed the Clarks of this and came to live at the Clarks' house. After about a year and a half, Mr Clark became dissatisfied with the arrangements and asked the Parkers to leave. The Parkers eventually left and sued the Clarks for damages for breach of contract.

Held there was a contract and the Parkers were entitled to recover the costs of moving and the third share of the Clarks' house which was to be left to Mrs Parker. *Per* Devlin J:

> A proposal between relatives to share a house and a promise to make a bequest of it may very well amount to no more than a family arrangement of the type considered in *Balfour v Balfour* [2.2.1] which the courts will not enforce. But, there is equally no doubt that arrangements of this sort, and in particular a proposal to leave property in a will, can be the subject of a binding contract ... The question must, of course, depend on the intention of the parties to be inferred from the language which they use and from the circumstances in which they use it.

In the circumstances, where the plaintiffs had to dispose of their own house to fulfil their side of the bargain, both sides must have believed that they were entering into a binding agreement.

Jones v Padavatton (1968) CA

The plaintiff, Mrs Jones, was the mother of the defendant, Mrs Padavatton. In 1962, the defendant daughter had a job in Washington, DC where she lived with her son. The mother persuaded the daughter to go to England and study for the Bar and promised her $200 per month for maintenance. The mother hoped that the daughter would qualify as a barrister and then come to practise and live in Trinidad, where the mother herself lived. In 1964, the mother bought a house in England in which the daughter lived along with paying tenants. The daughter was the mother's agent for the income and expenses of the house. By 1967, the daughter had not passed the first part of the two part Bar examinations and she had failed to provide her mother with accounts of the house. The mother therefore sought possession of the house against the daughter, which the daughter resisted on the ground that she had a contractual right to live there.

Held the mother should have possession as there was no binding contract between the parties. (I) *Per* Dankwerts LJ:

> ... the present case is one of those family arrangements which depend on the good faith of the promises which are made and are not intended to be rigid, binding agreements. *Balfour v Balfour* [2.2.1] was a case of husband and wife, but there is no doubt that the same principles apply to dealings between other relations, such as father and son and daughter and mother.

Fenton Atkinson LJ reached the same conclusion. (II) *Per* Salmon LJ:

> ... as a rule when arrangements are made between close relations, for example, between husband and wife, parent and child or uncle and nephew in relation to an allowance, there is a presumption against an intention of creating any legal relationship. This is not a presumption of law, but of fact ... Like all other presumptions of fact it can be rebutted.

In this 'exceptional' case, his lordship held that there was a binding agreement that the mother would pay $200 a week while the daughter read for the Bar. It was an implied term that the agreement would last for a reasonable time. The time that had elapsed from 1962 until the hearing in 1968 was too long and the agreement was therefore no longer valid. The daughter had failed to show that a new contract had been entered into in 1964.

Merritt v Merritt (1970) CA

The plaintiff wife and the defendant husband were married in 1941. They bought a house in 1949 in the husband's name and transferred it into their joint names in 1966. Then, the husband left home to live with another woman. The husband agreed to pay the wife £40 per month and left her to pay the remainder of the mortgage. At the wife's insistence, the husband wrote:

> In consideration of the fact that you will pay all charges in connection with the house ... when the mortgage has been completed I agree to transfer the property in to your sole ownership.

When the wife had paid off the mortgage, the husband refused to transfer the house.

Held the husband did have to transfer the house under the agreement made with his wife. Lord Denning MR and Widgery LJ both accepted that, although there was a presumption against an intention to form legal relations in the case of agreements between spouses living in amity, such a presumption did not apply to cases where the spouses were in the process of separation. *Per* Lord Denning MR, there was a presumption in favour of an intention to form legal relations in negotiations over a marital separation. Widgery LJ found it 'unnecessary to go so far' as that. Karminski LJ found that there was a binding contract by looking at the surrounding circumstances and did not refer to presumptions at all.

Heslop and Another v Burns and Another (1974) CA

In 1951, Mr Timms formed a romantic attraction for Mrs Burns. Mr Timms allowed the defendants, Mr and Mrs Burns, to live in a house he owned and he became godfather to their child. In 1954, Mr and Mrs Burns moved to another house belonging to Mr Timms. Mr Timms told Mrs Burns that he was buying the house for her and that it was hers. Until he became ill in 1968, Mr Timms visited Mr and Mrs Burns virtually every day. Mr and Mrs Burns remained in the house until Mr Timms died in 1970. Since Mr Timms had not left the house to Mr and Mrs Burns, his executors brought this action for possession of the house.

Held possession would be granted. There was no arrangement intended to create a legal relationship so the house remained the property of Mr

Timms. Mr and Mrs Burns occupied the house as licensees rather than as tenants. *Per* Stamp LJ:

> There was no contract, no arrangement, no statement by the deceased. The defendants, as I see it, were allowed to move into the property and occupy it simply as a result of the bounty of the deceased and without any arrangements as to the terms on which they should do so.

Per Scarman LJ:

> In the present case, I think one can find something very akin to a family arrangement. After all, we are considering the occupation of a house which is described by the lady most concerned [Mrs Burns] as the 'second home' of Mr Timms. We are certainly considering a whole course of dealing within the realm of friendship, and we are certainly faced with very great generosity shown over a long number of years by Mr Timms to the defendants' family.

2.2.2 Presumption in favour of the intention in commercial agreements

Rose and Frank Company v JR Crompton and Brothers Ltd and Others (1924) HL

The appellants were a US company which bought carbonising tissue, treated it and sold it. The respondents were two English companies whose business was to sell carbonising tissue. The parties entered into a written agreement under which the English companies would confine their sales of carbonising paper in North America and the appellants would only purchase carbonising paper from the English companies. Towards the end of the agreement was this clause:

> This arrangement is not entered into, nor is this memorandum written, as a formal or legal agreement, and shall not be subject to legal jurisdiction in the law courts either of the US or England, but it is only a definite expression and record of the purpose and intention of the three parties concerned, to which they each honourably pledge themselves with the fullest confidence – based on past business with each other – that it will be carried through by each of the three parties with mutual loyalty and friendly co-operation.

Some years later, disputes arose between the parties in the conduct of their business.

Held the clause was effective to make the contract one 'of honour only and unenforceable at law' (*per* Lord Phillimore). This did not prevent the parties taking legal action in respect of the rights and liabilities which accrued to them as a result of the individual transactions which took place during the currency of the contract, but the contract itself could not be enforced by the court.

Football pools coupons contain an 'honourable pledge' clause so that they cannot be sued upon.

Edwards v Skyways Ltd (1964) QB

See 2.1.2.

Esso Petroleum Co Ltd v Customs and Excise Commissioners (1975) HL

As a sales promotion scheme, the plaintiff company, Esso, produced millions of coins. Each coin showed the face, name and signature of one of the members of the England association football squad for the 1970 World Cup. There were 30 different coins to collect and the coins were given away free, one with every four gallons of Esso petrol purchased by a motorist. If the coins were 'produced ... for ... sale', they would have been subject to purchase tax, but not otherwise.

Held the coins were not produced for sale. (I) The four of their lordships who formed the majority all held that even if there was an enforceable contract, there was no sale. In the context of the Purchase Tax Act 1963, a 'sale' meant a sale for which the consideration was a money price. In this case the consideration for the coin was the entry by the motorist into another contract, to buy petrol. (II) The majority were split evenly on the question of whether there was the intention to form legal relations needed for a contract regarding the coins. (i) Lord Simon of Glaisdale, with whom Lord Wilberforce agreed, held that the circumstances of the transaction were commercial. He cited with approval *dicta* from *Rose and Frank Company v JR Crompton and Brothers Ltd and Others* (2.2.2) and *Edwards v Skyways Ltd* (2.1.2) to the effect that in commercial situations there is a presumption of an intention to form legal relations. He therefore held that the intention was present in the transactions between motorists and garages relating to the Esso coins. (ii) Viscount Dilhorne and Lord Russell of Killowen did not criticise the cases cited by Lord Simon of Glaisdale, but felt that there was no intention to create legal relations in this case largely because of the very small value of the coins. (III) Lord Fraser of Tullybelton, dissenting in the final result, held that there was the necessary intention to create legal relations and that the contract formed was for the sale of four gallons of petrol plus one coin at a certain price.

Q In this case, is there a majority for the intention to create legal relations together with a majority against a sale, or is there a majority against a sale together with *obiter dicta* on the subject of the intention?

3 Consideration

3.1 What does 'consideration' mean?

3.1.1 Judicial definitions

Thomas v Thomas (1842) CQB

The defendant was the surviving executor of the plaintiff's deceased husband. Before his death, the husband had expressed the wish that the plaintiff should have a life interest in a certain house of his in Merthyr Tydfil. After his death, his executors made a written agreement with the plaintiff in the following terms: in consideration of the deceased husband's wishes, the executors would convey the house to the plaintiff for life on various conditions, provided that the plaintiff pay the executors £1 per year towards the ground rent on the house and keep it in good repair. The defendant later refused to make such a conveyance and turned the plaintiff out of the house.

Held there was a good contract between the parties so the plaintiff must have the house. The deceased man's wishes were not good consideration, even though they were described as such in the agreement, because they did not move from the plaintiff. Both the promises of £1 per year and of keeping the house in good repair were sufficient consideration for the promise to convey a life interest. It did not matter that these promises were expressed in the form of a mere proviso in the agreement. It was also not important that £1 per year was not a full commercial rent for the house. *Per* Patteson J:

> Motive is not the same thing with consideration. Consideration means something which is of some value in the eye of the law, moving from the plaintiff: it may be some benefit to the defendant, or some detriment to the plaintiff; but at all events it must be moving from the plaintiff.

Currie and Others v Misa (1875) EC

The judgment of Lush J included the following definition of consideration:

> A valuable consideration, in the sense of the law, may consist either in some right, interest, profit, or benefit accruing to one party, or some forbearance, detriment, loss, or responsibility, given, suffered, or undertaken by the other.

The definition was also approved of by Lord Coleridge CJ in his dissenting judgment in the case.

Q Is the following a circular argument? If so, does it matter? 'A promise is consideration if it is a benefit or detriment. A promise is only a benefit or detriment if it is binding. A promise is binding if it is consideration.'

Dunlop Pneumatic Tyre Co Ltd v Selfridge and Co Ltd (1915) HL

See 4.1 for the summary of this case. *Per* Lord Dunedin:

> I am content to adopt from a work of Sir Frederick Pollock ... the following words as to consideration: 'An act or forbearance of one party, or the promise thereof, is the price for which the promise of the other is bought, and the promise thus given for value is enforceable.'

3.1.2 Consideration distinguished from a mere condition

Dickinson (Inspector of Taxes) v Abel (1968) Ch

Broadfields Farm was owned by Lloyds Bank Ltd as trustees. The taxpayer, Mr Abel, had family and local connections with the trust and the farm. The taxpayer had transmitted some offers to buy the farm to the bank. When Inns & Co Ltd were interested in buying the farm, their director, Mr Wallace, had a meeting with the taxpayer to discuss the matter. Mr Wallace offered £100,000 for the farm and the taxpayer explained that the offer must be made to the bank and gave Mr Wallace the bank's address. At the end of the meeting the taxpayer asked Mr Wallace 'what's in it for me?' to which Mr Wallace replied that his company would pay the taxpayer £10,000 if they purchased the farm for £100,000 or less. This was later confirmed in writing. The taxpayer telephoned the bank and told them of the offer. The bank asked for his opinion of it, and the taxpayer said that he personally would accept it and did not mention the promise of £10,000. The purchase went ahead and the taxpayer received £10,000. The issue was whether the £10,000 was taxable income for the taxpayer. It would be taxable only if it was paid under a binding contract.

Held the £10,000 was not taxable. The taxpayer could not have enforced the payment of £10,000 because he had given no consideration for it. The taxpayer had never been asked to recommend the offer, or do any other service for Inns and Co Ltd, in return for his money. The fact that the taxpayer had, in fact, recommended the offer did not mean he had given consideration, because there was no agreement for him to do so. The purchase of the farm for £100,000 or less was merely a condition of the gift, not consideration.

3.2 Consideration must be sufficient, but need not be adequate

Bainbridge v Firmstone (1838) CQB

The defendant asked to weigh the plaintiff's boilers and promised to return them to working order afterwards. The plaintiff agreed, but the defendant left the boilers in pieces. The defendant argued that the plaintiff could not obtain damages because he had not given any consideration.

Held, per Patteson J:

> The consideration is, that the plaintiff, at the defendant's request, had consented to allow the defendant to weigh the boilers. I suppose the defendant thought he had some benefit; at any rate, there is a detriment to the plaintiff from his parting with the possession for even so short a time.

Thomas v Thomas (1842) CQB

See 3.1.1.

Carlill v Carbolic Smoke Ball Co (1893) CA

See 1.4.1.

De La Bere v Pearson Ltd (1907) CA

The defendants owned a newspaper called 'MAP'. The paper had a regular page of financial advice given in response to readers' queries. A regular notice in the paper asked readers to send in their requests for financial advice. One reader was the plaintiff, who wrote to ask:

> ... how I can best invest £800 in two or three fairly safe securities to pay not less than 5% ... Please also name a good stockbroker.

The city editor of the newspaper passed the letter on to a broker who had been helping him with such queries for about six months. The city editor had not made any inquiries about the broker. The editor knew that the broker was not a member of the stock exchange, but did not know that he was an undischarged bankrupt. After some correspondence between the plaintiff and the broker, the plaintiff sent the broker £1,400 to invest in certain shares. The broker misappropriated the money to his own purposes.

Held the defendants would have to compensate the plaintiff for the £1,400 which had been lost as a result of the defendants' breach of contract. The defendants made an offer when they asked for letters seeking financial advice and the plaintiff accepted by writing the letter. The plaintiff's consideration was the letter written at the defendants' request, which might have benefited the defendants if they had printed it. The contract contained an implied term that the defendants would exercise reasonable care in choosing a broker, which they failed to do because of the city editor's failure to make any inquiries about the broker.

Note

In *Hedley Byrne v Heller*, Lord Devlin implied that this case should have been decided as a negligent misstatement case, rather than a breach of contract.

Chappell & Co Ltd and Others v The Nestlé Co Ltd and Others (1959) HL

Under s 8 of the Copyright Act 1956, it was not a breach of copyright to produce a record for retail sale so long as a certain percentage of the ordinary retail price was paid to the owner of the copyright. As part of a sales promotion scheme, the defendant, which was a chocolate manufacturing company, advertised certain records as being available to anyone who sent one shilling and six pence and three wrappers from the defendant's chocolate bars. The defendant had no use for the wrappers, which were thrown away when received. The usual price of records at the time was some six shillings and six pence and the copyright in one of the records was owned by the plaintiff. The defendant had offered the plaintiff the appropriate percentage of one shilling and six pence, but the plaintiff argued that the cash alone did not represent the ordinary retail price, so that the defendant had breached the plaintiff's copyright.

Held s 8 made an exception from breach of copyright only for sales where the consideration for a record is money. In this case, the consideration included non-monetary consideration, so there was no ordinary retail price. That meant that the defendant could not pay the plaintiff the required percentage, so the defendant had breached the plaintiff's copyright. Thus the majority thought that the wrappers were part of the consideration, despite their being of no intrinsic value to the defendant.

Lord Keith of Avonholm, dissenting, held that the wrappers were 'merely a qualification for purchasing the record' for the price of one shilling and six pence. Against this view, Lord Reid, in the majority, argued:

... where the qualification is doing something of value to the seller, and where the qualification only suffices for one sale and must be re-acquired before another sale, I find it hard to regard the repeated acquisitions of the qualification as anything other than parts of the consideration for the sales.

3.3   Consideration must move from the promisee

Tweddle v Atkinson (1861) CQB

The plaintiff was T's son who had married G's daughter. T and G had made a written agreement that T would pay the plaintiff £100 and G would pay him £200. They also agreed that the plaintiff 'has full power to sue the said parties ... for the aforesaid sums'. G did not pay the £200 and, since G had died, the plaintiff sued G's executor.

Held the plaintiff could not sue as he was not a party to the contract. *Per* Wightman J: '... it is now established that no stranger to the consideration can take advantage of a contract, although made for his benefit.' *Per* Crompton J:

> ... the consideration must move from the party entitled to sue upon the contract. It would be a monstrous proposition to say that a person was a party to the contract for the purpose of suing upon it for his own advantage, and not a party to it for the purpose of being sued.

3.4   Consideration need not move to the promisor

In Re Wyvern Developments Ltd (1972) Ch

Wyvern agreed to buy some land from Gresham. Wyvern did not have the money to complete the purchase and was wound up, with the Official Receiver as liquidator. The land remained vested in Gresham on trust for Wyvern subject to a vendor's lien in favour of Gresham of £20,598. Gresham could therefore only sell the land with the consent of Wyvern, given by the liquidator, or by applying to the court. The required consent was given by the Official Receiver when Gresham found a buyer, Winter, willing to pay £16,000. The whole of that sum would be paid to Gresham, since it was less than the vendor's lien. After contracts were exchanged between Gresham and Winter, the majority shareholder in Wyvern claimed there was another buyer willing to pay £35,000 and brought this action to prevent the official receiver executing on behalf of Wyvern the conveyance to complete the sale of the land to Winter.

Held the Official Receiver could not go back on his agreement to the sale. (I) The agreement of Wyvern to the sale, together with the correspondence between Gresham and Winter formed a tripartite contract which was binding on Wyvern. (i) *Per* Templeman J:

> On well established principles, it is not necessary for Wyvern to receive any part of the purchase price or any other consideration, provided that consideration moves from the promisees, Gresham and Winter.

(ii) In any event, there was consideration received by the Official Receiver for Wyvern.

> In my judgment, the implied promise of Gresham not to apply to the court to enforce its lien was consideration for the promise of the Official Receiver to execute the conveyance, thus making an application to the court unnecessary.

(II) Promissory estoppel (see 3.8.2) would apply to prevent the Official Receiver from going back on his promise to execute the conveyance. (III) As a trustee, a high standard of conduct would be required of the Official Receiver, so that he would not be allowed to break an undertaking in these circumstances.

3.5 Past consideration is no consideration

3.5.1 The general rule

Roscorla v Thomas (1842) CQB

In consideration that the plaintiff, at the request of the defendant, had earlier bought from the defendant a horse for the sum of £30, the defendant promised that it was sound and free from vice.

Held the promise of the horse's soundness did not give the defendant any contractual liability, because the plaintiff's consideration had already been given at the time of the defendant's promise.

In Re McArdle Deceased (1951) CA

The deceased Mr William McArdle died in February 1935 having left his estate to his five children, subject to the life interest of his widow, Holly. The deceased man's son, Monty, lived with his wife, Marjorie, in a bungalow that formed part of William McArdle's estate. Marjorie spent £488 on repairs to the bungalow which were completed in 1944. At Monty's request, all five of William McArdle's children signed a document in the following terms:

> To Mrs Marjorie McArdle ... In consideration of your carrying out certain alterations and improvements to the property ... we the beneficiaries under the Will ... hereby agree that the Executors ... shall repay to you from the said estate when so distributed the sum of £488 in settlement of the amount spent on such improvements. Dated April 30, 1945.

Holly died in 1948 and Marjorie requested the £488 in 1950, but William's children (except for Monty) now instructed the executors not to pay her.

Held Marjorie could not enforce the promise to pay her £488 because her consideration was past at the time of the agreement. The agreement was expressed as a valid contract which included a promise from Marjorie to carry out certain improvements. However, the fact that the work had already been completed turned the agreement into a gratuitous promise which could not be enforced in the courts.

3.5.2   Apparent exceptions

Lampleigh v Brathwait (1615)

The defendant had committed a murder and asked the plaintiff to try to obtain a pardon for him from the King. The plaintiff made several journeys in pursuance of this request and, afterwards, the defendant promised the plaintiff £100 in consideration of what the plaintiff had done for him. The defendant then failed to pay.

Held the plaintiff could recover the money:

A meer voluntary courtesie will not have a consideration to uphold an assumpsit [contract]. But if that courtesie were moved by a suit or request of the party that gives the assumpsit [the defendant], it will bind, for the promise, though it follows, yet it is not naked, but couples itself with the suit before.

In Re Casey's Patents: Stewart v Casey (1891) CA

In July 1887, the plaintiff and a partner registered two patents for ways of storing volatile or inflammable liquids. They then made arrangements with the defendant to take commercial advantage of the patents. On 29 January 1889, after the defendant had done various work on the ideas, the plaintiff and his partner wrote to the defendant:

We now have pleasure in stating that in consideration of your services as the practical manager in working both our patents ... we hereby agree to give you one third share of the patents above-mentioned, the same to take effect from this date.

The plaintiff's partner died in September 1889. In December 1889, the defendant made an entry in the Patents Register stating his claim to one third ownership in the two patents. This was an action to have that entry removed.

Held the entry must remain on the register as the defendant had a good claim to one third of the patents. One of the plaintiff's unsuccessful arguments was that the defendant could not enforce the letter of 29 January 1889 because his only consideration was work which he had already done at the time of the letter. *Per* Bowen LJ:

... the fact of a past service raises an implication that at the time it was rendered it was to be paid for, and, if it was a service which was to be paid for, when you get in the subsequent document a promise to pay, that promise may be treated either as an admission which evidences or as a positive bargain which fixes the amount of that reasonable remuneration on the faith of which the service was originally rendered.

Q (a) Does this case provide a satisfactory explanation for *Lampleigh v Brathwait* (3.5.2)? (b) In the passage cited above, Bowen LJ appears to have said that any past service raises an implication of an intention to pay for it: do you think that is what he meant to say? If so, was it correct?

Pao On and Others v Lau Yiu Long and Another (1979) PC

The plaintiffs, the Paos, owned all the shares in a Hong Kong private limited company, Shing On. Shing On's main asset was a building under construction. The defendants, the Laus, were majority shareholders in a Hong Kong public company, Fu Chip. Fu Chip was recently incorporated and was an investment company. On 27 February 1973, the parties and companies entered into two agreements. By the main agreement the Paos would sell all their shares in Shing On to Fu Chip. Fu Chip would pay $10.5m, which it would pay by issuing 4.2m shares in Fu Chip to the Paos, each share valued at $2.50. The completion date was to be 30 April 1973. The Paos undertook not to sell 2.5m of the 4.2m Fu Chip shares before May 1974. Because the Paos wanted to be protected against any fall in the value of the shares between February 1973 and May 1974, the subsidiary agreement was made which was a contract for the purchase of the 2.5m shares from the Paos by the Laus at a price of $2.50 per share on or before 30 April 1974.

After signing the agreements, the Paos realised that the subsidiary agreement deprived them of the chance to make any gains on the 2.5m shares. They therefore decided not to complete the main agreement unless the subsidiary agreement was replaced by a guarantee against loss on the 2.5m shares that the Paos had to retain. They wrote in these terms to Fu Chip on 25 April 1973. The Laus knew that if the Paos refused to complete the agreement, public confidence in Fu Chip would be severely damaged. They therefore acceded to the Paos' demand. On 4 May 1973, the second agreement was cancelled and a new agreement was made under which the Laus promised to compensate the Paos if Fu Chip shares were worth less than $2.50 by 30 April 1974. In the event, they fell to 36 cents at that date and the Laus argued that the guarantee was not enforceable by the Paos. The guarantee said:

> In consideration of your having at our request agreed to sell all of your shares of and in [Shing On] ... under an agreement ... dated the 27th day of February 1973, we [the Laus] hereby agree [to indemnify you against any fall in value of Fu Chip shares below $2.50 per share].

Held the guarantee was enforceable. (I) The Paos gave sufficient consideration to the Laus by promising to honour the main agreement with Fu Chip. (i) The Paos' expressly stated consideration was making the main agreement with Fu Chip, which had been done in the past. *Lampleigh v Brathwait* (3.5.2) and *In Re Casey's Patents: Stewart v Casey* (3.5.2) were to be followed. *Per* Lord Scarman, giving the judgment of the Board:

> An act done before the giving of a promise to make a payment or confer some other benefit can sometimes be consideration for the promise. The act must have been done at the promisor's request, the parties must have understood that the act was to be remunerated either by a payment or the conferment of some other benefit, and payment, or the conferment of a benefit, must have been legally enforceable had it been promised in advance. All three features are present in this case.

The Paos had promised at the Laus' request to retain the 2.5m shares and this was to be remunerated by a guarantee against loss. Once the subsidiary agreement was cancelled, there was no longer such a guarantee. (ii) (3.7.3) *Per* Lord Scarman:

> Their lordships do not doubt that a promise to perform, or the performance of, a pre-existing contractual obligation to a third party can be valid consideration.

The third party here was Fu Chip, the Laus not being a party to the main contract. (II) (10.1) The Laus were not subject to duress in signing the guarantee. However, *per* Lord Scarman (*obiter*):

> In their lordships' view, there is nothing contrary to principle in recognising economic duress as a factor which may render a contract voidable, provided always that the basis of such recognition is that it must amount to a coercion of will, which vitiates consent. It must be shown that the payment made or the contract entered into was not a voluntary act.

3.6 Forbearance may be consideration

3.6.1 Forbearance from a legal action known to be bad is not good consideration

Wade v Simeon (1846) CCP

The plaintiff began an action in the Court of Exchequer to recover £2,000 which he claimed the defendant owed him. The trial of the action was fixed for 7 December 1844, but, on 6 December, the defendant agreed to pay the money in return for the plaintiff staying the action. However, the action itself was ill founded in law and the plaintiff knew that he had no cause of action. The plaintiff now tried to recover the money from the defendant based on the agreement of 6 December.

Held the agreement of 6 December was not an enforceable contract because the plaintiff had not given good consideration. There is no benefit or detriment in forbearing from an action known to be bad. *Per* Tindal CJ:

It is almost *contra bonos mores*, and certainly contrary to all the principles of natural justice that a man should institute proceedings against another, when he is conscious that he has no good cause of action.

Q   Was there not a benefit to the defendant in having an action against him halted, even if the plaintiff knew it to be bad? Is this really a policy decision to prevent the abuse of court proceedings?

3.6.2   Forbearance from an action on a *bona fide* claim is good consideration

Cook and Others v Wright (1861) CQB

The plaintiffs were commissioners who had a statutory duty to ensure that property owners in the Whitechapel area of London carried out or paid for certain improvements. The defendant was a tenant who used to act as his landlady's agent for collecting the rent and paying the rates on three of her houses. The plaintiffs carried out paving works in front of the three houses and then demanded payment of £30 from the defendant as if he was the owner. The defendant believed that he did not have to pay but the plaintiffs threatened to sue him if he did not pay. The defendant therefore gave the plaintiffs promissory notes for three payments which would total the required £30. When the second and third promissory notes were due for payment, the defendant refused to pay them.

Held the defendant had to pay the plaintiffs the amounts of the notes because he had given them for good consideration. The defendant would not have been liable if he had given the notes under a mistake, believing himself to be liable to pay. However, in this case, the defendant did not give the notes because he thought he had a pre-existing liability to the plaintiffs, but only in order to prevent them suing him. So long as the plaintiffs had a reasonable claim which they *bona fide* intended to pursue, the compromise of that claim was good consideration, even where the plaintiffs had not yet started court action.

Callisher v Bischoffsheim (1870) CQB

The plaintiff believed that the Government of Honduras and others owed him money. The defendant promised the plaintiff certain bonds in return for the plaintiff's forbearance from suing his supposed debtors for a period. The defendant refused to hand over the bonds and claimed that when he had agreed to do so no money was actually owed to the plaintiff.

Held the plaintiff could enforce his agreement with the defendant even though his original claim against the Honduras Government and others was unfounded. The outcome would have been different if the plaintiff *had known* his claim was unfounded when he made it so that it had not been made *bona fide*.

3.6.3 Forbearance from legal action may be implied

The Alliance Bank Ltd v Broom (1864) CCh

The defendant had a loan account with the plaintiffs. When the defendant had borrowed over £22,000, the plaintiffs asked for security and the defendant agreed to give the plaintiffs a charge over certain goods. When the defendant did not complete the necessary documents, the plaintiffs sought an order to confirm their entitlement to a charge on the goods concerned.

Held the plaintiffs were entitled to the charge based on the agreement. The consideration given by the plaintiffs was their forbearance from taking action on the debt. This was not explicit in the agreement, but it could be implied that the defendant was getting the benefit of some amount of forbearance by the plaintiffs.

Miles v New Zealand Alford Estate Company (1886) CA

Mr Grant was chairman of the board of directors of the defendant company in which he owned 125 shares of £100 each. The company had been formed to buy the Alford Estate from Mr Grant. When the investment in the estate made losses, the other shareholders blamed Mr Grant. At an angry meeting of shareholders in March 1883, Mr Grant wrote out a guarantee that the company would pay out dividends of at least 5% for the following 90 years, failing which he personally would make up the shortfall in dividend payments. There were suggestions in the evidence that if Mr Grant had not given some such undertaking, the company would have taken legal action for rescission of the purchase of the estate from Mr Grant. In February 1884, Mr Grant was declared bankrupt. The plaintiff in this case was one of Mr Grant's creditors whose debt was secured on Mr Grant's shares in the company. However, the company itself had a first charge on the shares for any money owed to it by Mr Grant. The question therefore was whether the company had an enforceable claim in respect of the guarantee of dividends.

Held there was no sufficient evidence that the dividend guarantee was given for consideration. The majority would not infer that the company intended to take action against Mr Grant from which it forbore in consideration of the guarantee. They were strongly influenced by the lack of any documentation that showed the company to have bound itself to forbear from action against Mr Grant. The majority concluded that Mr Grant offered the guarantee in the hope and expectation that it would prevent legal action by the company or other shareholders, but, *per* Fry LJ, 'it is not right or competent for the court to turn an expectation into a contract'. Bowen LJ dissented, following the approach in *The Alliance Bank Ltd v Broom* (3.6.3), by inferring a forbearance from legal action on the part of the company.

3.6.4 Forbearance in domestic circumstances

White v Bluett (1853) CE

The plaintiff was the executor of the defendant's father. The deceased father had lent the defendant money which the plaintiff now sought to recover. The defendant said that he had complained to his father that the distribution of his favours among his children had disadvantaged the defendant. They had agreed that the defendant would not complain about that matter any more, in return for which his father would discharge him from liability for the money he had lent him.

Held the defendant was still liable for the debt because he had given no consideration for the promise to discharge him. (I) *Per* Pollock CB:

> The son had no right to complain, for the father might make what distribution of his property he liked; and the son's abstaining from doing what he had no right to do can be no consideration.

(II) *Per* Parke B: 'The agreement could not be enforced against the defendant.' It would therefore be one sided if it could be enforce by the defendant against his father's estate.

Combe v Combe (1951) CA

The parties married in 1915 and separated in 1939. In February 1943, the wife obtained a *decree nisi* of divorce. The wife's solicitor wrote to the husband's solicitor:

> With regard to permanent maintenance, we understand that your client is prepared to make [the wife] an allowance of £100 per year free of income tax.

The husband's solicitor wrote back confirming that agreement. In August 1943, the decree was made absolute. In July 1950, having received nothing from her former husband, the wife sued for the arrears of maintenance. The wife's income was some £700–800 per year and the husband's was £650 per year.

Held the wife could not enforce the agreement. (I) There was no consideration for the husband's promise to pay £100 per year. The wife's argument was that she had given an implied promise to forbear from proceedings for maintenance in the divorce courts. This was rejected because: (i) the wife could still have applied for maintenance at any time after the agreement; (ii) *per* Denning LJ:

> I cannot find any evidence of any intention by the husband that the wife should forbear from applying to the court for maintenance, or, in other words, any request by the husband, express or implied, that the wife should so forbear. He left her to apply, if she wished to do so. She did not do so, and I am not surprised, because it is very unlikely that the divorce court would have made an order in her favour, since she had a bigger income than her husband. Her forbearance was not intended by him, nor was it done at his request. It was, therefore, no consideration.

(II) (3.8.2) Promissory estoppel did not apply in this case, because *per* Denning LJ:

> Seeing that the principle never stands alone as giving a cause of action in itself, it can never do away with the necessity of consideration when that is an essential part of the cause of action.

Per Birkett LJ:

> I think that the description which was given by counsel for the husband in this court, namely, that the doctrine ... was, so to speak, a doctrine which would enable a person to use it as a shield and not as a sword, is a very vivid way of stating what, I think, is the principle underlying both those cases.

Per Asquith LJ, where the principle from *Central London Property Trust Ltd v High Trees House Ltd* (3.8.2) applies:

> ... the promisor cannot bring an action against the promisee which involves the repudiation of his promise or is inconsistent with it. It does not, as I read it, decide that a promisee can sue on the promise.

Horton v Horton (No 2) (1960) CA

The parties entered into a separation agreement under seal. This included a stipulation that the husband would pay the wife £30 per month. Some 10 months later, the wife wanted to make clear that she should receive £30 after any tax which should have been deducted by the husband. The parties therefore both signed a supplemental agreement to say that it had always been the intention of the parties that the wife should receive £30 per month after the deduction of tax. When the Inland Revenue claimed from the husband the tax which he should have deducted from the payments, he refused to pay any further amounts to the wife.

Held the original agreement was valid because it was under seal and the supplemental agreement was enforceable by the wife because she had given consideration for it. The purpose of the supplemental agreement was to correct the original agreement by bringing it into line with the parties' original intentions. Therefore, the wife could have taken action for the rectification of the original agreement if the supplemental agreement had not been made. The wife believed that she had a good claim for rectification and so her forbearance from such proceedings was her consideration, even though the husband's request for such forbearance was not explicit.

3.7 Promises to perform existing duties

3.7.1 Duties imposed by law

Collins v Godefroy (1831) CKB

The defendant subpoenaed the plaintiff, an attorney, as a witness in his case against his previous attorney. The plaintiff attended for six days, though he was not called on to give evidence, and asked the defendant for payment of six guineas, his normal daily rate.

Held a contract to pay a witness for attending court is not enforceable. *Per* Lord Tenterden CJ, even making the assumption that there was an express promise by the defendant to pay the plaintiff for attending:

> If it be a duty imposed by law upon a party regularly *subpoenaed*, to attend from time to time to give evidence, then a promise to give him any remuneration for loss of time incurred in such attendance is a promise without consideration. We think such a duty is imposed by law; and ... we are all of the opinion that a party cannot maintain an action for compensation for loss of time in attending a trial as a witness.

Ward v Byham (1956) CA

The plaintiff mother lived with the defendant father from 1949 and their daughter was born in October 1950. In May 1954, the father turned the mother out and employed a neighbour to care for the daughter for £1 per week. In July 1954, the mother found work as a housekeeper and asked the father for the daughter and for £1 per week maintenance. The father wrote to her:

> I am prepared to let you have [the child] and pay you up to £1 per week allowance for her providing you can prove that she will be well looked after and happy and also that she is allowed to decide for herself whether or not she wishes to come and live with you.

The child went to live with the mother on those terms. When, in February 1955, the mother married the man for whom she had been housekeeper, the father stopped paying the £1 a week.

Held the mother could enforce the father's promise to pay £1 per week for the maintenance of the daughter, even though the mother was under a statutory duty to look after her child regardless of any agreement. (I) *Per* Denning LJ:

> In looking after the child, the mother is only doing what she is legally bound to do. Even so, I think that there was sufficient consideration to support the promise. I have always thought that a promise to perform an existing duty, or the performance of it, should be regarded as good consideration, because it is a benefit to the person to whom it is given.

(II) *Per* Morris and Parker LJJ, the terms of the father's letter showed that there was consideration for the promise to pay £1. Neither of their lordships said which of the conditions laid out in the letter were the mother's consideration.

Q Is what Denning LJ has 'always thought' the law? Should it be?

Williams v Williams (1956) CA

The parties married in April 1945 and they had no children. In January 1952, the wife deserted the husband. In March 1952, they signed an agreement with three clauses:

> (1) The husband will pay to the wife for her support and maintenance a weekly sum of £1 10s to be paid every four weeks during the joint lives of the parties so long as the wife shall lead a chaste life ... (2) The wife will out of the said weekly sum or otherwise support and maintain herself and will indemnify the husband against all debts to be incurred by her and will not in any way at any time hereafter pledge the husband's credit. (3) The wife shall not so long as the husband shall punctually make the payments hereby agreed to be made commence or prosecute against the husband any matrimonial proceedings other than proceedings for dissolution of marriage ...

The husband obtained a divorce in 1955 on the grounds of his wife's desertion. The wife claimed some of the money due under the agreement which had not been paid by the husband.

Held the wife could enforce the husband's promise to pay her maintenance because she had given consideration for it. Clause (3) did not reveal any consideration because it was unenforceable as the wife could not alienate by contract her right to apply for maintenance. However, clause (2) did show consideration moving from the wife. (I) All three of their lordships held that by her desertion, the wife had suspended, but not extinguished, her husband's duty to maintain her. The agreement to accept a sum of £1 10s was therefore a benefit to the husband in case the wife later offered to return to him, when his duty to maintain her would be revived. (II) Denning LJ, but not Hodson or Morris LJJ, gave two further grounds for his decision:

[i] In promising to maintain herself whilst she was in desertion, the wife was only promising to do that which she was already bound to do. Nevertheless, a promise to perform an existing duty is, I think, sufficient consideration to support a promise, so long as there is nothing in the transaction which is contrary to the public interest.

(ii) The wife's promise not to pledge the husband's credit was consideration even though, while in desertion, the wife had no right to pledge the husband's credit. This was because it gave the husband an additional protection against the trouble of fighting false claims on him which could arise if the wife did purport to pledge his credit.

Q   Can you distinguish the consideration in (II)(ii) above from blackmail?

3.7.2   Public duties

Glasbrook Brothers Ltd v Glamorgan County Council and Others (1924) HL

The defendants owned a group of collieries near Swansea. The miners in these collieries refused to accept the terms of the settlement of the national coal strike which ended in July 1921. Remaining on strike, the men put pressure on the 'safety men' to stop work in their support. The job of the safety men was to operate the pumps which kept the mines free from the water which would otherwise flood them, causing great damage in a few days. When the safety men felt unable to work for fear of reprisals from the miners, the defendants went to the police to ask for protection for the safety men. The safety men would only return to work if a garrison of police was billeted at the colliery, but the police thought that a mobile group of police would give adequate protection against any trouble. The defendants agreed to pay the police to have 70 men billeted at the colliery. Within two months, the dispute came to a peaceful end and the defendants refused to pay the £2,200 demanded by the police authority.

Held the police authority could enforce the agreement for payment which was made for consideration and which was not against public policy. The defendants argued that if the police had a duty to act as they did then they gave no consideration for the promise to pay them, and if they had no such duty then it was against public policy to allow them to act thus for payment. However, a majority of their Lordships held that, *per* Viscount Cave LC:

> There may be services rendered by the police which, although not within the scope of their absolute obligations to the public, may yet fall within their powers, and in such cases public policy does not forbid their performance.

Per Viscount Finlay:

There was no duty on the police to give the special protection asked for, but it does not follow that it was their duty not to give it.

The majority felt that it was proper for the police to say, as they did, that they could guarantee the safety of the safety men without the need for a garrison, while the two dissenting judges held that the police did have a duty to provide a garrison because that was the only way to protect the colliery from damage caused by the withdrawal of the safety men.

Note

This decision was effectively confirmed by Parliament in s 15 of the Police Act 1964.

Harris v Sheffield United Football Club Ltd (1987) CA

The police regularly attended at football matches at the Club for which they sought a previously agreed payment from the Club. The Club argued that the police gave no consideration for the promise to pay so it could not be enforced.

Held the Club were bound to pay the charges agreed because the police duties at football matches were special police services and not merely the maintenance of law and order. The reasoning in *Glasbrook Brothers Ltd v Glamorgan County Council and Others* (3.7.2) was applied. The factors which led the court to conclude that these were special services were: that the police attended private premises; that attendance was not to deal with any actual or immediately imminent violence; that the event was of a partly private and partly public nature; and that the policing required was a considerable strain on the resources of the police force. These four factors meant that it was a legitimate use of discretion by the police to decide that duties at football matches were special duties and to charge for them.

3.7.3   Contractual duty owed to third party

Shadwell v Shadwell and Another (1860)

The defendants were the executor and executrix of the deceased Charles Shadwell. The plaintiff was Charles Shadwell's nephew. The plaintiff was engaged to be married and was starting a career at the bar when his uncle wrote a letter to him in these terms:

I am glad to hear of your intended marriage with Ellen Nicholl; and, as I promised to assist you at starting, I am happy to tell you that I will pay to you £150 yearly during my life and until your annual income derived from your profession of a Chancery barrister shall amount to 600 guineas.

The plaintiff claimed that 18 yearly sums became payable under that letter but that the uncle had only paid 12. He claimed the remaining six payments. The defendants argued that the plaintiff gave no consideration for the uncle's promise, and the plaintiff pleaded in reply that he went ahead with his marriage 'relying on the promise of' his uncle.

Held the plaintiff gave consideration for the payments by going ahead with the marriage. (I) Erle CJ, speaking for himself and Keating J, held that, in all the surrounding circumstances, a request from the uncle to complete the planned marriage could be inferred from the letter. The payments were promised as an inducement to marry. (II) Byles J dissented. He held: (i) There was no request by the uncle to the plaintiff to marry, only an expression of satisfaction at the engagement which had already taken place. (ii) Since the plaintiff was already legally bound to marry because he was engaged, a promise to do so could not be consideration. *Per* Byles J:

> The reason why doing what a man is already bound to do is no consideration, is, not only because such consideration is in judgment of law of no value, but because a man can hardly be allowed to say that the prior legal obligation was not his determining motive.

Note ───────────────────────────────────

In *Jones v Padavatton* (see 2.2.1), Salmon LJ said, *obiter*, of *Shadwell v Shadwell and Another* that it 'was a curious case. It was decided ... on a pleading point, and depended largely upon the true construction of a letter written by an uncle to his nephew. I confess that I should have decided it without hesitation in accordance with the views of Byles J'.

Scotson and Others v Pegg (1861)

The plaintiffs agreed with third parties to carry a cargo of coal to the order of the third parties. The third parties ordered the plaintiffs to deliver the coal to the defendant. The plaintiffs then made an agreement with the defendant that the plaintiffs would deliver the coal to the defendant and the defendant would unload it at the rate of 49 tons a day. The defendant failed to unload quickly enough and the plaintiffs sued for damages. The defendant argued that the plaintiffs had not given good consideration for the defendant's promise to unload at a certain rate.

Held the plaintiffs' consideration was good so the plaintiffs could enforce the contract. The plaintiffs' promise to deliver the coal to the defendant was a benefit to the defendant because it was possible that the plaintiffs' obligation to the third parties to deliver the coal to the defendant was disputed by the plaintiffs. *Per* Wilde B:

> ... there is no authority for the proposition that where there has been a promise to one person to do a certain thing, it is not possible to make a valid promise to another to do the same thing.

The New Zealand Shipping Co Ltd v AM Satterthwaite & Co Ltd: *The Eurymedon* (1974) PC

The carrier shipped a drilling machine from Liverpool to Wellington consigned to the plaintiff consignee. The carrier was a wholly owned subsidiary of the defendant stevedore which carried out all the unloading of loads carried by the carrier to Wellington. In August 1964, the stevedore negligently damaged the drill during unloading. By that time, the drill was owned by the consignee who held the bill of lading which was the consignee's contract with the carrier. The bill of lading gave the carrier exemption from any liability for damaging the drill unless an action was started against them within one year. This action was only started in April 1967. The bill of lading said that all exemptions of the carrier would apply to every servant or agent of the carrier and that, for these purposes:

> ... the carrier is or shall be deemed to be acting as agent or trustee on behalf of and for the benefit of all persons who are or might be his servants or agents from time to time (including independent contractors ...) and all such persons shall to this extent be or be deemed to be parties to the contract in or evidenced by this bill of lading.

Held the stevedore could rely on the exemption from actions started after more than a year. (I) *Scruttons Ltd v Midland Silicones Ltd* (4.1) left open the possibility that a third party could benefit from a clause in a contract where one of the parties contracted as agent for the third party. In this case, the carrier contracted as agent for the stevedore. (II) (3.3) The stevedore could rely on the exemption in the bill of lading only if it had given consideration. *Per* Lord Wilberforce, delivering the majority judgment:

> ... the bill of lading brought into existence a bargain initially unilateral but capable of becoming mutual, between the shippers and the stevedore, made through the carrier as agent. This became a full contract when the stevedore performed services by discharging the goods. The performance of these services for the benefit of the shipper was the consideration for the agreement by the shipper that the stevedore should have the benefit of the exemptions and limitations contained in the bill of lading.

(III) Although it was assumed that the stevedore was obliged to unload by some contract with the carrier, *per* Lord Wilberforce:

> An agreement to do an act which the promisor is under an existing obligation to a third party to do, may quite well amount to valid consideration and does so in the present case: the promisee obtains the benefit of a direct obligation which he can enforce. This proposition is illustrated and supported by *Scotson and Others v Pegg* [3.7.3] which their lordships consider to be good law.

Pao On and Others v Lau Yiu Long and Another (1979) PC

See 3.5.2.

3.7.4 Contractual duty owed to promisor

Stilk v Myrick (1809)

The plaintiff agreed to act as a seaman on a voyage from London to the Baltic and back for £5 per month. During the voyage, two seamen deserted and the captain agreed to share the wages of the two deserters between the remaining nine seamen if they would remain to take the ship back to London. The plaintiff claimed his share of the additional wages which the defendant resisted paying.

Held the plaintiff could not enforce the agreement which was, *per* Lord Ellenborough, 'void for want of consideration'. The plaintiff could recover only the £5 per month due under the original contract. The seamen 'had undertaken to do all they could under all the emergencies of the voyage' and:

> ... the desertion of a part of the crew is to be considered an emergency of the voyage as much as their death, and those who remain are bound by the terms of their original contract to exert themselves to the utmost to bring the ship in safely to her destined port.

Hartley v Ponsonby (1857)

The plaintiff and 35 others agreed to serve as seamen on a return voyage from Liverpool to last up to three years. The plaintiff was to receive £3 per month. After three months, the ship reached Australia where 17 of the crew were imprisoned for refusing to work. The defendant, who was the ship's master, could not find further crew members at a reasonable price, but he hoped to do so in Bombay. He persuaded the remaining 19 men to continue to Bombay by promising to pay some of them extra money when they got back to Liverpool. He made a written promise to pay the plaintiff £40 'providing he assist in taking [the ship] from this port to Bombay with a crew of nineteen hands'. When they got back, the defendant failed to pay the additional £40.

Held the plaintiff could enforce the promise to pay him an extra £40. This was because it was so dangerous to sail the ship with such a small crew, that it was unreasonable to expect the crew to continue. Thus the plaintiff was not obliged to help under his original contract so he was free to make a new agreement. Although the plaintiff drove a hard bargain, there was no duress.

Note ─────────────────────────

The original contract between the parties could be said to have been frustrated (for frustration, see Chapter 8).

North Ocean Shipping Co Ltd v Hyundai Construction Co Ltd and Another: The Atlantic Baron (1978) QB

In April 1972, the defendant yard agreed to build a vessel for the plaintiff owners. The price was US$30,950,000 to be paid in five instalments. In February 1973, the US dollar was devalued by 10%. In April 1973, the yard demanded that the four instalments not yet paid be increased by 10% to compensate them for the devaluation of the dollar. The owners resisted the increase for which there was no legal basis. In May 1973, unknown to the yard, the owners agreed a three year time charterparty for the vessel with Shell. The yard continued to insist on the price increase and, on 26 June 1973, they threatened to terminate the contract if the owners did not agree by 30 June. The owners, who did not want to lose their deal with Shell, sent a telex saying:

> Although we are convinced we are under no obligation to make additional payments which you ask, we are prepared as you demand ... and in order to maintain an amicable relationship and without prejudice to our rights, to make an increase of 10% in instalments payable subsequent to 12 February 1973. No doubt you will arrange for corresponding increases in the letter of credit.

The letter of credit provided security for the repayment to the owners of money paid to the yard if the yard defaulted in performance of the contract. The owners paid the extra costs and the vessel was delivered on 27 November 1974. The owners wanted to recover the extra 10% they had paid and they made their claim to do so on 30 July 1975.

Held by Mocatta J the owners could not recover the additional payments: (I) There was consideration for the increased price. (i) Following *Stilk v Myrick* (3.7.4) the yard's completion of the boat in accordance with the contract of April 1972 could not be consideration moving from the yard, nor could the maintenance of an amicable relationship. (ii) The increase of the letter of credit was consideration for the increased payments. (II) (10.1) The yard's threat to break its contract was economic duress and it was this duress which forced the owners to agree to the price increase. The contract for the price increase was therefore voidable by the owners for duress. (III) By delaying between 27 November 1974 and 30 July 1975, the owners affirmed the agreement and lost their right to avoid it.

Q   Could the economic duress argument (which was a novelty in a decided case in 1978) be applied to *Stilk v Myrick* (3.7.4)?

Williams v Roffey Bros and Nicholls (Contractors) Ltd (1989) CA

The defendants were the main contractors in the refurbishment of a block of 27 flats. The defendants engaged the plaintiff as sub-contractor to undertake the carpentry work on the flats and some of the work on the roof. By an agreement between the parties made on 21 January 1986, the plaintiff would be paid £20,000. The timing of payments was not specified. By the end of March 1986, the plaintiff had completed much of the work and had received £16,200. However, the plaintiff had run into financial problems for two reasons: (i) the price of £20,000 was too low to allow him to make a profit. The defendants' own surveyor said that a reasonable price would be £23,783; (ii) the plaintiff failed to supervise his workmen adequately. On 9 April 1986, the parties made an oral agreement that the defendants would pay an additional £10,300, to be paid in instalments of £575 on the completion of the plaintiff's work on each of the 18 flats which were not already finished. By the end of May 1986, the plaintiff stopped work having substantially but not completely finished work in another eight flats and having been paid a further £1,500.

Held the plaintiff was entitled to payment under the terms of the agreement of 9 April. (I) Following *Hoenig v Isaacs* (12.1.2), substantial completion entitled the plaintiff to payment after making a deduction for the incomplete parts. (II) The plaintiff could enforce the agreement of 9 April, as he had given consideration for it. (i) *Per* Glidewell LJ:

(i) If A has entered into a contract with B to do work for, or to supply goods or services to, B in return for payment by B and (ii) at some stage before A has completely performed his obligations under the contract B has some reason to doubt whether A will, or will be able to, complete his side of the bargain and (iii) B thereupon promises A an additional payment in return for A's promise to perform his contractual obligations on time and (iv) as a result of giving his promise B obtains in practice a benefit, or obviates a disbenefit, and (v) B's promise is not given as a result of economic duress or fraud on the part of A, then (vi) the benefit to B is capable of being consideration for B's promise, so that the promise will be legally binding.

This refines and limits the application of the principle in *Stilk v Myrick* (3.7.4) but leaves it unscathed. (ii) *Per* Russell LJ:

In the late 20th century, I do not believe that the rigid approach to the concept of consideration to be found in *Stilk v Myrick* is either necessary or desirable. Consideration there must still be but in my judgment the courts nowadays should be more ready to find its existence ... where the bargaining powers are not unequal and where the finding of consideration reflects the true intention of the parties.

Getting the work finished by the plaintiff and having a more formalised scheme of payments were in this case good consideration received by the defendants. (iii) *Per* Purchas LJ:

Prima facie this would appear to be a classic *Stilk v Myrick* case ... With some hesitation ... I consider that the modern approach to the question of consideration would be that where there were benefits derived by each party to a contract of variation even though one party did not suffer a detriment this would not be fatal to the establishing of sufficient consideration to support the agreement ... On the facts found by the judge [in the court below], he was entitled to reach the conclusion that consideration existed and in those circumstances I would not disturb that finding.

3.7.5 Part payment of a debt

Pinnel's Case (1602) CCP

The defendant owed the plaintiff £8 10s due to be paid on 11 November 1600. The defendant had paid £5 2s 2d on 1 October at the request of the plaintiff who had accepted the early payment in full satisfaction of the debt. The plaintiff now sought the £16 due under a bond if the defendant had not paid the debt in full.

Held paying the debt before it was due at the creditor's request was sufficient consideration for the discharge of the whole debt in this case. However, *obiter*:

> ... payment of a lesser sum on the day in satisfaction of a greater, cannot be any satisfaction for the whole ... but the gift of a horse, hawk, or robe, etc in satisfaction is good ... If I am bound ... to pay you £10 at Westminster and you request me to pay you £5 at the day in York, and you will accept it in full satisfaction of the whole £10 it is a good satisfaction for the whole.

Note

(a) The 'rule in *Pinnel's Case*' is the *dictum* that payment of a lesser sum on the same day (or later) and at the same place as the original debt was due is not sufficient consideration for the discharge of the whole debt. (b) The case was decided for the plaintiff because of a technical deficiency in the defendant's pleadings.

Foakes v Beer (1884) HL

The plaintiff obtained a court judgment against the defendant for £2,090 19s in August 1875. In December 1876, the parties made a written agreement which stated that the plaintiff had agreed to the defendant's request for time to pay. The plaintiff accepted £500 at the time of the agreement 'in part satisfaction' of the debt; and, on the condition that the defendant would pay sums of £150 every six months until the £2,090 19s was paid, the plaintiff promised not to 'take any proceedings whatever on the said judgment'. The agreement did not mention interest to which the plaintiff was entitled by statute at the rate of 4% per year. In June 1882, the plaintiff brought the action to confirm that she was still entitled to interest from the defendant even though the defendant had made all the payments due under the agreement of December 1876.

Held the plaintiff was still entitled to the interest. (I) The agreement was a unilateral contract by which the plaintiff promised to accept the instalments if the defendant chose to pay them. (i) *Per* the Earl of Selborne LC and Lord Blackburn, the agreement must be construed as a promise by the plaintiff to accept instalments to the total of £2,019 19s as full satisfaction of both the debt and interest, that is, to accept payment without any interest. (ii) Lord Watson and Lord Fitzgerald construed the agreement as including a promise by the plaintiff to accept the instalments as satisfaction of only the judgment sum itself and not of any interest. They therefore found for the plaintiff on the basis that she had never agreed any compromise of her right to receive interest. However, they went on to consider argument (II) in case their view on argument (I) was wrong. (II) Applying the rule in *Pinnel's Case* (3.7.5), the defendant had given no consideration for the plaintiff's promise to forgive the interest. The promise of a lesser sum (£2,090 19s), paid later than it was due, could not be consideration for the discharge of a greater sum (£2,090 19s plus interest at 4%). All of the judges expressed some doubt as to whether the rule was a good thing, but they were not prepared to change a rule that had been accepted for so long, even though it had rarely been the *ratio decidendi* of authoritative decisions. Lord Blackburn's judgment amounted to an argument against the rule, but he bowed to the views of the other three judges in the final result. *Per* Lord Blackburn:

> All men of business, whether merchants or tradesmen, do every day recognise and act on the ground that prompt payment of a part of their demand may be more beneficial to them than it would be to insist on their rights and enforce payment of the whole.

Q How is the later development of promissory estoppel (3.8) to be reconciled with this case?

Hirachand Punamchand and Others v Temple (1911) CA

The defendant, an officer in the British army in India, borrowed money from the plaintiffs, Indian moneylenders, giving them a bond and a promissory note. When the defendant could not repay them, the plaintiffs wrote to the defendant's father in London asking for the money. After some correspondence, the defendant's father sent banker's drafts for a lesser sum which it was clear that he intended in full settlement of the debt. The plaintiffs wrote back demanding the rest of the money and saying that they would cash the drafts and credit the amount to the account. Having cashed the drafts, they sued the defendant for the remaining debt.

Held the plaintiffs could not recover any further sums from the defendant. The plaintiffs could not be heard to say that they had cashed the drafts without accepting the terms upon which they were sent as to have done so would have been dishonest. So, it had to be presumed that the plaintiffs had accepted the drafts from the defendant's father in full settlement. The principle which then applied was that when a creditor accepts a lesser sum from a third party the creditor can no longer proceed for the rest of the debt. Their lordships gave several reasons for this principle. (I) *Per* Vaughan Williams LJ: (i) in equity, any further money received by the creditor would be held on trust for the third party and the third party was opposed to insisting on further payment; (ii) even at common law it would be a 'fraud upon the stranger' to insist on further payment. (II) *Per* Fletcher Moulton LJ either (i) 'there is an extinction of the debt'; or (ii) 'it would be an abuse of the process of the court to allow the creditor under such circumstances to sue'.

Vanbergen v St Edmunds Properties Ltd (1933) CA

The plaintiff owed a sum of money to the defendants. The defendants promised not to proceed to serve a bankruptcy notice on the plaintiff if he paid them by 7 July 1932. On 6 July, the plaintiff telephoned the defendants' solicitor saying that he could not get the money in time, but that he could borrow it at Eastbourne on Friday, 8 July. The defendants' solicitor therefore agreed to allow the plaintiff until midday on 8 July to get the money to the defendants and required the plaintiff to pay it in at Eastbourne for the credit of the solicitor's account at the law courts branch of the Bank of England. This would make the money available to the defendants in London on 8 July. The plaintiff did obtain the money and paid it as required on 8 July. However, the plaintiff's letter to the solicitor telling him of the payment did not arrive. The solicitor therefore sent a clerk to the plaintiff's office at 6.00 pm on 8 July and the clerk served a bankruptcy notice on the plaintiff. One of the plaintiff's business associates heard the discussion through a partly open door and the plaintiff lost the chance of dealing with the associate on credit terms as a result. The plaintiff therefore sued for damages consequent on the breach of the agreement by the defendants not to serve the notice if the plaintiff paid the money at Eastbourne by 8 July.

Held the plaintiff had given no consideration so he could not enforce the agreement. Payment of a debt at a certain place (Eastbourne) was not consideration where, as in this case, the place was a 'voluntary indulgence' given by the creditors for the benefit of the debtor. The creditors gained no advantage from payment in Eastbourne so *Foakes v Beer* (3.7.5) would be followed.

In Re Selectmove Ltd (1993) CA

See 1.2.4.

3.8 Waiver and estoppel

3.8.1 Waiver

Hartley v Hymans (1920) KB

The plaintiff and the defendant made a written contract that the plaintiff would sell to the defendant 11,000 lb of cotton yarn to be delivered at 1,100 lb per week starting in the first week of September 1918. The defendant's right to cancel in the event of the plaintiff failing to deliver on time was specified in the contract. The plaintiff made deliveries much later and in smaller quantities than the contract required. The defendant repeatedly wrote urging the plaintiff to deliver as soon as possible and reminding the plaintiff that the defendant could cancel the contract if he chose. In March 1919, when the plaintiff was finally ready to deliver the remainder of the order, the defendant, without giving any final warning or demand, refused to accept any further deliveries.

Held by McCardie J the plaintiff was entitled to damages for the defendant's refusal to take delivery. (I) By his letters, the defendant had waived his right to insist on delivery within the contract time. Because the plaintiff had acted at great expense in reliance on the waiver, the defendant could not assert his former rights. (II) 'I hold that (in so far as estoppel differs from waiver) the defendant is estopped from saying that the period for delivery expired on 15 November 1918, or from asserting that the contract ceased to be valid on that date.' (III) A new agreement would be implied that the contract should extend until the defendant gave the plaintiff a notice requiring delivery within some reasonable period, which he had never done.

Charles Rickards Ltd v Oppenheim (1950) CA

In July 1947, the defendant ordered a car from the plaintiffs to be built to his specification. Time was important to the defendant and the plaintiffs found a sub-contractor, JBC, who promised to complete the work in six or seven months which promise the plaintiffs passed on to the defendant. After seven months expired, the defendant pressed for delivery from the plaintiffs and from JBC, the plaintiffs having authorised the defendant to deal directly with JBC regarding the specifications of the work. On 28 June 1948, JBC promised the defendant that the car would be ready in two weeks. On the next day, the defendant wrote to JBC that he would not accept delivery of the car after 25 July. The plaintiffs received a copy of the letter from JBC on 6 or 7 July. The car was finished on 18 October 1948 and the defendant refused delivery.

Held the defendant was entitled to refuse to receive or pay for the car. The defendant had waived his specification of a seven month contract period by pressing for delivery after the seven months had expired and he could no longer rely on his rights under that contract. However, the defendant was entitled to reassert that time was of the essence by giving reasonable notice. In all the circumstances, the defendant's letter of 29 June was reasonable notice to both JBC and the plaintiffs that they must deliver the car by a certain date which they failed to do.

3.8.2 Promissory estoppel

Jorden v Money (1854) HL

The plaintiff, jointly with two others, borrowed £1,200 from the defendant's brother in 1841, giving the lender a bond. The defendant's brother died in 1843 leaving the plaintiff's bond to the defendant. The defendant let the plaintiff know that she believed that the plaintiff had been exploited in borrowing the money and that it would not be just or honourable to enforce the bond. In 1845, the plaintiff became engaged to marry and wanted to be sure that the bond would not be enforced against him. The defendant promised several times that she would never enforce the bond against the plaintiff but wanted to keep it in case she could enforce it against the other two debtors. Relying on the promises, the plaintiff married his fiancée. This action was brought by the plaintiff some years later, after the defendant had herself married, for a declaration that the bond had been abandoned and could not now be enforced.

Held the defendant could still enforce the bond if she chose to do so. Lord Cranworth LC confirmed the rule of law and equity known as estoppel that a person who makes a false representation of a fact which is acted on by another cannot afterwards deny that fact in proceedings against that other person. The rule applied even where the representor did not know that the representation was false, but it was limited to cases where the representor had reasonable grounds for supposing that the representee would act upon the representation. However, *per* Lord Cranworth LC:

> ... the doctrine does not apply to a case where the representation is not a representation of fact, but a statement of something which a party intends or does not intend to do.

The defendant in this case never represented that she had executed a legal release from the debt, but only that she intended not to enforce it. She could change her mind at will, so the plaintiff could not have the declaration he sought.

Hughes v Metropolitan Railway Company (1877) HL

The defendants were tenants of a group of houses which they held from the plaintiff on a 99 year lease. The lease allowed the landlord to give notice to the tenant of repairs which the tenant would have to carry out within six months of the notice. On 22 October 1874, the plaintiff gave the defendants such a notice to repair. On 28 November, the defendants wrote to the plaintiff suggesting that the plaintiff might want to buy out the defendants' remaining interest in the lease and saying 'we propose to defer commencing the repairs until we hear from you as to the probability of an arrangement such as we suggest'. The plaintiff replied on 1 December asking the defendants to suggest a price. On 30 December, the defendants wrote suggesting a price of £3,000. On 31 December, the plaintiffs wrote back:

> We think the price asked for is out of all reason. We must therefore request you to reconsider the question of price, having regard to our previous observations, and to the fact that the company have already been served with notice to put the premises in repair, and we shall be glad to receive in due course a modified proposal from you.

On 19 April 1875, the defendants told the plaintiff that, since no sale had been agreed, they would now make the necessary repairs. On 22 April 1875, the six months expired and, on 28 April, the plaintiff began proceedings for possession of the property based on the defendants' failure to repair in time. The repairs were completed in mid-June 1875.

Held by entering negotiations following the defendants' letter of 28 November, the plaintiff had agreed to suspend the time running on the six month notice to repair. The negotiations continued at least until 31 December 1874 and the defendants had until six months from that date to complete the repairs. *Per* Lord Cairns LC:

> ... if parties who have entered into definite and distinct terms involving certain legal results – certain penalties or legal forfeiture – afterwards by their own act or with their own consent enter upon a course of negotiation which has the effect of leading one of the parties to suppose that the strict rights arising under the contract will not be enforced, or will be kept in suspense, or held in abeyance, the person who otherwise might have enforced those rights will not be allowed to enforce them where it would be inequitable having regard to the dealings which have thus taken place between the parties.

Central London Property Trust Ltd v High Trees House Ltd (1946) KB

The defendants were a wholly owned subsidiary company of the plaintiffs. In 1937, the plaintiffs let a block of flats to the defendants for 99 years at a rent of £2,500 per year. By the outbreak of the war in September 1939, the block was one-third occupied. Because of the war, the defendants could not find enough tenants to cover the rent they were to pay to the plaintiffs. The plaintiffs therefore, in January 1940, reduced the rent to £1,250 per year. In 1941, a receiver was appointed to manage the affairs of the plaintiffs. From early 1945 the block was fully occupied. In September 1945, the receiver realised that the full rent was not being paid and he brought an action to test the effect of the plaintiffs' agreement to a reduction in rent. The claim was for the arrears from July 1945.

Held by Denning J, the rent reduction was a promise to charge the reduced rent for so long as war conditions prevented the full occupation of the block. In the event, this period ended in early 1945 when the block was occupied. Therefore, the arrears claimed were recoverable at the rate of £2,500 per year. *Obiter*, the plaintiffs would not have succeeded if they had sought to claim the full rent for the period between January 1940 and early 1945.

> Promises which were intended to create legal relations and which, in the knowledge of the person making the promise, were going to be acted on by the party to whom the promise was made, and have in fact been so acted on ... must be honoured.

Denning J distinguished *Jorden v Money* (3.8.2):

> ... because there the promisor made it clear that she did not intend to be legally bound,

and cited *Hughes v Metropolitan Railway Company* (3.8.2) in support of the principle which he had outlined. He also stated that:

> ... the logical consequence, no doubt, is that a promise to accept a smaller sum in discharge of a larger sum, if acted on, is binding not withstanding the absence of consideration.

Q   (a) How far does the decision in *Hughes v Metropolitan Railway Company* (3.8.2) support the principle stated by Denning J in this case? (b) How is the conflict between Denning J's remarks about the acceptance of a smaller sum in discharge of a larger and the case of *Foakes v Beer* (3.7.5) to be resolved? (c) How persuasive is Denning J's attempt to distinguish *Jorden v Money* (3.8.2)?

Combe v Combe (1951) CA

See 3.6.4.

Tool Metal Manufacturing Co Ltd v Tungsten Electric Co Ltd (1955) HL

The plaintiff company, TMMC, granted the defendant company, TECO, certain rights over some of TMMC's patents by an agreement made in April 1938. TECO agreed to pay specified fees, including onerous 'compensation' if they sold more than a certain quantity of the metal alloys which were the subject of the agreement. From April 1942, TECO stopped paying the amounts due for compensation. TMMC said that they would not claim the compensation payments pending a re-negotiation of the contract between the parties. In September 1944, TECO rejected an amended agreement suggested by TMMC and, in January 1945, TECO sued TMMC claiming that the agreements had been made through fraud on TMMC's part. In March 1946, TMMC denied the fraud and counterclaimed for the compensation due from June 1945. (TMMC did not seek to claim the compensation for the three years up to the end of the war.) In 1950, the Court of Appeal decided the case holding that the fraud was not proved and that the counter-claim must fail. The counterclaim failed because of TMMC's promise not to enforce payment of compensation which gave rise to an equity as in *Hughes v Metropolitan Railway Company* (3.8.2). Later in 1950, this action was started by TMMC who now claimed the compensation payments from January 1947.

Held after TMMC had suspended their right to claim the compensation payments, they had to give TECO reasonable notice before their rights could be resumed. TMMC's counterclaim made in March 1946 was a 'clear intimation' that they would seek to enforce their rights in the future. Nine months was a reasonable time to allow TECO to take account of the new situation, so TMMC must succeed in their claim for payments from January 1947 onwards. *Per* Viscount Simonds:

> The gist of the equity lies in the fact that one party has by his conduct led the other to alter his position. I lay stress on this, because I would not have it supposed, particularly in commercial transactions, that mere acts of indulgence are apt to create rights ...

D and C Builders Ltd v Rees (1965) CA

The plaintiffs were a two man building company which did some work on the defendant's shop in May and June 1964. After some payments, a balance of over £480 remained unpaid. In November 1964, the defendant offered £300 in full settlement. The plaintiffs were close to bankruptcy, which the defendant knew, and so they reluctantly accepted the defendant's cheque for £300. The plaintiffs now sued for the remaining £180.

Held the plaintiffs could claim the £180. (I) All three of their lordships held that at common law the rule in *Pinnel's Case* (3.7.5) and *Foakes v Beer*

(3.7.5) applied to allow the plaintiffs to claim the balance of the debt. (II) *Per* Lord Denning MR, promissory estoppel could apply in this case to prevent the plaintiffs insisting on their rights, but it was not equitable to apply the doctrine because the defendant extracted the plaintiffs' promise by holding the plaintiffs 'to ransom'.

WJ Alan Ltd v El Nasr Export and Import Co (1972) CA

The parties made two written contracts, each for the sale of 250 tons of coffee at a price of 262 shillings per hundredweight. At the time, the Kenyan shilling was equal in value to the UK shilling, but, on its true construction, the contract was held to refer to Kenyan shillings. Payment for the coffee was expressed to be 'by confirmed irrevocable letter of credit'. The defendant buyers set up a letter of credit which was expressed in sterling and which did not conform to the contract in various other respects. Following two shipments of coffee, totalling 279 tons, the plaintiff sellers issued two invoices expressed in sterling which were paid by the buyers' bank. A third shipment of the remaining 221 tons was made and the sellers made out an invoice expressed in sterling. Then they heard that sterling had been devalued, but the Kenyan shilling was not devalued. The sellers claimed that they were entitled to payment in Kenyan shillings under the contract and sued the buyers for the difference caused by the devaluation of sterling.

Held the sellers could not claim the difference. By making use of the sterling letter of credit, the sellers had accepted the use of sterling despite the contract's reference to the Kenyan currency. (I) (i) *Per* Lord Denning MR, the sellers had waived their right to be paid in Kenyan shillings. It was an instance of the principle of waiver 'first enunciated by Lord Cairns LC in *Hughes v Metropolitan Railway Company* (3.8.2), and rescued from oblivion in *Central London Property Trust Ltd v High Trees House Ltd* (3.8.2)'. (ii) Megaw LJ held that the change from Kenyan shillings to sterling was a variation in the contract, binding both parties. Because either party could gain or lose from the change at the time it was made, both gave consideration for the variation. Megaw LJ also held that if there were not a variation, the buyers would still succeed on the basis of waiver. (iii) Stephenson LJ held that there was either variation for consideration or waiver. (II) Lord Denning MR commented that while a waiver sometimes merely suspends strict rights, 'there are cases where no withdrawal is possible. It may be too late to withdraw; or it cannot be done without injustice to the other party. In that event he is bound by his waiver'. Megaw LJ held that the waiver in this case was effective once and for all, not merely temporarily. (III) Lord Denning MR held that waiver could apply whenever the promisee has acted on the belief induced by the other party, even where the promisee has not suffered any detriment thereby.

Stephenson LJ held that there was detriment in this case and declined to express a view on whether waiver could apply without detriment.

Société Italo-Belge pour le Commerce et l'Industrie SA v Palm and Vegetable Oils (Malaysia) Sdn Bhd: *The Post Chaser* (1981) QB

The plaintiff sellers agreed to sell 250 tons of Malayan Palm Oil at $792.50 per ton to the defendant buyers. The sellers obtained the oil from K who were shipping it to Rotterdam. The practice in the market was that a string of traders who had previously contracted with each other would each declare the shipment to the next within a few hours of receiving their own declaration. K declared the shipment to the sellers on 16 December 1974. However, the sellers only declared to the buyers on 10 January 1975. This delay was a breach of their agreement with the buyers. The buyers made no protest, and declared to Conti who declared to L&P who declared to IPP who declared to NOGA. On 14 January, NOGA rejected the shipment because of the delay in declaring it. On 20 January, Conti told the buyers that they would insist on maintaining the string and asked the buyers to arrange for them to receive the documents in Rotterdam. The buyers therefore sent a message to K that day asking K to give the documents directly to Conti. This was done, but NOGA still refused the shipment and this rejection was passed up the string to the sellers on 22 January. The sellers sold the shipment for only $460 per ton and now claimed the difference between that price and $792.50 per ton from the buyers as damages.

Held the loss was due to the default of the sellers who could not recover it from the buyers. (I) The buyers' lack of protest on 10 January was not an unequivocal representation that the buyers would waive their rights to reject the shipment because of the sellers' delay. However, the buyers' message of 20 January was an unequivocal representation that they would accept the documents and the shipment. (II) For equitable estoppel to apply to the representation, it had to be shown that the sellers had acted in reliance upon the buyers' representation in such a way that it became inequitable for the buyers to go back on it. *Per* Robert Goff J: 'To establish such inequity, it is not necessary to show detriment.' In this case, the sellers acted in reliance upon the representation by presenting the documents through K, but, given that only two days passed between the representation (on 20 January) and its withdrawal (on 22 January), the sellers suffered no prejudice from relying on the representation and there was nothing to make the buyer's withdrawal of their representation inequitable.

Allied Marine Transport Ltd v Vale do Rio Doce Navegacao SA:
The Leonidas D (1985) CA

See 1.2.4.

In Re Selectmove Ltd (1993) CA

See 1.2.4.

3.8.3 Proprietary estoppel

Crabb v Arun District Council (1975) CA

The plaintiff owned a piece of land which was divided into two portions. He intended to sell the two portions separately for development. The first portion had a right to access to the public road but the second did not. The plaintiff therefore met with the defendant council in July 1967 and obtained agreement for an access point for the second portion. The agreement was never reduced to writing and the council did not ask for any payment from the plaintiff. That winter, the council put up a fence along the land's boundary leaving two gaps for the two access points. In February 1968, the council ordered the construction of a gate at each of the two access points. In autumn 1968, the plaintiff sold the first portion without reserving any right of way for the owner of the second portion, as he relied on the access point available since the oral agreement of July 1967. In January 1969, the plaintiff padlocked the gate of the second portion, which so incensed the council that they tore the gate down and put up a fence in the gap. The council then demanded £3,000 to give the plaintiff access to the public road for the second portion.

Held the plaintiff was entitled to access without having to pay the council. Where A acts in reliance on encouragement from B that A has a right in land while B knows that B has a right (at common law) in the land which conflicts with the right A believes himself to have, B will be estopped (in equity) from denying the right which he has encouraged A to act on. This kind of estoppel, unlike promissory estoppel, may found a cause of action for A, not merely a defence.

3.8.4 Estoppel by convention

Amalgamated Investment and Property Co Ltd (in liquidation) v Texas Commerce International Bank Ltd (1981) CA

The plaintiff, AIP, wholly owned a Bahamas company, ANPP. ANPP needed a loan of $3,250,000 for a property development in the Bahamas. The loan was negotiated between the defendant bank and AIP. AIP signed a guarantee of all moneys lent by the bank to ANPP. The bank made the loan through its own Bahamas subsidiary company, Portsoken. Later AIP itself borrowed money in England from the bank. Both loans were secured on the properties they concerned as well as by guarantees. When AIP was unable to meet the loan repayments, the bank sold the properties in England and in the Bahamas. The proceeds from the property in the Bahamas were not sufficient to meet the loan to ANPP and the bank made up the shortfall of $750,000 from the surplus on the sale of AIP's English properties. The liquidator of AIP now claimed that the surplus on the sale of the AIP properties in England should not be used to meet the shortfall on the ANPP property in the Bahamas because the guarantee only applied to money lent to ANPP by the bank itself and not to money lent by the bank's subsidiary, Portsoken.

Held the bank could keep the money. (I) The guarantee should be construed in the light of the surrounding correspondence and circumstances. In that light, the guarantee was intended to include loans from Portsoken which was no more than, *per* Lord Denning MR, the '*alter ego* of the bank'. (II) If their lordships were wrong about point (I), then AIP would be estopped from denying that it had guaranteed the loan from Portsoken to ANPP. They had dealt for some years on the common assumption that the guarantee applied to the loan from Portsoken and the bank had given indulgences to and refrained from exercising its full rights against AIP as a result. *Per* Lord Denning MR:

> ... where the parties to a contract are both under a common mistake as to the meaning or effect of it and thereafter embark on a course of dealing on the footing of that mistake, thereby replacing the original terms of the contract by a conventional basis on which they both conduct their affairs, then the original contract is replaced by the conventional basis.

3.8.5 The relationship between waiver and equitable estoppel

Motor Oil Hellas (Corinth) Refineries SA v Shipping Corporation of India: The Kanchenjunga (1990) HL

In this case, Lord Goff of Chieveley, in a speech with which the other members of the House of Lords agreed, took the opportunity to state the general principles of the law of waiver and of promissory estoppel and to relate them to each other.

Held per Lord Goff:

> It is a commonplace that the expression 'waiver' is one which may, in law, bear different meanings. In particular, it may refer to a forbearance from exercising a right or to an abandonment of a right. Here, we are concerned with waiver in the sense of abandonment of a right which arises by virtue of a party making an election. Election itself is a concept which may be relevant in more than one context. In the present case, we are concerned with an election which may arise

in the context of a binding contract, when a state of affairs comes into existence in which one party becomes entitled, either under the terms of the contract or by the general law, to exercise a right, and he has to decide whether or not to do so.

...

Election is to be contrasted with equitable estoppel, a principle associated with the leading case of *Hughes v Metropolitan Railway Co* [3.8.2]. Equitable estoppel occurs where a person, having legal rights against another, unequivocally represents (by words or conduct) that he does not intend to enforce those rights; if in such circumstances the other party acts, or desists from acting, in reliance upon that representation, with the effect that it would be inequitable for the representor thereafter to enforce his legal rights inconsistently with his representation, he will to that extent be precluded from doing so.

There is an important similarity between the two principles, election and equitable estoppel, in that each requires an unequivocal representation, perhaps because each may involve a loss, permanent or temporary, of the relevant party's rights. But, there are important differences as well. In the context of a contract, the principle of election applies when a state of affairs comes into existence in which one party becomes entitled to exercise a right, and has to choose whether to exercise the right or not. His election has generally to be an informed choice, made with knowledge of the facts giving rise to the right. His election once made is final; it is not dependent upon reliance on it by the other party. On the other hand, equitable estoppel requires an unequivocal representation by one party that he will not insist upon his legal rights against the other party, and such reliance by the representee as will render it inequitable for the representor to go back upon his representation. No question arises of any particular knowledge on the part of the representor, and the estoppel may be suspensory only. Furthermore, the representation itself is different in character in the two cases. The party making his election is communicating his choice whether or not to exercise a right which has become available to him. The party to an equitable estoppel is representing that he will not in future enforce his legal rights. His representation is therefore in the nature of a promise which, though unsupported by consideration, can have legal consequences; hence it is sometimes referred to as promissory estoppel.

4 Privity

Note

If the Contracts (Rights of Third Parties) Bill is made into law, it will allow third parties to sue directly on contracts which confer rights upon them. The Bill passed the House of Lords in June 1999 and was set to proceed in the House of Commons at the time this edition went to press.

4.1 The basic rule of privity

Tweddle v Atkinson (1861) CQB

See 3.3.

Dunlop Pneumatic Tyre Co Ltd v Selfridge & Co Ltd (1915) HL

The plaintiffs made an agreement with Dew & Co that Dew & Co could buy the tyres made by the plaintiffs at a discount in return for a promise not to sell them on for less than the plaintiffs' list prices. Dew & Co were allowed to give a discount to certain customers, including the defendants, but only if they obtained from the customer the same promise as to maintaining the list price as they had made themselves. Dew & Co sold some tyres to the defendants at a discount and they obtained from the defendants the promise as to list price. When the defendants broke that promise by selling the tyres for less than the list price, the plaintiffs sued them.

Held the plaintiffs could not sue the defendants as there was no agreement between them. The plaintiffs argued that Dew & Co had contracted with the defendants as agents for the plaintiffs. Their lordships were divided as to whether that argument could succeed, but were unanimous in holding that in any case the plaintiffs had given no consideration for the defendants' promise. All the consideration was from Dew & Co, so only they could sue the defendants. *Per* Viscount Haldane LC:

> In the law of England, certain principles are fundamental. One is that only a person who is a party to a contract can sue on it ... A second principle is that if a person with whom a contract not under seal has been made is to be able to enforce it consideration must have been given by him to the promisor or to

some other person at the promisor's request ... A third proposition is that a principal not named in the contract may sue upon it if the promisee really contracted as his agent. But again, in order to entitle him to sue, he must have given consideration either personally or through the promisee, acting as his agent in giving it.

Scruttons Ltd v Midland Silicones Ltd (1961) HL

A drum of chemicals was shipped from New York to London consigned to the plaintiffs. The bill of lading governing the carriage of the drum (the contract between the plaintiffs and the third party ship owner) included a limitation of the liability of 'the carriers' to $500 (some £179) per package unless a higher value was declared before the voyage. The defendants were stevedores who were used as sub-contractors by the ship owner to unload the goods from the ship. The defendants negligently dropped the drum of chemicals causing damage worth over £593. The defendants argued that they were entitled to the benefit of the limitation of liability to $500.

Held the defendants could not claim the benefit of a clause in a contract to which they were not a party. (I) The phrase 'the carriers' referred only to the ship owner and did not include the defendants. (II) The ship owner did not contract as agent for the defendants. (III) There was no implied contract between the defendants and the plaintiffs that the defendants should have the benefit of the limitation of liability clause in the contract between the plaintiff and the ship owner. (IV) There was, *per* Viscount Simonds, a 'fundamental' principle, as Viscount Haldane LC called it, in *Dunlop Pneumatic Tyre Co Ltd v Selfridge & Co Ltd* (4.1), an:

> ... elementary principle, as it has been called times without number, that only a person who is a party to a contract can sue on it ... The exceptions to the rule in *Tweddle v Atkinson* (3.3) are apparent rather than real.

Per Lord Reid:

> Although I may regret it, I find it impossible to deny the existence of the general rule that a stranger to a contract cannot in a question with either of the contracting parties take advantage of the provisions of the contract even where it is clear from the contract that some provision in it was intended to benefit him. That rule appears to have been crystallised a century ago in *Tweddle v Atkinson* [4.1] and finally established in this House in *Dunlop Pneumatic Tyre Co Ltd v Selfridge & Co Ltd* [4.1].

(V) Lord Denning dissented arguing: (i) an exemption clause benefits not only one of the parties to the contract but also that party's servants or agents who handled the goods for the party; (ii) the ship owner carried the goods as bailee and the plaintiffs had given the ship owner implied permission to pass the goods on similar terms to the defendants by way of sub-bailment.

Lord Denning repeated his argument (V) (ii) on different facts in the Court of Appeal in *Morris v CW Martin & Sons Ltd* (see 4.2.3).

Beswick v Beswick (1967) HL

The plaintiff's husband had a business as a coal merchant. In March 1962, the plaintiff's husband gave the business to the defendant, his nephew, in return for the defendant's promise to pay him £6 10s per week and to pay the plaintiff £5 per week after he died. The plaintiff's husband died in November 1963 and the defendant refused to honour his commitment to pay the plaintiff £5 per week. The plaintiff sued the defendant both in her personal capacity and as administratrix of her husband's estate.

Held (I) The plaintiff could not succeed in her personal capacity because she was not a party to the contract. Contrary to the views of Lord Denning MR in the Court of Appeal, s 56(1) of the Law of Property Act 1925 had not overturned the traditional doctrine of privity of contract. (II) As representative of her late husband's estate, the plaintiff could enforce the contract. The plaintiff would therefore be granted an order for specific performance of the contract.

4.2 Exceptions to the basic rule

4.2.1 The promise may be held on trust for the third party

Les Affréteurs Réunis SA v Leopold Walford (London) Ltd (1919) HL

The defendant ship owners made a charterparty with the third party charterers. The plaintiffs, Leopold Walford (London) Ltd, acted as brokers between the owners and the charterers. The charterparty included this clause: 'A commission of 3% on the estimated gross amount of hire is due to Leopold Walford (London) Ltd, on signing this charter (ship lost or not lost).' Before the charterparty took effect, the French Government requisitioned the ship. The brokers now sued the ship owners to recover their commission under the charterparty. By agreement, the action was treated as if the charterers had been joined as plaintiffs. The owners argued that there was a trade custom that brokerage commission was only payable out of hire charges and that since, because of the requisitioning, no hire charges had been paid under the charterparty, the brokers could not be paid either.

Held the brokers could recover the commission due to them under the charterparty. (I) Even though the brokers were not party to the agreement, the promise to benefit them could be enforced because it was held on trust for them by the charterers who were a party. *Per* Lord Birkenhead LC:

> In these cases, the broker, on ultimate analysis, appoints the charterer to contract on his behalf. I agree therefore ... that, in such cases, charterers can sue as trustees on behalf of the broker.

(II) (5.4) A trade custom could not override the clear meaning of an express term of the contract.

Darlington Borough Council v Wiltshier Northern Ltd (1994) CA

See 4.2.6.

4.2.2   The third party might benefit under a trust of the property

In Re Flavell (1883) CA

Mr Flavell was a solicitor who carried on business in partnership with a Mr Bowman. They both signed a partnership agreement in 1875. This provided that, in the event of the death of a partner, his executors or administrators would receive certain annual sums out of the profits of the business. The agreement provided that:

> ... any yearly sum which may under this present article for the time being become payable to the executors or administrators of a deceased partner to be applied in such manner as such partner shall by deed or will direct for the benefit of his widow ... and in default of such direction to be paid to such widow, if living, for her own benefit ...

Mr Flavell made no direction regarding the annuity, but he left all of his estate to his wife. He died in 1883 not leaving enough to pay all his debts. The plaintiff receiver was appointed to collect in Mr Flavell's assets for the benefit of his creditors. The question in this case was whether the annuity formed part of the general estate, in which case it would go to the creditors, or was paid under a trust, in which case Mrs Flavell would keep it.

Held the money was paid under a trust. The money never became part of Mr Flavell's assets but came to his representatives 'impressed with a trust'.

In Re Schebsman (1943) CA

The debtor was employed by two companies. His employment ended on 31 March 1940. On 20 September 1940, he made a written agreement with the two companies which included a promise by the companies to pay the debtor an annual sum for a number of years. If the debtor died, certain sums specified in the agreement would be paid to his widow. In March

1942, the debtor was made bankrupt and, in May 1942, he died. This action was an application by the debtor's trustee in bankruptcy that the sums payable to his widow under the agreement should form part of his estate and so be available for his creditors.

Held the payments were not part of the debtor's estate. (I) The contract did not establish any trust over the payments. It was a contract between two parties (the debtor and the companies) to benefit a third (the widow). *Per* du Parcq LJ:

> Unless an intention to create a trust is clearly to be collected from the language used and the circumstances of the case, I think that the court ought not to be astute to discover indications of such an intention.

(II) The money at no point belonged to the debtor and he had no right to tell the companies to make payments other than in accordance with the contract. Therefore the trustee in bankruptcy also had no right to call for the money.

Q Is there any real difference between this case and *In Re Flavell* (above), or does this case illustrate the reluctance of modern courts to find implied trusts in contracts?

4.2.3 The third party may have rights as a bailor or sub-bailee

Morris v CW Martin & Sons Ltd (1965) CA

The plaintiff owned a long white mink stole which she sent to a furrier, Mr Beder, to be cleaned. The plaintiff gave Mr Beder permission to send the stole to the defendants, a large firm of cleaners. Mr Beder and the defendants contracted on the defendants' standard terms which included a number of clauses limiting or excluding the defendants' liability for damage to the items to be cleaned. The defendants gave the fur to an employee, Morrissey, to clean it. Morrissey stole the stole which was not recovered. The plaintiff now sought damages from the defendants for its loss.

Held the plaintiff could recover the value of the lost fur from the defendants. (I) To hand over a fur for cleaning is a bailment. The defendants were therefore sub-bailees of the plaintiff. A sub-bailee for reward, like a bailee for reward, has duties to the bailor independently of, though capable of being overridden by, any contract between them. The defendants delegated their duties in respect of this stole to their servant, Morrissey, who breached the bailee's duty not to convert the bailed goods. The defendants were therefore liable to the plaintiff for breach of their duty as sub-bailees. (II) None of the exclusion clauses in the defendants' contract with Beder covered the facts in this case. (III) *Per* Lord Denning MR, *obiter*, if the exclusion clauses had covered the facts, they would have protected the defendants because the plaintiff had consented to the bailee (Mr Beder) making a sub-bailment on the usual terms in the trade, which is what he had done. Diplock LJ said 'I deliberately refrain from expressing an opinion about this'. Salmon LJ said:

> As at present advised, I am strongly attracted by the view expressed on this topic by Lord Denning MR, but I have formed no concluded opinion on it.

Q   If Lord Denning MR's argument at (III) did not apply in *Scruttons Ltd v Midland Silicones Ltd* (see 4.1), in which he was in the minority in the House of Lords, is there any distinguishing factor to enable it to apply in this case?

The KH Enterprise (1993) PC

The plaintiffs (the bailors) shipped goods under terms which allowed the carriers (the bailees) to 'sub-contract on any terms the whole or any part of' the carriage of the goods. A part of the carriage was sub-contracted by the carriers to the defendant ship owners (the sub-bailees) on terms which included that the contract of carriage would be governed by the law of Taiwan. The ship owners' vessel sank with the loss of the plaintiffs' goods. The plaintiffs allowed the limitation period in Taiwanese law to go by and then tried to sue the defendants in the High Court of Hong Kong arguing that they were not bound by the jurisdiction clause in the contract between the carriers and the ship owners.

Held the action would be stayed because the plaintiffs were bound by the terms of the contract between the carriers and the defendants. The judgment of their lordships was given by Lord Goff of Chieveley. (I) He said that:

> English law still maintains, though subject to increasing criticism, a strict principle of privity of contract, under which as a matter of general principle only a person who is a party to a contract may sue upon it. The force of this principle is supported and enhanced by the doctrine of consideration, under which as a general rule only a promise supported by consideration will be enforceable at common law. How long these principles will continue to be maintained in all their strictness is now open to question ... The present case is concerned with the question whether the law of bailment can here be invoked by the ship owners to circumvent this difficulty.

(II) Applying the principle set out by Lord Denning MR in *Morris v C W Martin & Sons Ltd* (4.2.3), their lordships held that a bailor is bound by the terms of a sub-bailment if and only if the bailor gave permission, which may be express or implied, for the sub-bailment. (III) The sub-bailee is only liable as bailee to the bailor 'if he has sufficient notice that a person other than the bailee is interested in the goods so that it can properly be said that (in addition to his duties to the bailee) he has, by taking the goods into his custody, assumed towards that other person the responsibility for the goods which is characteristic of a bailee'.

4.2.4 The third party may benefit from a collateral contract including a warranty

Shanklin Pier Ltd v Detel Products Ltd (1951) KB

The plaintiffs owned the pier at Shanklin in the Isle of Wight. The pier fell into disrepair during the war, and, in 1946, the plaintiffs decided to repair and re-paint the pier. The plaintiffs appointed contractors to carry out the work, with the plaintiffs reserving the right to vary the specifications of the paint. The defendants told the plaintiffs that one of the paints manufactured by the defendants, called DMU, would be suitable for painting the pier. Relying on this, the plaintiffs exercised their right under their contract with their contractors to instruct the contractors to use DMU. The contractors bought and used DMU which turned out not to be suitable and which soon had to be replaced.

Held the plaintiffs could recover their losses from the defendants even though the plaintiffs were not a party to the contract for the purchase of the paint. The defendants had given the plaintiffs a warranty that their paint was suitable which was enforceable because the plaintiffs had given consideration by causing (or by promising to cause) their contractors to buy the defendants' paint. *Per* McNair J:

> If, as is elementary, the consideration for the warranty in the usual case is the entering into of the main contract in relation to which the warranty is given, I see no reason why there may not be an enforceable warranty between A and B supported by the consideration that B should cause C to enter into a contract with A or that B should do some other act for the benefit of A.

Wells (Merstham) Ltd v Buckland Sand and Silica Co Ltd (1963) QB

The plaintiffs were in business as growers of chrysanthemums. The defendants sold sand. The plaintiffs asked the defendants whether the defendants had any sand suitable for growing chrysanthemums in. The defendants said that their 'BW' sand was suitable and told the plaintiffs its analysis. The plaintiffs then asked a builders materials firm, H, to buy some BW sand from the defendants and deliver it to the plaintiffs. This was because H provided a cheaper way to buy and transport the sand than if the plaintiffs bought it and transported it themselves. The sand turned out to have an iron content well in excess of that stated in the analysis given to the plaintiffs and as a result it destroyed a crop of chrysanthemums.

Held the plaintiffs could recover their losses from the defendants even though the sale contracts were made by the defendants with H, without the defendants knowing of the plaintiffs' involvement at the time of the sales. *Per* Edmund Davies J:

> As between A (a potential seller of goods) and B (a potential buyer), two ingredients, and two only, are in my judgment required in order to bring about a collateral contract containing a warranty: (1) a promise or assertion by A as to the nature, quality or quantity of the goods which B may reasonably regard as being made *animo contrahendi*; and (2) acquisition by B of the goods in reliance on that promise or assertion.

4.2.5 The contract may be made by the promisee as agent for the third party

The New Zealand Shipping Co Ltd v AM Satterthwaite & Co Ltd: *The Eurymedon* (1974) PC

See 3.7.3.

4.2.6 In contracts for the benefit of third parties, the promisee may recover damages for the third parties' loss

Jackson v Horizon Holidays Ltd (1974) CA

The plaintiff arranged through the defendants a four week package holiday in Ceylon for himself, his wife and their three year old twins. He stated a number of specific requirements for the hotel which the defendants promised to satisfy. The hotel that the plaintiff had booked was not built in time for the holiday so the defendants found another hotel and reduced the price of the holiday from £1,432 to £1,200. The replacement hotel turned out to be dirty, mouldy and unsuitable in other ways. The plaintiff and his family spent two weeks there and two weeks at the still unfinished hotel which he had first booked. The plaintiff recovered damages of £1,100 and the defendants, who admitted liability, appealed against the sum awarded.

Held the award was correct. (I) *Per* Lord Denning MR, the award was too high to compensate the plaintiff for only his own distress and losses but it was correct as compensation for the distress and losses of the whole family. The plaintiff did not contract as agent for his family, the children being too young to have acted as principals, and there was no trust. Nonetheless, the plaintiff could recover for the third parties for the benefit of whom he had contracted. (II) Orr and James LJJ agreed that the damages of £1,100 were appropriate but did not give their reasoning in detail.

Woodar Investment Development v Wimpey Construction UK Ltd (1980) HL

The parties made a contract in February 1973 for the sale of some land at Cobham, Surrey. The negotiations were carried out for the plaintiffs, Woodar, by Mr Cornwell who was also associated with Transworld Trade Ltd. At first, a price of £1,000,000 was agreed, but, in the final contract, the price was £850,000 and there was a special condition that, on completion, the defendants, Wimpey, would pay £150,000 to Transworld. It was at Mr Cornwell's request that the promise was made to make a payment to Transworld. However, there was no evidence that Woodar contracted as agent or trustee for Transworld. Under special condition E(a)(iii) of the contract, Wimpey could withdraw from the transaction if compulsory purchase proceedings were commenced before completion. Wimpey served a notice of withdrawal because of compulsory purchase proceedings in March 1974. In fact, it was held, the proceedings did not fall within special condition E(a)(iii). Woodar now claimed that by erroneously invoking the special condition Wimpey had wrongfully repudiated the contract entitling Woodar to damages both for its own loss and on behalf of Transworld.

Held (I) (3:2) Wimpey's notice did not amount to a repudiation so damages would not be awarded. (II) *Obiter*, their lordships considered the question of what damages would have been recovered in respect of the £150,000 payable to Transworld if they had decided point (I) differently. They noted that an order of specific performance of the obligation to pay £150,000 as in *Beswick v Beswick* (4.1) was not possible because the contract was no longer in force. (i) *Per* Lord Wilberforce, with whom Lord Salmon agreed on this point, the decision in *Jackson v Horizon Holidays Ltd* (above) did not apply to this case; but:

It may be supported either as a broad decision on the measure of damages [*per* James LJ] or possibly as an example of a type of contract, examples of which are persons contracting for family holidays, ordering meals in restaurants for a party, hiring a taxi for a group, calling for special treatment.

What damages Woodar could recover was 'a question of great doubt and difficulty, no doubt open in this House, but one on which I prefer to reserve my opinion'. (ii) *Per* Lord Russell of Killowen Woodar could have recovered 'no more than nominal damages'. (iii) *Per* Lord Keith of Kinkel, *Jackson v Horizon Holidays Ltd*:

... is capable of being regarded as rightly decided on a reasonable view of the measure of damages due to the plaintiff as the original contracting party, and not as laying down any rule of law regarding the recovery of damages for the benefit of third parties.

In some contracts where, as a consequence of the plaintiff's loss, third parties do not obtain a benefit that they should have had under the contract, the plaintiff could recover for the expense of recompensing the third parties for their deprivation. (iv) *Per* Lord Scarman:

> If the opportunity arises, I hope the House will reconsider *Tweddle v Atkinson* [4.1] and the other cases which stand guard over this unjust rule [the denial of *jus quaesitum tertio*, the right of a third party under a contract]. Likewise, I believe it open to the House to declare that, in the absence of evidence to show that he has suffered no loss, A, who has contracted for a payment to be made to C, may rely on the fact that he required the payment to be made as *prima facie* evidence that the promise for which he contracted was a benefit to him and that the measure of his loss in the event of non-payment is the benefit which he intended for C but which has not been received.

Linden Gardens Trust Ltd v Lenesta Sludge Disposals Ltd and Others, St Martins Property Corp Ltd and Another v Sir Robert McAlpine & Sons Ltd (1993) HL

Appeals in these two cases were heard together by their lordships.

In the first case, Stock Conversion had a leasehold interest in a property. Stock Conversion made a contract with the defendant contractors that the defendants would remove asbestos from the property. Clause 17(1) of the contract provided: 'The employer shall not without the written consent of the Contractor assign this Contract.' The work was completed in 1980. In 1985, Stock Conversion sold their interest in the property to the plaintiffs, Linden Gardens. In 1987 and 1988, Linden Gardens found asbestos in the property which the defendants should have removed. Linden Gardens paid to have the asbestos removed. Without the defendants' permission, Stock Conversion purported to assign their right of action to Linden Gardens, and the latter sued the contractors for the losses caused by the fact that asbestos remained in the property.

In the second case, the first plaintiffs, Corporation, entered into a building contract in 1974 with the defendants, McAlpines. Clause 17 of the contract was like that in the first case. In 1976, Corporation assigned the property concerned to the second plaintiffs, Investments, and purported to assign to Investments the benefit of the construction contract. It was alleged (and assumed for the purposes of the appeal) that there were breaches of contract by McAlpines which took place after the assignment to Investments. The cost of remedial works was paid by Corporation which recovered it from Investments.

Held (I) the benefit of the contract could not be assigned because of clause 17(1). This meant that Investments could not succeed in its claim in the second case. (II) Clause 17 also prevents the assignment of accrued rights of action, so that Linden Gardens' claim in the first case must fail. (III) Corporation could recover substantial damages in the second case even though it did not retain an interest in the property when the breaches took place and it was not out of pocket because the costs of remedial work had been refunded by Investments. (i) Lord Keith of Kinkel, Lord Bridge of Harwich and Lord Ackner rested their decisions on the grounds given by Lord Browne-Wilkinson, who said:

> In my judgment, the present case falls within the rationale of the exceptions to the general rule that a plaintiff can only recover damages for his own loss. The contract was for a large development of property which, to the knowledge of both Corporation and McAlpines, was going to be occupied, and possibly purchased, by third parties and not by Corporation itself. Therefore, it could be foreseen that damage caused by breach would cause loss to a later owner and not merely to the original contracting party, Corporation. [That later owner was to have no direct right of action against McAlpines.] In such a case, it seems to me proper, as in the case of the carriage of goods by land, to treat the parties as having entered into the contract on the footing that Corporation would be entitled to enforce contractual rights for the benefit of those who suffered from defective performance but who, under the terms of the contract, could not acquire any right to hold McAlpines liable for the breach. It is truly a case in which the rule provides 'a remedy where no other would be available to a person sustaining loss which under a rational legal system ought to be compensated by the person who caused it'.

(ii) Lord Keith of Kinkel and Lord Bridge of Harwich expressed sympathy for the broader grounds upon which Lord Griffiths founded his opinion. *Per* Lord Griffiths, one who makes a contract for work and labour should be able to recover substantial damages regardless of whether that person has a proprietary interest in the property upon which the work is carried out:

> In such cases as the present, the person who places the contract has suffered financial loss because he has to spend monies to give him the benefit of the bargain which the defendant had promised but failed to deliver.

It did not matter who actually paid for the repairs. So long as they are carried out, the defendant, who broke his contract, should pay for them.

Darlington Borough Council v Wiltshier Northern Ltd (1994) CA

The plaintiff Council wanted to build a new recreation centre. However, for reasons related to local authority funding, the contracts with the defendant builders were entered into, not by the Council, but by a private company, Morgan Grenfell (Local Authorities Services) Ltd. The centre when built would be owned by the Council and at no stage passed to Morgan Grenfell. The contract expressly contemplated an assignment of Morgan Grenfell's rights of action for breach of contract to the Council.

Such an assignment was made and the Council sued the builders for defective building works. The builders argued that Morgan Grenfell would not have suffered any loss because it had no proprietary interest in the defective centre and thus that the Council could not recover substantial damages as Morgan Grenfell's assignee.

Held (I) *Per* Dillon, Steyn and Waite LJJ, by extension of the rule expressed by Lord Browne-Wilkinson in *St Martin's Property Corpn Ltd v Sir Robert McAlpine & Sons Ltd* (4.2.6), Morgan Grenfell could have sued for the Council's loss, which right of action it had assigned to the Council. (II) (4.2.1) *Per* Dillon and Waite LJJ, the Council was also entitled to succeed on the ground that Morgan Grenfell held the benefit of its rights under the building contract on constructive trust for the Council. The only reasons directed at this point were given by Dillon LJ who said that any damages which Morgan Grenfell had recovered in relation to losses suffered by the Council would have been held on constructive trust for the Council. Steyn LJ did not find it necessary to consider the constructive trust point. (III) Steyn LJ would have also decided the case under Lord Griffiths' wider principle from *St Martin's Property Corp Ltd v Sir Robert McAlpine & Sons Ltd* (4.2.6) which Steyn LJ expressly approved. Dillon and Waite LJJ did not comment upon Lord Griffiths' wider principle. (IV) *Obiter*, *per* Steyn LJ:

> The case for recognising a contract for the benefit of a third party is simple and straightforward. The autonomy of the will of the parties should be respected. The law of contract should give effect to the reasonable expectations of contracting parties. Principle certainly requires that a burden should not be imposed on a third party without his consent. But, there is no doctrinal, logical or policy reason why the law should deny effectiveness to a contract for the benefit of a third party where that is the expressed intention of the parties ... The genesis of the privity rule is suspect. It is attributed to *Tweddle v Atkinson* [3.3]. It is more realistic to say that the rule originated in the misunderstanding of *Tweddle v Atkinson* ... While the privity rule was barely tolerable in Victorian England, it has been recognised for half a century that it has no place in our more complex commercial world.

4.2.7 A purchaser of property may be bound by a negative covenant of which he has notice

Tulk v Moxhay (1848)

The plaintiff owned Leicester Square and some of the houses around it. In 1808, he sold the square itself to a purchaser by a conveyance which included a covenant by the purchaser that he, his heirs and assigns would maintain the square as a garden and pleasure ground. By various subsequent conveyances, the square came into the ownership of the defendant. Although the conveyance by which the defendant purchased the square did not include the covenant to maintain it, the defendant knew of the covenant in the conveyance of 1808. The plaintiff now sought an injunction to prevent the defendant from carrying out a proposal to convert the square to other purposes.

Held the covenant attached an equity to the property which bound all who took the property with notice of the covenant. Therefore, the plaintiff, who retained the houses around the square which would be affected by the proposed change in the square, was entitled to the injunction he sought.

Lord Strathcona Steamship Co Ltd v Dominion Coal Co Ltd (1925) PC

The plaintiff charterers arranged for a steamship to be built to their specification and agreed in a charterparty that they would charter the ship for 10 successive years with options to renew the charter for a further eight years. The ship came into service in 1916. By 1920, it had changed hands several times and the new owners refused to perform the charterparty although they had known of it when they acquired the ship. The charterers sued the defendant owners and the latter argued that they were not a party to the contract.

Held the owners would be restrained by injunction from using the ship inconsistently with the charterparty. The principle of *Tulk v Moxhay* (above) applied to other property as well as to land. A purchaser of property who knows that the vendor has contracted with a third party for a particular use of the property cannot use the property inconsistently with that contract. Although the third party cannot obtain an order for specific performance of the contract against the purchaser (so positive covenants relating to the property cannot be enforced), an injunction prohibiting the purchaser from using the property inconsistently with the vendor's covenant will be granted. The plaintiff can only enforce the contract so long as he continues to have an interest in the property.

4.3 Interaction of the rule of privity with the law of torts

4.3.1 The third party may have a remedy in the tort of negligence

White and Another v Jones and Another (1995) HL

The testator instructed the defendant solicitors to prepare a new will for him. The new will, unlike his previous will, would have benefited the testator's two daughters, the plaintiffs. The solicitors negligently failed to carry out the testator's instructions before the testator died. The plaintiffs therefore did not receive any legacy from the testator because of the defendants' failure to carry out properly their contract with the testator.

Held the plaintiffs could recover damages from the defendants for the tort of negligence. The main question was whether the defendants owed a duty of care to the plaintiffs in this case. One of the factors which influenced the majority who answered that question in the affirmative was that the defendants would have no other remedy if their claim in negligence failed.

4.3.2 The third party may commit a tort if he interferes with contractual rights

British Motor Trade Association v Salvadori and Others (1948) Ch

All British car manufacturers and their authorised dealers were members of the plaintiff Association. Since the government did not allow cars to be imported, the members of the Association were the only source of new cars in Britain. The Association enforced a system of list prices which in many cases were below the price a car could fetch on the open market. Every purchaser of a new car signed an agreement with the dealer and the Association not to sell the car within a year without the Association's consent. The defendants were car dealers outside the Association who operated in the 'Warren Street kerb market'. Each defendant would find a person (A) who was willing to buy a new car from a member of the Association (B) and then sell it to the defendant. The defendant would then sell the car usually to another dealer who would sell it to a member of the public. At each step the price of the car increased.

Held each defendant, by agreeing to buy a car in the knowledge that the seller (A) would be breaching a contract (with B), was guilty of the tort of wrongful interference in contractual rights. The Association could therefore obtain damages in tort from the defendants even though the defendants were not parties to the contracts the breach of which was the Association's complaint.

5   Terms

5.1   The terms of a contract in writing bind a signatory

L'Estrange v F Graucob Ltd (1934) KBDC

The plaintiff owned a café in Llandudno; the defendants manufactured and sold slot machines. Two of the defendants' representatives called on the plaintiff who agreed to buy a cigarette machine from the defendants. The plaintiff signed a document headed 'Sales agreement' which she believed was an order form for the machine. She had not read the document and was not aware of its full contents. When the machine failed to operate properly, the plaintiff attempted to withdraw from the contract and claimed a refund of her deposit. The plaintiff argued that there was an implied term in the contract that the machine would be reasonably fit for its purpose. The defendants counter claimed for the £70 remaining purchase price of the machine arguing that there was no implied term because the contract included (in what Maugham LJ called 'regrettably small print') this clause:

> This agreement contains all the terms and conditions under which I agree to purchase the machine specified above and any express or implied condition, statement, or warranty, statutory or otherwise not stated herein is hereby excluded.

Held the defendants could rely on the clause to exclude the implied term as to fitness for purpose and therefore must succeed in their counter claim. *Per* Scrutton LJ:

> When a document containing contractual terms has been signed, then, in the absence of fraud, or, I will add, misrepresentation, the party signing it is bound, and it is wholly immaterial whether he has read the document or not ... The plaintiff, having put her signature to the document and not having been induced to do so by any fraud or misrepresentation, cannot be heard to say that she is not bound by the terms because she has not read them.

5.2 A warranty or term distinguished from a mere representation

5.2.1 Could the representor have been assumed to have had knowledge of the fact represented, or did the representee have expertise in the matter?

Routledge v McKay and Others (1954) CA

The fifth party seller sold a motor cycle combination to the fourth party buyer in 1949. In reply to a question from the buyer as to the date of the combination, the seller said that it was 'late 1941 or 1942' and produced the registration book which was dated in 1941. Although the seller was not responsible for altering the registration book, he knew that the combination was older than stated in the book. A week later, the buyer and the seller signed a document drafted by the buyer which said:

> It is agreed between [the buyer] ... and [the seller] ... that a ... motor cycle ... now [owned by the buyer] to be exchanged for a ... combination motor cycle owned by [the seller] and further [the buyer] will pay the sum of £30 to complete the transaction. It is understood that when the £30 is paid over this transaction is closed.

Later, the buyer sold the motor cycle combination to the third party who sold it to the defendant who sold it to the plaintiff. It turned out that the combination was first registered in 1930. The seller, who could not issue an indemnity notice against the person who sold the combination to him because his claim would be statute barred, denied having given a warranty as to the motor cycle combination's age.

Held the buyer could not recover damages from the seller who had not given a warranty. (I) (5.2.3) The written agreement showed that the contract did not include a warranty as to the age of the combination. (II) The warranty could not be a collateral contract because it was made a week before the sale agreement came into existence. (III) (5.2.3) *Per* Denning LJ:

> The seller, unless he is the first owner, is not the originator of the statement about the year. He has to accept it from the registration book, and cannot be expected to warrant its accuracy unless he in express terms makes himself responsible.

Oscar Chess Ltd v Williams (1956) CA

In March 1954, the defendant's mother bought a second hand Morris car on the footing that it was a 1948 model. The registration book appeared to show that the car was first registered in 1948. The defendant often used the car to give a lift to a car salesman who worked for the plaintiffs. In May

1955, the defendant told the salesman that he wanted to buy a new car and offered the Morris in part exchange. The defendant told the salesman that it was a 1948 model and showed him the registration book. The salesman looked up the current second-hand value of the car and made the defendant an offer which was accepted. Some eight months after the deal was done the plaintiffs sent the chassis and engine numbers to Morris Motors Ltd who told them that the car was made in February 1939. The appearance of Morris cars had not changed between 1939 and 1948. The plaintiffs now sued for the difference in value between the 1939 car and a 1948 model.

Held the plaintiffs' claim could not succeed. (I) The plaintiffs had not acted promptly enough to have the contract set aside in equity on the grounds of mistake. (See *Leaf v International Galleries*, 6.4.1.) (II) The statement that the car was a 1948 model was not a warranty, but a mere innocent misrepresentation for which there was no remedy. (See Chapter 6 on misrepresentation.) *Per* Denning LJ:

> The question whether a warranty was intended depends on the conduct of the parties, on their words and behaviour, rather than on their thoughts. If an intelligent bystander would reasonably infer that a warranty was intended, that will suffice ... It must have been obvious to both [parties] that the seller had himself no personal knowledge of the year when the car was made. He only became owner after a great number of changes. He must have been relying on the registration book ... In these circumstances, the intelligent bystander would, I suggest, say that the seller did not intend to bind himself so as to warrant that the car was a 1948 model.

It was also relevant that the plaintiffs were themselves experts in the car trade. *Per* Hodson LJ:

> The defendant was stating an opinion on a matter of which he had no special knowledge or on which the buyer might be expected also to have an opinion and exercise his judgment.

(III) Morris LJ dissented holding that the representation was vital to the contract and so should be viewed as a term of the contract.

Dick Bentley Productions Ltd and Another v Harold Smith (Motors) Ltd (1965) CA

The plaintiff, Mr Bentley, told the defendant that he was looking for a Bentley car. The defendant said that he was able to find out the history of cars. The defendant found a car which he said had done 20,000 miles since it had had a new engine and gearbox. The odometer showed only 20,000 miles. The car was disappointing and turned out to have done more than the stated number of miles. The plaintiff sought damages arguing that the mileage was a warranty by the defendant.

Held the mileage being no more that 20,000 miles was a warranty by the defendant. *Per* Lord Denning MR:

> If a representation is made in the course of dealings for a contract for the very purpose of inducing the other party to act on it, and it actually induces him to act on it by entering into the contract, that is *prima facie* ground for inferring that the representation is a warranty ... Here we have a dealer, Mr Smith, who was in a position to know, or at least to find out, the history of the car. He could get it by writing to the makers. He did not do so ... When the history of this car was examined, his statement turned out to be quite wrong. He ought to have known better. There was no reasonable foundation for it.

5.2.2 Was the fact represented of special importance to the representee?

Bannerman v White and Others (1861) CCP

It became the practice to use sulphur in the cultivation of hops. The brewers began to fear that the sulphur affected the quality of their beer, so, in 1854, they announced that they would only buy hops that were guaranteed to have been cultivated without sulphur. In 1860, the plaintiff, a hop grower, offered his growth for the year to the defendants, who were hop merchants. The plaintiff showed the defendants samples and, before the price was discussed, the defendants asked the plaintiff whether sulphur had been used; the plaintiff said it had not. At the time of the purchase of the hops, the plaintiff gave the defendants this note:

> I hereby guarantee Messrs Wigan, White and Wigans against any loss by my 1860 hops through the mode of treatment on the poles or curing, and hold myself liable to pay them any damage caused them thereby.

It transpired that sulphur had been used on five acres of the 300 acres from which the growth had been picked and that all the hops had been mixed together. The plaintiff had forgotten the sulphur when negotiating with the defendants.

Held the fact that the hops had not been treated with sulphur was a warranty. *Per* Erle CJ, delivering the judgment of the court:

> ... the defendants required, and the plaintiff gave his undertaking, that no sulphur had been used. This undertaking was a preliminary stipulation; and, if it had not been given, the defendants would not have gone on with the treaty which resulted in the sale. In this sense it was the condition upon which the defendants contracted ... The intention of the parties governs in the making and in the construction of all contracts. If the parties so intend the sale may be absolute, with a warranty superadded; or the sale may be conditional to be null if the warranty is broken. And, upon this statement of facts, we think that the intention appears that the contract should be null if sulphur had been used.

5.2.3 Was the representation overridden by a later contract on different terms?

Hopkins v Tanqueray (1854) CCP

The defendant sent his horse, 'California', for sale at auction. On Sunday, the day before the auction, the defendant found the plaintiff kneeling down examining California's legs. The defendant said 'You need not examine his legs; you have nothing to look for: I assure you he is perfectly sound in every respect'. The plaintiff got up and replied 'If you say so, I am perfectly satisfied'. On the next day, the plaintiff bought the horse at the auction, where it was well known that the horses were not warranted. The horse was not sound, although it was accepted that the defendant had spoken in good faith.

Held the defendant's statement was, *per* Jervis CJ, 'a representation only, and not a warranty'. *Per* Maule J:

> The fact of that conversation passing between the plaintiff and the defendant at the time when it was known to both that the sale was to take place by public competition on the following day, affords to my mind a very strong reason for thinking that the defendant could not have intended what he then said to be imported as a warranty into the transaction.

Per Cresswell J:

> If the representation ... had been made at the time of the sale, so as to form part of the contract, it might have amounted to a warranty.

Schawel v Reade (1912) HL

The plaintiff was buying horses for the Austrian government and he bought from the defendant a horse called 'Mallow Man' which turned out to be unsound. When the plaintiff was inspecting the horse the defendant said to him 'You need not look for anything; the horse is perfectly sound. If there was anything the matter with the horse, I should tell you'. Later on the same day, the plaintiff bought the horse from the defendant without any additional warranty.

Held per Lord Macnaghten, 'that is about as plain a warranty of the soundness of the horse as could be given'. *Per* Lord Atkinson:

> A statement is made, it is acted upon, and it is made by the person who makes it for the purpose of the sale, that is, with the intention of bringing about the sale. I do not know what other ingredient is necessary to create a warranty.

Per Lord Moulton the representation was made:

> ... in order that the plaintiff might purchase the horse, and the plaintiff acted upon that representation, and desisted from his personal examination of that horse ... Now, it would be impossible, in my mind, to have a clearer example of

an express warranty where the word 'warrant' was not used. The essence of such warranty is that it becomes plain by the words, and the action, of the parties that it is intended that in the purchase the responsibility of the soundness shall rest upon the vendor.

Q Does Lord Atkinson's recipe for a warranty distinguish it from a mere representation?

Heilbut, Symons & Co v Buckleton (1912) HL

The defendants, who were well known rubber merchants, underwrote an issue of shares in a new company, the Filisola Rubber and Produce Estates Ltd. The plaintiff telephoned the defendants' agent and said 'I understand you are bringing out a rubber company'. The defendants' agent replied 'We are' and the plaintiff asked if the agent had any prospectuses. He did not have any and the plaintiff then asked 'if it was all right', to which the agent answered 'We are bringing it out'. The plaintiff said 'That is good enough for me' and subsequently bought 6,000 shares in Filisola. Later, the estate turned out not to contain as many rubber trees as had been thought and the shares lost their value. The plaintiff brought this action for a breach of warranty that the company was a rubber company. The jury found for the plaintiff that Filisola could not be properly described as a rubber company and that the defendants had warranted that it was one.

Held as a matter of law, there was no warranty by the defendants, so even if Filisola was not a rubber company, the plaintiff could not obtain damages from the defendants. The contract for the purchase of the shares was in writing and did not include any warranty upon which the plaintiff could found his action. Any warranty to be found in the telephone conversation would therefore amount to a collateral contract. *Per* Lord Moulton:

> It is evident ... that there may be a contract the consideration for which is the making of some other contract ... It is collateral to the main contract, but each has an independent existence, and they do not differ in respect of their possessing to the full the character and status of a contract. But, such collateral contracts must from their very nature be rare [because it is more natural to amend the main contract instead]. [They] are therefore viewed with suspicion by the law. They must be proved strictly. Not only the terms of such contracts but the existence of an *animus contrahendi* on the part of all the parties to them must be clearly shown.

Couchman v Hill (1946) CA

The plaintiff bought the defendant's heifer at an auction. The heifer was described in the catalogue as 'unserved' and at the auction, when the heiffer was in the ring, the plaintiff asked both the defendant and the auctioneer to confirm that the heifer was unserved which they did. The heifer was later found to be carrying a calf and it died from the strain of doing so at too young an age. The defendant relied on one of the published conditions of sale at the auction:

> The lots are sold with all faults, imperfections, and errors of description, the auctioneers not being responsible for the correct description, genuineness, or authenticity of, or any fault or defect in, any lot, and giving no warranty whatever.

Held any claim based on the description given in the catalogue would be defeated by the auctioneer's conditions which successfully excluded any liability for such descriptions. However, the oral statements of both the defendant and the auctioneer at the sale were intended by the parties to be warranties in return for which the plaintiff agreed to bid. *Per* Scott LJ, with whom Tucker and Bucknill LJJ agreed, the plaintiff's questions to the defendant and the auctioneer meant:

> I am frightened of contracting on your published terms, but I will bid if you will tell me by word of mouth that you accept full responsibility for the statement in the catalogue that the heifers have not been served, or, in other words, give me a clean warranty. That is the only condition on which I will bid.

Since the warranty was part of the description of the goods, it was a condition rather than a mere warranty.

Note

Although *Hopkins v Tanqueray* (5.2.3) was not cited in this case, in *Harling v Eddy* (below), Sir Raymond Evershed MR and Denning LJ both noted that *Hopkins v Tanqueray* was distinguishable from this case because, *per* Denning LJ, 'there was there no warranty at all'.

Harling v Eddy (1951) CA

The defendant was a cattle dealer who offered a large number of Guernsey heifer cows for sale by auction on 30 June 1950 which were described in the catalogue as 'tuberculin-tested'. They had in fact been tested, with satisfactory results, shortly before the sale. The catalogue also contained conditions of sale including this one:

> (12) No animal, article, or thing is sold with a "warranty" unless specially mentioned at the time of offering, and no warranty so given shall have any legal force or effect unless the terms thereof appear on the purchaser's account.

When animal number 9 came into the ring, no one made any bid. The defendant then said that:

> There was nothing wrong with the heifer, that he would absolutely guarantee her in every respect, and he would be willing to take her back if she turned out not to be what he stated she was.

The plaintiff bought the cow but she gave little milk and finally died of tuberculosis in October.

Held the plaintiff could recover damages from the defendant. (I) (5.7.2) Although condition of sale (12) excluded warranties, the statement by the defendant was a condition, not a mere warranty. To claim damages, the plaintiff must treat the breached condition as if it were a warranty, but that did not bring it within condition of sale (12). (II) Even if the defendant's statement was only a warranty and not a condition, in the circumstances the defendant implied that the statement was intended to apply to the exclusion of condition (12), so that the plaintiff would still succeed. (III) *Per* Denning LJ:

> The law is that if a seller of goods by auction gives an express oral warranty, he cannot escape from his responsibility for it by saying that the catalogue contained an exempting clause.

Routledge v McKay and Others (1954) CA

See 5.2.1.

5.3   Incorporation of express terms

5.3.1   Ticket cases

Parker v The South Eastern Railway Company (1877) CA

The defendants owned a railway station where they operated a left luggage cloak room. The plaintiff paid 2d to leave a bag at the cloak room and was handed a paper ticket. On the front of the ticket were a number, the date, details of the opening times of the cloakroom and the words 'see back'; on the back of the ticket were several clauses including one which said 'The company will not be responsible for any package exceeding the value of £10'. The plaintiff's bag, which was worth more than £10, was lost by the defendants and the defendants denied liability on the ground of the exclusion printed on the back of the ticket. The plaintiff admitted knowing that there was writing on the back of the ticket but said that he had not read it and did not realise that it contained conditions.

Held the action would have to be retried before a jury as the trial judge had not put the correct questions of fact before the original jury. (I) *Per* Mellish LJ, the right direction is:

> ... that if the person receiving the ticket did not see or know that there was any writing on the ticket, he is not bound by the conditions; that if he knew there was writing, and knew or believed that the writing contained conditions, then he is bound by the conditions; that if he knew there was writing on the ticket,

but did not know or believe that the writing contained conditions, nevertheless he would be bound, if the delivering of the ticket to him in such a manner that he could see there was writing upon it, was, in the opinion of the jury, reasonable notice that the writing contained conditions.

Thus, the plaintiff would be bound in cases where the defendants could expect the plaintiff to know the ticket contained conditions, such as where the ticket is a bill of lading, but not where the plaintiff might think the ticket is merely a receipt such as one he might get after paying a toll. (II) *Obiter, per* Baggallay LJ, if there had been no ticket the defendants would have been liable under common law as bailees for reward of the bag. (III) *Obiter, per* Bramwell LJ (who dissented on the main question, holding that as a matter of law the plaintiff accepted the conditions), the plaintiff would not have been bound by a condition on the ticket that he had not read if it was unreasonable or irrelevant to the deposit of the bag.

Thompson v London Midland and Scottish Railway Co (1929) CA

The plaintiff went on an excursion by the defendants' train with her daughter and her niece. The niece bought all three tickets, the plaintiff not being able to read. The tickets were special excursion tickets at half the normal price. On the front of each ticket were the words 'Excursion, For conditions, see back'. On the back of each ticket was a notice: 'Issued subject to the conditions and regulations in the company's time tables and notices and excursion and other bills.' On the excursion bill was a notice referring to the conditions shown in the time table. In the time table on page 552 were these words:

Excursion tickets and tickets issued at fares less than the ordinary fares are issued subject to ... the condition that neither the holders nor any other person shall have any right of action against the company ... in respect of ... injury (fatal or otherwise) loss, damage or delay however caused.

The booking office held one copy of the timetable and there was a charge of 6d to buy a copy. Without inquiring as to the conditions, the plaintiff went on the excursion. The train stopped so that, when the plaintiff got down from i,t she was right at the end of the platform. She slipped over the end of the platform and now sued for damages for the injuries she suffered.

Held the defendants could rely on their exclusion clause to avoid any liability for the plaintiff's injuries. In *Parker v South Eastern Railway Company* (5.3.1), the contract was one which could have been made without any written ticket, which is why there was a question of fact as to whether the defendants gave reasonable notice that the ticket contained conditions. In this case, it was clear to all parties that a ticket would be issued. Since the ticket clearly referred to conditions, the plaintiff was bound by the conditions whether she actually knew of them or not so long as she accepted the ticket. The defendants had done all they could reasonably be expected to do in the circumstances to bring the conditions to the plaintiff's notice. It did not avail the plaintiff that she could not read. It also did not help the plaintiff that the conditions themselves could only be found from the ticket by a circuitous route. *Per* Lawrence and Sankey LJJ, the plaintiff would not have been bound by an unreasonable condition, but this was, *per* Lawrence LJ, 'a reasonable condition, which need not have special attention directed to it'. *Per* Sankey LJ, the plaintiff would not have been bound if the conditions in the time table were printed in Chinese.

Q (a) Was this condition reasonable? (b) Why does it matter what language a condition is printed in if the plaintiff does not try to read it and cannot read even English?

5.3.2 A receipt or a notice may come too late to import contractual terms

Chapelton v Barry Urban District Council (1940) CA

The plaintiff went to the beach at Cold Knap, a place within the defendant council's area. There was a pile of deck chairs with a notice saying 'Barry Urban District Council. Cold Knap. Hire of chairs, 2d per session of three hours. The public are respectfully requested to obtain tickets properly issued from the automatic punch in their presence from the chair attendants'. There was an attendant nearby who gave the plaintiff a chair and a ticket. The plaintiff did not read the ticket, but put it in his pocket and took the chair to the beach. When the plaintiff sat down, the canvass gave way and the plaintiff suffered a severe jar. The injury was caused by the council's negligence in providing such a chair, but the council relied on some words printed on the ticket:

> Available for three hours. Time expires where indicated by cut off and should be retained and shown on request. The council will not be liable for any accident or damage arising from hire of chair.

Held the council must pay damages for the plaintiff's injury because the ticket was a mere receipt and not a contractual document. In these circumstances, the notice by the chairs was an offer by the council which the plaintiff accepted by taking a chair. The express terms of the contract were therefore those on the notice. The plaintiff had no reason to think that the ticket would contain conditions, but was entitled to believe that it would be a receipt which would show for how long he could use the chair. He therefore had no obligation to read it. It was significant that someone could take the chair and, if the attendants were busy, he might only get a ticket some time later.

Q Would it make a difference to the outcome of this case if the plaintiff *had* read the ticket (a) before, or (b) after taking the chair, or would the ticket have remained a mere receipt because he *might* not have read it?

Olley v Marlborough Court Ltd (1948) CA

The plaintiff stayed at the defendants' hotel from May 1945 until February 1947. This case concerned an incident in November 1945 when a thief came into the hotel, took the plaintiff's room key from the key board in the office and stole some of the plaintiff's belongings from her room. It was held that the defendants were negligent in letting the key be taken and that they were *prima facie* liable for the plaintiff's loss. The defendants argued (*inter alia*) that they were protected from liability by a notice in the plaintiff's bedroom which said 'The proprietors will not hold themselves responsible for articles lost or stolen, unless handed to the manageress for safe custody'.

Held the defendants were liable to compensate the plaintiff for her loss. (I) (12.2.1) The notice should be construed as denying the defendants' liability so long as loss was not caused by negligence on the part of the defendants. (II) The plaintiff's contract with the defendants was formed at the reception desk before she first saw her room. The price of the room was paid weekly in advance, but each new week's payment was not made under a new contract. There was just one contract, made before the plaintiff had seen the notice, which was of indefinite duration.

McCutcheon v David MacBrayne Ltd (1964) HL

The plaintiff lived on Islay, but was staying on the mainland. He asked his brother-in-law, Mr McSporran, to send him his car. Mr McSporran took the plaintiff's car to the defendants' office as they ran the only freight shipping service to the mainland. One of the defendants' employees quoted a price which Mr McSporran paid and gave him a receipt. The employee omitted to ask Mr McSporran to sign a risk note which the defendants required for all shipping contracts. On the voyage, the defendants' boat sank due to their negligence and the plaintiff's car was lost. The defendants argued that their liability was excluded by exclusion clauses which were: (I) incorporated by the receipt; (II) contained in their printed conditions which were displayed in the office; and (III) contained in the risk note which the plaintiff had signed on four previous occasions when he had sent freight by the defendants' boat.

Held the defendants could not rely on their exclusion clauses and would have to pay for the plaintiff's car. (I) The receipt was not a contractual document. *Per* Lord Hodson:

The receipt was handed over ... after the contract was completed and cannot be treated as an offer. It played no part on the formation of the contract and there was no reason to suppose that it referred to conditions.

(II) Neither the plaintiff, not his agent, Mr McSporran, read the notices on the walls and they did not form part of the contract made. (III) (5.3.3) Although the plaintiff had signed the risk note on four previous occasions when he had sent freight by the defendants' service, he had never read the 3,000–4,000 word document and did not know that it included a total exclusion of the defendants' liability. In this case, the parties made an oral contract without the defendants' usual conditions and the plaintiff could take advantage of that, just as the defendants would have taken advantage of the written contract (contained in the risk note) if it had been made. The fact that one party did not know what a clause said made it harder to find that that clause was incorporated into a contract by a course of dealing.

Thornton v Shoe Lane Parking Ltd (1970) CA

The plaintiff drove his car into the defendants' multi-storey car park. A light at the entrance turned from red to green and the ticket machine pushed out a ticket which the plaintiff took. The plaintiff parked his car and returned later to collect it. While he was loading his belongings into the boot of the car, an accident occurred which injured the plaintiff and which the defendants were found to have caused by their negligence. The defendants claimed that they were not liable because of the statement on the ticket issued to the plaintiff, 'This ticket is issued subject to the conditions of issue as displayed on the premises'. There was a long list of conditions posted on one of the columns in the car park which included an exemption from liability for any injury to customers however caused.

Held the defendants could not rely on the exemption clause among the conditions. (I) The ticket was no more than a receipt. Because it was issued from an automatic machine, with no human attendant, it was not possible for the plaintiff to return the ticket after he had taken it. Therefore, the ticket came too late to incorporate any new contractual terms. (II) Even if the machine was the equivalent of a booking clerk so that the ticket cases applied to this case, the defendants did not give the plaintiff reasonable notice (see *per* Mellish LJ in *Parker v The South Eastern Railway Company* (5.3.1)) that this condition was in the contract. Because the clause was, *per* Lord Denning MR, 'so wide and so destructive of rights', the defendants had to draw it to the plaintiff's attention:

> ... in the most explicit way ... In order to give sufficient notice, it would need to be printed in red ink with a red hand pointing to it, or something equally startling.

Interfoto Picture Library Ltd v Stiletto Visual Programmes Ltd (1987) CA

On 5 March 1984, the defendants, an advertising agency, telephoned the plaintiffs, a picture library, seeking some pictures of the 1950s to use in a presentation to a client. The plaintiffs said they would see if they had anything suitable. That day, the plaintiffs sent to the defendants 47 transparencies together with a delivery note. The delivery note included nine conditions; condition 2 read:

> All transparencies must be returned to us within 14 days from the date of posting/delivery/collection. A holding fee of £5.00 plus VAT per day will be charged for each transparency which is retained by you longer than the said period of 14 days save where a copyright licence is granted or we agree a longer period in writing with you.

The defendants, who did not read the conditions rang the plaintiffs to say that they might use one or two of the pictures and that they would get back to them. In fact, the defendants did not use the transparencies but only returned them to the plaintiffs on 2 April, despite telephone calls from the plaintiffs on 20 March and 23 March. The plaintiffs therefore claimed £3,783.50 (£5 x 47 transparencies x 14 days x 115% to include VAT) as the holding charge after the pictures were returned on 2 April.

Held condition 2 was not incorporated in the contract between the parties and the plaintiffs would therefore be awarded a *quantum meruit* holding charge of £3.50 per week per picture (that is, a total of £378.35) in place of £5.00 per day. (I) The contract was formed when the defendants accepted the pictures and telephoned the plaintiffs to say they would get back to them later. It must be assumed that the defendants recognised there was writing on the delivery note which was likely to contain contractual terms, though the defendants were assumed not to have read the conditions. *Per* Bingham LJ:

> To the extent that the conditions ... were in common form or usual terms regularly encountered in this business, I do not think the defendants could successfully contend that they were not incorporated into the contract.

However, condition 2 was 'unreasonable and extortionate' so that, to ensure incorporation, the plaintiffs would have had to have taken special steps to bring it to the defendants' attention, which they had failed to do. (II) *Obiter*, the clause was probably void as a penalty clause (14.1.3), but that had not been argued, so the point was not decided.

5.3.3 Incorporation by course of dealing

McCutcheon v David MacBrayne Ltd (1924) HL

See 5.3.2.

Hollier v Rambler Motors (AMC) Ltd (1971) CA

The plaintiff telephoned the defendants and asked if they would repair his car. The defendants said they would carry out the repairs if the plaintiff sent the car to them. The plaintiff agreed and sent his car to the defendants' garage. While it was there, it was damaged in a fire which was found to have been caused by the defendants' negligence. In the preceding five years, the defendants had repaired other cars belonging to the plaintiff three or four times. On at least two of those occasions, the plaintiff had signed a form headed 'Invoice' at the bottom of which appeared the words 'The company is not responsible for damage caused by fire to customers' cars on the premises'. The defendants argued that that exclusion clause was incorporated into their contract with the plaintiff.

Held the defendants could not rely on the exclusion clause and must pay for the damage to the plaintiff's car. (I) The clause was not incorporated into the contract by a course of dealing. *Per* Salmon LJ:

> If it was impossible to rely on a course of dealing in *McCutcheon v David MacBrayne Ltd* (5.3.2), still less would it be possible to do so in this case, when the so called course of dealing consisted only of three or four transactions in the course of five years.

(II) (12.2.1) Even if it were incorporated, the clause would not be effective to exclude liability for the defendants' negligence. Where a type of damage could have many causes, a party who wishes to exclude liability for that type of damage caused by his own negligence must use plain language to do so. The ordinary man or woman would understand this clause to be a warning that the defendants would not be liable for damage caused by fires caused other than by the defendants' negligence.

British Crane Hire Corporation Ltd v Ipswich Plant Hire Ltd (1973) CA

Both parties were in the business of hiring out cranes and other equipment. The defendants were doing some work on marshy land in Suffolk and they had an urgent need for a dragline crane. They telephoned the plaintiffs who agreed to hire them out a crane for an agreed price. The crane was delivered to the defendants and the plaintiffs sent their usual printed form shortly afterwards with a request that the defendants should sign the form and return it to the plaintiffs. Then the crane sank in the marshy ground and had to be extracted at a considerable cost. Under the conditions on the printed form, that cost would be born by the defendants, but as the defendants had not signed the form they refused to pay. The plaintiffs argued that the conditions should be incorporated by a course of dealing that involved two hirings in the previous year in respect of each of which the defendants had signed the form.

Held the conditions were incorporated into the contract and so the defendants must pay the costs of saving the crane. *Per* Lord Denning MR:

... the parties were both in the trade and were of equal bargaining power ... The defendants themselves knew that firms in the plant-hiring trade always imposed conditions in regard to the hiring of plant; and that their conditions were on much the same lines ... I would not put it so much on the course of dealing, but rather on the common understanding which is to be derived from the conduct of the parties, namely, that the hiring was to be on the terms of the plaintiffs' usual conditions.

Q If the conditions had not been incorporated, would it have made any difference to who had to pay the costs?

Circle Freight International Ltd v Medeast Gulf Exports Ltd (1988) CA

The plaintiffs were freight forwarding agents. The defendants were exporters of goods to the Middle East. On at least 11 occasions between March and August 1983, the defendants used the services of the plaintiffs to export goods. On each occasion, the contract was made orally by telephone. The plaintiffs sent invoices to the defendants on each occasion after they had taken the goods to their warehouse. Each invoice stated:

All business is transacted by the company under the current trading conditions of the Institute of Freight Forwarders [IFF] a copy of which is available on request.

In August 1983, a quantity of the defendants' dresses was stolen from the plaintiffs' van because of negligence on the part of the plaintiffs. The plaintiffs argued that their liability was limited by one of the conditions of the IFF. The defendants said that those conditions were not incorporated in the contract in respect of the dresses. The defendants knew that there would be some terms but had not realised what they were or seen that they would be the IFF conditions.

Held the IFF conditions were incorporated in the contract for the carriage of the dresses by the course of dealings between the parties. *Per* Taylor LJ:

Here, the parties were commercial companies. There had bee a course of dealing in which at least 11 invoices had been sent giving notice that business was conducted on the IFF terms at a place on the document where it was plain to be seen ... The IFF conditions are not particularly onerous or unusual and, indeed, are in common use. In these circumstances, ... I consider that reasonable notice of the terms was given by the plaintiffs. Putting it another way, I consider that the defendants' conduct in continuing the course of business after at least 11 notices of the terms and omitting to request a sight of them would have led and did lead the plaintiffs reasonably to believe the defendants accepted their terms. In those circumstances, it is irrelevant that in fact [the defendants] did not read the notices.

5.4 Terms implied by custom

Hutton v Warren (1836) CE

The plaintiff was the tenant of the defendant's farm until the defendant gave the plaintiff notice to quit. *Per* Parke B:

> It was proved that, by a custom of the country, a tenant was bound to farm according to a certain course of husbandry for the whole of his tenancy, and at quitting was entitled to a fair allowance for seed and labour on the arable land, and was obliged to leave the manure, if the landlord would purchase it. In October 1833, after the notice to quit, the defendant, his agent, and the plaintiff, had an interview; and the agent insisted that the plaintiff should sow the arable land, and that he was bound to keep the farm in regular course. The plaintiff accordingly did, afterwards, sow the arable land, for which he claimed the compensation in question.

Held the plaintiff could claim payment for the seeds and labour he had spent on the land even though it was not explicit in the lease that he could do so. *Per* Parke B, giving the judgment of the court:

> We are of the opinion that this custom was by implication imported into the lease. It has long been settled, that, in commercial transactions, extrinsic evidence of custom and usage is admissible to annex incidents to written contracts, on matters with respect to which they are silent.

Les Affréteurs Réunis SA v Leopold Walford (London) Ltd (1919) HL

See 4.2.1.

5.5 Terms implied by the court

The Moorcock (1889) CA

The parties agreed that the plaintiff's ship should be discharged and loaded at the defendants' wharf. For that purpose, the ship would be moored alongside the jetty, where it would be grounded at low tide. Although the defendants made no charge for mooring the ship at their jetty, they received fees for their loading and unloading work. The ship came alongside the jetty as agreed, but when low tide came, it was damaged owing to the centre of the vessel settling on a ridge of hard ground beneath the mud. The plaintiff now claimed the cost of repairs from the defendants who denied liability.

Held the defendants were liable for the damage because there was an implied term in the parties' contract that the defendants would take reasonable care to check that the river bed near the jetty was in good condition or to inform the plaintiff if it was not. *Per* Lord Esher MR:

> The owners of the wharf and jetty are there always, and if anything happens in front of their wharf they have the means of finding it out, but persons who come in their ships to this wharf have no reasonable means of discovering what the state of the bed of the river is until the vessel is moored and takes the ground for the first time.

Per Bowen LJ:

> The implication which the law draws from what must obviously have been the intention of the parties, the law draws with the object of giving efficacy to the transaction and preventing such a failure of consideration as cannot have been within the contemplation of either side ... In business transactions such as this, what the law desires to effect by the implication is to give such business efficacy to the transaction as must have been intended at all events by both parties who are business men.

Note

The judgment of Bowen LJ in this case is the source of the 'business efficacy' test for the implication of a term.

Shirlaw v Southern Foundries Ltd (1939) CA (affirmed by HL)

The plaintiff was employed by the defendants as their managing director. His agreement was to serve as managing director for 10 years from 1933. In 1936, the defendants were taken over by another company, Federated, and adopted new articles of association which empowered Federated to remove any of the defendants' directors. In 1937, Federated exercised their power to remove the plaintiff as a director of the defendants. As a consequence, the plaintiff ceased to be managing director. The plaintiff sought compensation for the breach of an implied term in his contract with the defendants that the defendants would not change their articles to allow him to be removed as a director.

Held there was such an implied term upon which the plaintiff could rely to obtain damages. *Per* MacKinnon LJ:

> Too often ... such an invitation [to find the existence of an implied term] is backed by the citation of a sentence or two from the judgment of Bowen LJ in *The Moorcock* [above]. They are sentences from an extempore judgment as sound and sensible as all the utterances of that great judge; but I fancy that he would have been rather surprised if he could have foreseen that these general remarks of his would come to be a favourite citation of a supposed principle of law ...

For my part, I think there is a test that may be at least as useful as such generalities. If I may quote from an essay which I wrote some years ago, I then said:

Prima facie that which in any contract is left to be implied and need not be expressed is something so obvious that it goes without saying; so that, if, while the parties were making their bargain, an officious bystander were to suggest some express provision for it in their agreement, they would testily suppress him with a common 'Oh, of course!' At least it is true, I think, that if a term were never implied by a judge unless it could pass that test, he could not be held to be wrong.

Q Does the last sentence of MacKinnon LJ's *dictum* quoted above mean that a judge who always follows his test would never be wrong, or only that such a judge would never wrongly imply a term, but might still wrongly refuse to do so?

Luxor (Eastbourne) Limited v Cooper (1940) HL

See 1.4.4.

Liverpool City Council v Irwin (1976) HL

The defendant tenants lived on the ninth and tenth floors of a tower block in Everton that was owned by the plaintiff council. The tower block had a staircase and two lifts. There was also a chute through which the tenants' rubbish passed to the ground floor for collection. There was no written lease or tenancy agreement, but only a document headed 'Conditions of Tenancy'. This document simply contained a list of obligations on the tenants and it was signed only by the tenants. The block was in a bad condition owing to vandalism, alleged non-cooperation by the tenants and neglect by the council. Following a rent strike, the council took proceedings for possession. The tenants counter-claimed for damages and an injunction to stop the council neglecting the block. The tenants alleged that the council was in breach of terms to be implied in the agreements between the council and the tenants.

Held the council had an implied obligation to take reasonable care to keep the staircase, lifts and rubbish chute in a state of reasonable repair and usability. (I) *Per* Lord Wilberforce there were four categories of implied terms: (i) Where 'the courts are spelling out what both parties know and would, if asked, unhesitatingly agree to be part of the bargain'. (ii) 'In other cases, where there is an apparently complete bargain, the courts are willing to add a term on the ground that the contract will not work – this is the case, if not of *The Moorcock* (5.5) itself on its facts, at least of the doctrine of *The Moorcock* as usually applied.' (iii) The implication of terms because they are reasonable, as suggested by Lord Denning MR in the

Court of Appeal in this case, should be rejected as extending 'a long, and undesirable, way beyond sound authority'. (iv) This case is in a fourth category:

> The court here is simply trying to establish what the contract is, the parties not having themselves fully stated the terms. In this sense, the court is searching for what must be implied ... In my opinion, such obligation should be read into the contract as the nature of the contract itself implicitly requires, no more, no less; a test in other words of necessity.

(II) Lord Cross of Chelsea combined the test from *The Moorcock* with the officious bystander test. (III) *Per* Lord Salmon, a term should be implied where it was necessary, for example in the situation where without the term the contract would be 'inefficacious, futile and absurd'. (IV) Four of their lordships expressly disapproved of Lord Denning MR's suggestion that a term could be implied merely because it was reasonable to do so, while the fifth simply agreed with Lord Wilberforce.

Q   Does a test of necessity amount to anything more objective than a test of what is necessary for one of the parties?

Shell UK Ltd v Lostock Garage Ltd (1976) CA

The defendant garage had a solus agreement with the plaintiffs, Shell, under which the garage agreed to buy all its petrol from Shell. The agreement could be terminated by either side on 12 months' notice. In 1975, the oil crisis dramatically increased the price of petrol so that motorists economised and used less. By December 1975, there was a price war. The garage had four local competitors each of which cut its price to 70p per gallon. Lostock could not afford to sell below 75p per gallon and lost most of its business. Two of the competing garages were free from ties and so were able to buy from cheaper suppliers. The other two were tied to Shell. Those two benefited from a support scheme by which Shell kept the retail price at 70p, but the scheme only applied to large garages. The defendant garage was too small to benefit from the support scheme. On 28 January 1976, the garage went to a cheaper supplier, Mansfield, in order to stay in business. However, on 6 March, Mansfield stopped supplying the garage because Shell had threatened Mansfield with an action for interference with Shell's contractual rights (see *British Motor Trade Association v Salvadori and Others*, 4.3.2). The support scheme ended in April. Shell now sued the garage for damages for Shell's loss of profit on the supplies which the garage bought from Mansfield and sought injunctions to enforce the solus agreement until the 12 month notice period expired. The garage argued that the support scheme was a breach of an implied term in the solus agreement that Shell would not abnormally discriminate against the garage.

Held no such term could be implied, but Shell could not enforce the solus agreement or obtain damages for other reasons. (I)(i) *Per* Lord Denning MR, following *Liverpool City Council v Irwin* (5.5):

> ... there are two broad categories of implied terms. The first category comprehends all those relationships which are of common occurrence, such as the relationship of seller and buyer, owner and hirer, master and servant, landlord and tenant ... In all those relationships, the courts have imposed obligations on one party or the other, saying they are implied terms. These obligations are not founded on the intention of the parties, actual or presumed, but on more general considerations ... In these relationships, the parties can exclude or modify the obligation by express words, but unless they do so, the obligation is a legal incident of the relationship which is attached by the law itself and not by reason of any implied term ... The second category comprehends those cases which are not within the first category ... In these cases, the implication is based on an intention imputed to the parties from their actual circumstances ... Such an imputation is only to be made when it is necessary to imply a term to give efficacy to the contract and make it a workable agreement in such manner as the parties would clearly have done if they had applied their mind to the contingency which has arisen. These are the 'officious bystander' type of case.

Since the suggested term in this case cannot be brought within either category, it cannot be implied. (ii) *Per* Ormrod LJ, following *Liverpool City Council v Irwin*:

> ... the court should only imply a term or terms if it is 'necessary' to do so. This necessity test is a stringent one and, in my judgment, the proposed terms go well beyond the bounds of necessity.

(II) It was not equitable to grant Shell the enforcement of the tie by injunctions or by specific performance. Shell could not have damages because they could not prove that the garage would have bought significant amounts of petrol from Shell if the garage had not bought any from Mansfield, so Shell could not show that they had suffered loss.

Q   Are the approaches of Lord Denning MR and Ormrod LJ in this case equivalent to each other? If not, which more correctly represents the House of Lords' decision in *Liverpool City Council v Irwin*?

Bournemouth and Boscombe Athletic Football Club Co Ltd v Manchester United Football Club Ltd (1980) CA

By a written contract signed on 27 September 1972, a football player, Edward John MacDougall, was transferred from Bournemouth to Manchester United for a fee of £175,000 plus a further payment of £25,000 when the player had scored 20 goals for Manchester United in first class football. Up to December 1973, the player scored four goals in 11 matches. Then the manager of Manchester United was changed and the new manager, Tommy Docherty, did not wish to retain the player. The player was sold shortly afterwards to West Ham for £170,000. Bournemouth now claimed their additional payment of £25,000 arguing that Manchester United had breached an implied term in their contract that Manchester United would give the player a reasonable opportunity to score the 20 goals.

Held some such term had to be implied to give business efficacy to the contract. Bournmouth were entitled to the £25,000.

Eyre v Measday (1985) CA

The plaintiff, a married woman with three children, asked the defendant, a doctor, to sterilise her. The defendant agreed to carry out a laparoscopy sterilisation and the plaintiff signed a consent form for that procedure. The defendant explained how the operation worked and that it was irreversible. The operation was performed successfully, but, after about a year, the plaintiff discovered she was pregnant. The defendant, in line with common practice, had not told the plaintiff that there was a risk of between two and six in every 1,000 that a pregnancy could occur after an apparently successful laparoscopy.

Held the contract was that the defendant would perform a certain kind of operation, which he did. Although a term may be implied that the defendant would carry out the operation with reasonable skill and care, it could not be implied that the defendant warranted that the operation would have the desired result. Although both parties *thought* the operation would have that result, the defendant had not done anything which should have caused the plaintiff to think that he *guaranteed* the result. This was because medical procedures are by their nature uncertain, so that a surgeon would have to be explicit if such a guarantee were to be found.

Marcan Shipping (London) Ltd v Polish Steamship Co: *The Manifest Lipkowy* (1989) CA

The defendants wanted to sell a vessel. The plaintiffs negotiated the sale for them. The sale agreement provided 'Commission to be deducted from the purchase price at time of payment ...'. The agreement gave the buyers a right to cancel if the ship was delivered late. A collateral contract was made between the plaintiffs and the defendants which provided:

> ... that on the agreed ... purchase price ... a commission of ... US$262,305 ... shall be deducted from the purchase price and be paid to [the plaintiffs].

The ship was not delivered on time and the buyers cancelled the transaction. The plaintiffs now argued that there was an implied term of the collateral contract that the defendant sellers would not break the sale agreement so as to deprive the plaintiffs of their commission.

Held there was no such implied term. In a contract like this one, the broker took the risk that he would receive nothing if the contract was not completed. *Per* May LJ, with whom Ralph Gibson LJ agreed:

> For my part, I think that reference to the officious bystander frequently does not assist in deciding whether or not a term is to be implied. Officious bystanders may well take different views depending on which side they happen to be standing. In my judgment, it is quite clear from such cases as *Liverpool City Council v Irwin* [5.5] that the real basis upon which a term can be implied in contracts in cases such as this is that they are necessary in order to make the contract work.

Per Bingham LJ:

> I take it to be well established law that a term will be implied only where it is necessary in a business sense to give efficacy to a contract, or where the term is one which the parties must obviously have intended.

5.6 Terms implied by statute

5.6.1 Sale of Goods Act 1979

Section 12 Implied terms about title, etc

(As amended by Sale and Supply of Goods Act 1994)

(1) In a contract of sale, other than one to which sub-s (3) below applies, there is an implied term on the part of the seller that, in the case of a sale, he has a right to sell the goods, and, in the case of an agreement to sell, he will have such a right at the time when the property is to pass.

(2) In a contract of sale, other than one to which sub-s (3) below applies, there is also an implied term that:

    (a) the goods are free, and will remain free until the time when the property is to pass, from any charge or encumbrance not disclosed or known to the buyer before the contract is made; and

    (b) the buyer will enjoy quiet possession of the goods except so far as it may be disturbed by the owner or other person entitled to the benefit of any charge or encumbrance so disclosed or known.

(3) This sub-section applies to a contract of sale in the case of which there appears from the contract or is to be inferred from its

circumstances an intention that the seller should transfer only such title as he or a third person may have.

(4)   In a contract to which sub-s (3) above applies, there is an implied term that all charges or encumbrances known to the seller and not known to the buyer have been disclosed to the buyer before the contract is made.

(5)   In a contract to which sub-s (3) above applies, there is also an implied term that none of the following will disturb the buyer's quiet possession of the goods, namely:

(a)   the seller;

(b)   in a case where the parties to the contract intend that the seller should transfer only such title as a third person may have, that person;

(c)   anyone claiming through or under the seller or that third person otherwise than under a charge or encumbrance disclosed or known to the buyer before the contract is made.

(5A)   As regards England and Wales and Northern Ireland, the term implied by sub-s (1) above is a condition and the terms implied by sub-ss (2), (4) and (5) above are warranties.

Section 13 Sale by description

(As amended by Sale and Supply of Goods Act 1994.)

(1)   Where there is a contract for the sale of goods by description, there is an implied term that the goods will correspond with the description.

(1A)   As regards England and Wales and Northern Ireland, the term implied by sub-s (1) above is a condition.

(2)   If the sale is by sample as well as by description, it is not sufficient that the bulk of the goods corresponds with the sample if the goods do not also correspond with the description.

(3)   A sale of goods is not prevented from being a sale by description by reason only that, being exposed for sale or hire, they are selected by the buyer.

Section 14 Implied terms about quality or fitness

(As amended by Sale and Supply of Goods Act 1994.)

(1)   Except as provided by this section and s 15 below and subject to any other enactment, there is no implied term about the quality or fitness for any particular purpose of goods supplied under a contract of sale.

(2)   Where the seller sells goods in the course of a business, there is an implied term that the goods supplied under the contract are of satisfactory quality.

(2A) For the purposes of this Act, goods are of satisfactory quality if they meet the standard that a reasonable person would regard as satisfactory, taking account of any description of the goods, the price (if relevant) and all the other relevant circumstances.

(2B) For the purposes of this Act, the quality of goods includes their state and condition and the following (among others) are in appropriate cases aspects of the quality of the goods:

(a) fitness for all the purposes for which goods of the kind in question are commonly supplied;

(b) appearance and finish;

(c) freedom from minor defects;

(d) safety; and

(e) durability.

(2C) The term implied by sub-s (2) above does not extend to any matter making the quality of goods unsatisfactory:

(a) which is specifically drawn to the buyer's attention before the contract is made;

(b) where the buyer examines the goods before the contract is made, which that examination ought to reveal;

(c) in the case of a contract for sale by sample, which would have been apparent on a reasonable examination of the sample.

(3) Where the seller sells goods in the course of a business and the buyer, expressly or by implication, makes known:

(a) to the seller; or

(b) where the purchase price or part of it is payable by instalments and the goods were previously sold by a credit broker to the seller, to that credit broker,

any particular purpose for which the goods are being bought, there is an implied term that the goods supplied under the contract are reasonably fit for that purpose, whether or not that is a purpose for which such goods are commonly supplied, except where the circumstances show that the buyer does not rely, or that it is unreasonable for him to rely, on the skill or judgment of the seller or credit broker.

(4) An implied condition or warranty about quality or fitness for a particular purpose may be annexed to a contract of sale by usage.

(5) The preceding provisions of this section apply to a sale by a person who in the course of a business is acting as agent for another as they apply to a sale by a principal in the course of a business, except

where that other is not selling in the course of a business and either the buyer knows that fact or reasonable steps were taken to bring it to the notice of the buyer before the contract is made.

(6) As regards England and Wales and Northern Ireland, the terms implied by sub-ss (2) and (3) above are conditions.

Section 15 Sale by sample

(As amended by Sale and Supply of Goods Act 1994)

(1) A contract of sale is a contract for sale by sample where there is an express or implied term to that effect in the contract.

(2) In the case of a contract for sale by sample, there is an implied term:

   (a) that the bulk will correspond with the sample in quality;

   [(b) is deleted;]

   (c) that the goods will be free from any defect, making their quality unsatisfactory, which would not be apparent on reasonable examination of the sample.

(3) As regards England and Wales and Northern Ireland, the term implied by sub-s (2) above is a condition.

Section 15A Modifications of remedies for breach of conditions in
non-consumer cases

(Inserted by Sale and Supply of Goods Act 1994)

(1) Where in the case of a contract of sale:

   (a) the buyer would, apart from this sub-section, have a right to reject goods by reason of a breach on the part of the seller of a term implied by ss 13, 14 or 15 above; but

   (b) the breach is so slight that it would be unreasonable for him to reject them,

then, if the buyer does not deal as a consumer, the breach is not to be treated as a breach of condition but may be treated as a breach of warranty.

(2) This section applies unless a contrary intention appears in, or is to be implied from, the contract.

(3) It is for the seller to show that a breach fell within sub-s (1)(b) above.

Section 55 Exclusion of implied terms

(1) Where a right, duty or liability would arise under a contract of sale of goods by implication of law, it may (subject to the Unfair Contract Terms Act 1977) be negatived or varied by express agreement, or by the course of dealing between the parties, or by such usage as binds both parties to the contract.

(2)   An express term does not negative a term implied by this Act unless inconsistent with it.

Harlingdon and Leinster Enterprises Ltd v Christopher Hull Fine Art Ltd (1989) CA

Both parties were art dealers. The defendants, who did not specialise in German expressionists, were asked to sell two paintings which were attributed to the German expressionist, Gabriele Münter. The defendants knew that the plaintiffs did deal in such pictures and so contacted them. Mr Runkel of the plaintiffs visited the defendants and spoke there to Mr Hull of the defendants. *Per* Nourse LJ:

> Mr Hull said that he did not know much about the paintings, that he had never heard of Gabriele Münter and that he thought little of her paintings. He made it absolutely plain that he was not an expert in them. By some form of words which neither party could precisely remember at the trial, Mr Hull to a certain extent made it clear he was relying on Mr Runkel.

Mr Runkel himself had no special training or expertise to enable him to identify the painter. Mr Runkel agreed to buy one of the paintings from the defendants for £6,000. The plaintiffs sold the painting to a buyer who found that it was a fake. The plaintiffs refunded the price paid by their buyer and now sought the return of the £6,000 from the defendants, arguing that there was a sale by description within s 13 of the Sale of Goods Act 1979 (5.6.1) and that the painting was not of merchantable quality, the test which s 14 of the Sale of Goods Act 1979 imposed at that time because the painting was not fit for its purpose.

Held the plaintiffs could not succeed on either ground. (I) *Per* Nourse and Slade LJJ, Stuart-Smith LJ dissenting, there was no sale by description in these circumstances where the buyer did not rely on the description of the painting as being by Münter in making his decision to buy. (II) The painting remained fit for the purpose of resale even though it could only be sold for a much lower price. In addition, it was still fit for the purpose of aesthetic appreciation. Stuart-Smith LJ dissented on this point as well, holding:

> ... both parties knew perfectly well that the purpose of the sale was resale as dealers, and not merely putting the picture on the wall and enjoying its aesthetic qualities. I cannot think that it is a reasonable expectation in these circumstances that a fake which is virtually worthless is fit for the purpose of being sold as a painting by Münter at a price of £6,000.

(III) *Per* Nourse LJ, *obiter*:

> I desire to add some general observations about sales of pictures by one dealer to another where the seller makes an attribution to a recognised artist ... the

astuteness of lawyers ought to be directed towards facilitating, rather than impeding, the efficient working of the market. The court ought to be exceedingly wary in giving a seller's attribution any contractual effect. To put it in lawyers' language, the potential arguability of almost any attribution, being part of the common experience of the contracting parties, is part of the factual background against which the effect if any, of an attribution must be judged.

Q Does the change to s 14 since this case so that price is now specifically made a matter to be included in assessing whether the goods are of satisfactory quality strengthen Stuart-Smith LJ's dissenting argument in (II) above for any future cases like this one?

Slater v Finning Ltd (1996) HL

The defenders supplied camshafts to the pursuers which the defenders knew would be used in the engine of the pursuers' vessel, *The Aquarius II*. The camshafts wore out excessively quickly and the pursuers claimed damages for breach of the term implied by s 14(3) of the Sale of Goods Act 1979 (5.6.1). The cause of the problem was never established in detail. However, it was held by the court at first instance that the cause of the trouble was external to both the engine and the camshafts.

Held there was no breach of the term implied by s 14(3) of the Sale of Goods Act 1979 in this case. *Per* Lord Keith of Kinkel:

As a matter of principle ... it may be said that where a buyer purchases goods from a seller who deals in goods of that description there is no breach of the implied condition of fitness where the failure of the goods to meet the intended purpose arises from an abnormal feature or idiosyncrasy, not made known to the seller, in the buyer or in the circumstances of the use of the goods by the buyer. That is the case whether or not the buyer is himself aware of the abnormal feature or idiosyncrasy.

Per Lord Steyn:

Outside the field of private sales, the shift from *caveat emptor* to *caveat venditor* in relation to the implied condition of fitness for purpose has been a notable feature of the development of our commercial law. But to uphold the present claim would be to allow *caveat venditor* to run riot.

5.6.2 Supply of Goods and Services Act 1982

Section 13 Implied term about care and skill

In a contract for the supply of a service where the supplier is acting in the course of a business, there is an implied term that the supplier will carry out the service with reasonable care and skill.

Section 14 Implied term about time for performance

(1)   Where, under a contract for the supply of a service by a supplier acting in the course of a business, the time for the service to be carried out is not fixed by the contract, left to be fixed in a manner agreed by the contract or determined by the course of dealing between the parties, there is an implied term that the supplier will carry out the service within a reasonable time.

(2)   What is a reasonable time is a question of fact.

Section 15 Implied term about consideration

(1)   Where, under a contract for the supply of a service the consideration for the service is not determined by the contract, left to be determined in a manner agreed by the contract or determined by the course of dealing between the parties, there is an implied term that the party contracting with the supplier will pay a reasonable charge.

(2)   What is a reasonable charge is a question of fact.

Section 16 Exclusion of implied terms, etc

(1)   Where a right, duty or liability would arise under a contract for the supply of a service by virtue of this Part of this Act, it may (subject to sub-s (2) below and the Unfair Contract Terms Act 1977) be negatived or varied by express agreement, or by the course of dealing between the parties, or by such usage as binds both parties to the contract.

(2)   An express term does not negative a term implied by this Act unless inconsistent with it.

(3)   Nothing in this Part of this Act prejudices:

(a)   any rule of law which imposes on the supplier a duty stricter than that imposed by s 13 or 14 above; or

(b)   subject to para (a) above, any rule of law whereby any term not inconsistent with this Part of this Act is to be implied in a contract for the supply of a service.

(4)   This Part of this Act has effect subject to any other enactment which defines or restricts the rights, duties or liabilities arising in connection with a service of any description.

5.7 Conditions, warranties and innominate terms

5.7.1 Sale of Goods Act 1979

Section 10 Stipulations about time

(1)   Unless a different intention appears from the terms of the contract, stipulations as to time of payment are not of the essence of a contract of sale.

(2)   Whether any other stipulation as to time is or is not of the essence of the contract depends on the terms of the contract.

(3)   In a contract of sale, 'month' *prima facie* means calendar month.

Section 11 When condition to be treated as warranty

(2)   Where a contract of sale is subject to a condition to be fulfilled by the seller, the buyer may waive the condition, or may elect to treat the breach of the condition as a breach of warranty and not as a ground for treating the contract as repudiated.

(3)   Whether a stipulation in a contract of sale is a condition, the breach of which may give rise to a claim for damages, but not to a right to reject the goods and treat the contract as repudiated, depends in each case on the construction of the contract; and a stipulation may be a condition, though called a warranty in the contract.

(4)   Where a contract of sale is not severable and the buyer has accepted the goods or part of them, the breach of a condition to be fulfilled by the seller can only be treated as a breach of warranty, and not as a ground for rejecting the goods and treating the contract as repudiated, unless there is an express or implied term of the contract to that effect.

(6)   Nothing in this section affects a condition or warranty whose fulfilment is excused by law by reason of impossibility or otherwise.

5.7.2 The cases

Wallis, Son and Wells v Pratt and Haynes (1911) HL

The parties made a written agreement for the sale of 'common English sainfoin' seed. The defendant sellers delivered giant sainfoin instead. The plaintiff buyers did not realise the error, accepted the seed and sold it on to others. The buyers had to pay damages to those who had bought the seed from them and sought to recover their loss from the sellers. The sellers argued that they were protected by a clause in the parties' contract which provided that 'Sellers give no warranty expressed or implied as to growth, description or any other matters'.

Held the sellers had to pay damages for the buyers' loss. It was clear from several sections of the Sale of Goods Act 1893 (now the Sale of Goods Act 1979, see 5.7.1) that there was a distinction between a warranty and a condition and that the description of goods was a condition. A breach of that condition was therefore not covered by the exclusion clause.

Aerial Advertising Co v Bachelors Peas Ltd (1938) KB

The defendants, who sold tinned peas, agreed with the plaintiffs, who flew advertising aeroplanes, that the plaintiffs would make two tours with an aeroplane trailing a streamer bearing the words 'Eat Bachelor's Peas' for a total price of £500. Each tour was to last 25 hours of time spent over towns. The times and places of each flight were to be approved by the defendants in advance. During the first tour, the weather was poor and the plaintiffs' pilot was in daily contact with the defendants. On 9 November 1937, the pilot agreed his flight for 9 and 10 November. However, on 11 November, he flew without consulting the defendants. He flew during the morning over Manchester and Salford, including passing over the main squares which were crowded with people. The crowds were commemorating Remembrance Day by keeping two minutes silence and they were horrified by the advertising aeroplane flying over them. The defendants immediately received many telephone calls and letters condemning them for desecrating Remembrance Day and promising to boycott their goods. Despite taking advertisements to apologise in the newspapers, the defendants felt they could not allow the second tour to go ahead as it would merely remind their customers of the incident on 11 November.

Held the defendants were entitled to treat the contract as repudiated and refuse to pay for a second tour. *Per* Atkinson J:

> There must be implied in that contract a term that the flying under the contract would be carried out with reasonable skill and with reasonable care, having regard to the object of the contract, and in whatever precise words the implied obligation is expressed, it must be, I think, certainly wide enough to exclude flying in a way which would bring the advertisers into hatred and contempt.

The plaintiffs breached that term in a way which meant that the defendants could no longer have their choice of flying times and places, which had been the main benefit of the contract, because they were constrained not to return to the North of England in the foreseeable future. It was thus 'commercially wholly unreasonable' for the defendants to carry on with the contract, so they were entitled to consider themselves no longer bound by it.

Q   Is the term implied by the court in this case a condition or a term like that considered in *Hong Kong Fir Shipping Co Ltd v Kawasaki Kisen Kaisha Ltd* (below)?

Harling v Eddy (1951) CA

See 5.2.3.

Hong Kong Fir Shipping Co Ltd v Kawasaki Kisen Kaisha Ltd (1961) CA

The defendant charterers chartered a ship from the plaintiff owners by a charterparty that included a term (the seaworthiness term) that the ship was 'in every way fitted for ordinary cargo service'. Various problems arose with the ship which meant that she was docked for repairs for about 20 weeks during and after an eight week voyage between Liverpool and Osaka. The charterers wrote to the owners repudiating the contract and claiming damages for the delays. The owners claimed damages for wrongful repudiation by the charterers. At first instance, it was found that the ship was unseaworthy with regard to the engine room staff who were not sufficiently skilled or experienced.

Held for the owners, the breach of the seaworthiness term did not give the charterers a right to repudiate the contract. *Per* Upjohn LJ, the seaworthiness term could not be a condition because a very minor breach, such as a missing nail, could not have been intended by the parties to give the charterer a right to end the contract. It is open to the parties to specify that a certain term is to be treated as a condition, but they had not done so here. The delays would only have given the charterers a right to cancel if they were so serious as to have frustrated the contract (see Chapter 8 on frustration). *Per* Diplock LJ, a party who still has obligations to perform under a contract obtains a right to treat the contract as being at an end when an event happens which deprives that party of 'substantially the whole benefit which it was the intention of the parties as expressed in the contract that he should obtain as the consideration for performing those undertakings'. This rule applies whether the event is caused by the default of the other party (breach of contract) or without the default of either party (frustration). Therefore, not all terms can be classified as conditions and warranties. There are many terms, some breaches of which will give rise to an event justifying the ending of the contract and other breaches of which will not do so. The correct approach in respect of such terms is not to consider whether the clause is a condition or a warranty but rather to look at the effect of the particular breach which happened. The division of terms into warranties and conditions is not exhaustive.

Note

Terms like the one discussed in this case are now called innominate or intermediate terms. Diplock LJ's judgment in this case is usually credited with being the first explicit judicial recognition of the existence of such terms.

Maredelanto Compania Naviera SA v Bergbau-Handel GmbH: The Mihalis Angelos (1970) CA

A charterparty included a provision in clause 1 that the vessel was 'expected ready to load under this charter about 1 July 1965'. In fact, the plaintiff owners had no reason to expect that the vessel could be ready by that date, which indeed it was not. The defendant charterers repudiated the contract on 17 July 1965 and the question in this case was whether the owners' breach of clause 1 gave the charterers a right to repudiate the contract, that is, whether clause 1 was a condition of the contract or not.

Held this clause was a condition, the breach of which gave the charterers a right to treat the contract as repudiated. (I) Similar clauses had been held to be conditions in the past and nothing in *Hong Kong Fir Shipping Co Ltd v Kawasaki Kisen Kaisha Ltd* (5.7.2) prevented the same result being reached. (II) There should be certainty in the law. (III) Since such a clause can only be breached by the ship owner giving an assurance dishonestly or without reasonable grounds, the owners could not suffer injustice by the charterers being allowed to end the contract. (IV) It did not defeat the charterers' acceptance of repudiation that at the time they made it, they gave an invalid ground for it. A valid ground, in this case the breach of clause 1, could be relied on even if it was only raised some time after the repudiation was accepted.

L Schuler AG v Wickman Machine Tool Sales Ltd (1973) HL

Schuler were manufacturers of machine tools and other engineering products. On 1 May 1963, they made a written contract with Wickman under which Wickman received rights to sell Schuler's products in the UK. The contract included the following terms:

7(b) It shall be a condition of this Agreement that – (i) [Wickman] shall send its representatives to visit the six firms whose names are listed in the Schedule hereto at least once every week for the purpose of soliciting orders for panel presses; (ii) that the same representative shall visit each firm on each occasion unless there are unavoidable reasons preventing the visit being made by that representative in which case the visit shall be made by an alternate representative and [Wickman] will ensure that such a visit is always made by the same alternate representative ... 11(a) ... Schuler or [Wickman] may by notice in writing to the other determine this agreement forthwith if – (i) the other shall have committed a material breach of its obligations hereunder and shall have failed to remedy the same within 60 days of being required in writing so to do ...

Wickman committed some minor breaches of the requirements of clause 7(b) and Schuler repudiated the contract. The question was whether Schuler had a right to repudiate.

Held Schuler did not have a right to repudiate the contract for a minor breach of clause 7(b). Schuler contended that the word 'condition' used in clause 7(b) had a technical legal meaning (a term of which any breach gives the innocent party a right to treat the contract as repudiated), particularly since the Sale of Goods Act 1893 (now the Sale of Goods Act 1979, see 5.7.1) and particularly in a document, which, like this one, had been drawn up by lawyers. This contention was rejected on the ground that the word 'condition' had several possible meanings and that to ascribe to it here the technical legal meaning would produce an absurd result because minor breaches of the clause were almost inevitable and would not go to the root of the contract. In the light of clause 11(a), the use of the word 'condition' in clause 7(b) could be made sense of by construing it as meaning that any breach of clause 7(b) would be treated as a material breach of obligations within the meaning of clause 11(a). *Per* Lord Reid:

The fact that a particular construction leads to a very unreasonable result must be a relevant consideration. The more unreasonable the result the more unlikely it is that the parties can have intended it, and, if they do intend it, the more necessary it is that they shall make that intention abundantly clear.

Note ———————————————————————————

The result of this case is that even the description of a term as a condition in the contract is not, by itself, sufficient to ensure that the term is treated as a condition by the court.

A/S Awilco v Fulvia SpA di Navigazione: *The Chikuma* (1981) HL

By clause 5 of a charterparty, payment by the charterers to the owners of the hire charge was:

... to be made ... in cash in US currency, monthly in advance ... otherwise failing the punctual and regular payment of the hire ... the Owners shall be at liberty to withdraw the vessel from the service of the Charterers.

It was also provided that the payment was to be made to the owners' bank in Italy. A monthly payment was due on 22 January 1976. On 21 January, the charterers instructed their Norwegian bank to make a credit transfer to the owners. On 22 January, the Norwegian bank sent a telex to the Italian bank asking them to credit the owners' account and this the Italian bank did. However, under Italian banking law and practice, although the owners had use of the money, interest would not start to run on it until 26 January and, had they withdrawn the money before 26 January, they would have had to pay interest upon it. On 24 January, the owners withdrew the vessel from the charterers on the ground that they had failed to pay the instalment due on 22 January.

Held the owners were entitled to withdraw from the charterparty under clause 5. To comply with clause 5, the payment must be as good as cash. The payment made on 22 January was not as good as cash because it could not earn interest. It was only the equivalent of an overdraft facility. Although the breach of clause 5 was very minor, it was a breach and therefore the owners could withdraw the ship from the charterers. Ship owners and charterers have approximately equal bargaining power. In this situation, the courts should allow them to contract freely and in construing their contracts should, *per* Lord Bridge of Harwich with whom all of their lordships agreed:

> ... strive to follow clear and consistent principles and steadfastly refuse to be blown off course by the supposed merits of individual cases.

Bunge Corporation v Tradax SA (1981) HL

The parties made a written contract for the sale of 15,000 long tons of US soya bean meal to be delivered in three 5,000 ton shipments. The clause regarding the date of delivery for the first shipment was in these terms:

> PERIOD OF DELIVERY – During June 1975 at Buyers' call. Buyers shall give at least 15 consecutive days' notice of probable readiness of vessel(s), and of the approximate quantity required to be loaded. Buyers shall keep Sellers informed of any changes in the date of probable readiness of the vessel(s).

The buyers gave notice of the ship to be used on 17 June. On 20 June, the sellers withdrew from the contract on the ground that the notice came less than 15 days before the end of June so that the notice was late. The buyers argued that, following Diplock LJ's judgment in *Hong Kong Fir Shipping Co Ltd v Kawasaki Kisen Kaisha Ltd* (5.7.2), their breach did not deprive the sellers of substantially the whole benefit of the contract and so it could not justify the sellers' repudiation of the contract.

Held the clause regarding delivery time was a condition and so the sellers were entitled to withdraw from the contract when the buyers had breached it. (I) The test of such clauses has two steps. First, it must be considered whether the clause was intended to be a condition or a warranty, or if it is an innominate (or intermediate) term. Only then, and only if it is an innominate term, is the test of depriving the innocent party of substantially the whole benefit applied. In *Hong Kong Fir Shipping Co Ltd v Kawasaki Kisen Kaisha Ltd* (5.7.2), Diplock LJ was not giving a new way of recognising a condition, but only giving the test to determine the consequences of a breach of a term which had been held to be neither a warranty nor a condition. (II) Time clauses in mercantile contracts would usually be treated as conditions. In this case, the clause was important to the sellers and the general rule that such a clause is a condition would apply.

Cie Commerciale Sucres et Denrées v C Czarnikow Ltd: *The Naxos* (1990) HL

In a contract for the sale of 12,000 metric tons of sugar some standard sugar trading rules were incorporated, including rule 14: '... the Seller shall have the sugar ready to be delivered to the Buyer at any time within the contract period ...' The buyers called for delivery on 29 May, a date which was held to have been within the contract period. When the sellers had not produced the sugar on 3 June, the buyers withdrew from the contract and bought sugar from a third party at a higher price.

Held the buyers had been entitled to treat the contract as repudiated and could recover from the sellers the amount the buyers had lost by buying the sugar at a higher price. Rule 14 was a condition of the contract. The reasons were: (I) Rule 14 was a time clause of a mercantile contract, so the principle expressed in *Bunge v Tradax SA* (5.7.2) applied to make it likely that the rule was a condition. (II) The availability of the sugar in accordance with Rule 14 was of crucial importance to the buyers, which also made it likely that the parties had intended the rule to be a condition when they made the contract.

6   Misrepresentation

6.1   What is a misrepresentation?

6.1.1   A statement which is literally true may be a misrepresentation

Dimmock v Hallett (1866) CLJ

The plaintiff seller sold an estate of 934 acres at auction to the defendant buyer on 25 January 1866. The buyer relied on several statements by the seller. Two of them were as follows. (I) Two farms of together 246 acres were described as being let to yearly Lady Day tenants for a total of £290 per year. This was strictly true, but the seller did not mention that at the date of the sale the two tenants had given notice that they would be quitting at Lady Day (25 March) 1866. (II) A farm of 300 acres was described as 'lately in the occupation of Mr R Hickson, at an annual rent of £290 15s. Now in hand'. Again, this was strictly true, but two other facts were not mentioned: (i) Hickson came in at Midsummer (24 June) 1863 and left at Michaelmas (29 September) 1864. Although he paid £290 15s for the last year, he paid only £1 for the first quarter; (ii) since Hickson left, the seller had agreed to let the farm to someone else for £225 per year. Although that deal had later fallen through, it was an indication of the falling value of the farm.

Held both of the statements did amount to material misrepresentations giving the buyer a right to be discharged from the agreement. (I) The buyer would have assumed that the tenants had not given notice, especially since the seller stated that some other tenants on the estate had given notice. Therefore, the buyer would have assumed that his rent was safe until Lady Day 1867 when the tenants would next have the opportunity to quit. (II) Both of the missing facts noted above made the second statement a material misrepresentation as well. It would lead the buyer to expect that the farm could be let for about £290 15s which was not true.

6.1.2   A statement about an intention may be a misrepresentation

Edgington v Fitzmaurice and Others (1884) CA

The defendants were directors of a company in which the plaintiff held some shares. The company sent a prospectus to the plaintiff for some new debentures which it proposed to issue (that is, loans which it sought to raise). The prospectus stated that the objects of the debenture issue were:

(1) To enable the society to complete the present alterations and additions to the buildings and to purchase their own horses and vans, whereby a large saving will be effected in the cost of transport. (2) To further develop the arrangements at present existing for the direct supply of cheap fish from the coast, which are still in their infancy.

Relying on this statement and on a mistaken belief that his loan would be secured, the plaintiff bought £1,500 worth of the debentures. In fact, the directors knew that they would have to use the bulk of the loan to pay off the company's pressing creditors. A few months later, the company was wound up and the debenture holders could not be repaid. The plaintiff now sought damages for his losses on the ground of fraudulent misrepresentation (deceit).

Held the statements of objects were statements of fact which the defendants knew to be untrue when they made them so the plaintiff could recover from them the money he had lost on the debentures. (I) *Per* Bowen LJ:

The state of a man's mind is as much a fact as the state of his digestion. It is true that it is very difficult to prove what the state of a man's mind at a particular time is, but, if it can be ascertained, it is as much a fact as anything else. A misrepresentation as to the state of a man's mind is, therefore, a misstatement of fact.

(II) (6.2) *Per* Cotton LJ:

It is not necessary to show that the misstatement was the sole cause of his acting as he did. If he acted on that misstatement, though he was also influenced by an erroneous supposition, the defendants will be still liable.

6.1.3 A statement of opinion may involve a misrepresentation or even a warranty, but a mere opinion is not a misrepresentation

Smith v Land and House Property Corporation (1884) CA

The plaintiff vendors put up for sale an hotel at Walton-on-the-Naze which they described in the particulars of sale as being let to a Mr Fleck who they said was a 'most desirable' and 'very desirable' tenant. The defendant buyers entered into a contract to buy the hotel. In fact, the tenant was behind with his rent at that time and he had been late to pay it before. The buyers then refused to complete the purchase of the hotel and the vendors brought this action for specific performance. The buyers counterclaimed for rescission of the contract.

Held the description of the tenant as desirable was a misrepresentation which entitled the buyers to rescind the contract. *Per* Bowen LJ:

> If the facts are not equally known to both sides, then a statement of opinion by the one who knows the facts best involves very often a statement of a material fact, for he impliedly states that he knows facts which justify his opinion ... [The vendor's statement] is not a guarantee that the tenant will go on paying his rent, but it is to my mind a guarantee of a different sort, and amounts at least to an assertion that nothing has occurred in the relations between the landlords and the tenant which can be considered to make the tenant an unsatisfactory one.

Bisset v Wilkinson and Another (1926) PC

The defendant buyers bought some land at Avondale in New Zealand from the plaintiff vendor for the purpose of sheep farming. The vendor told the buyers that, 'if the place was worked as I was working it, with a good six horse team, my idea was that it would carry 2,000 sheep'. The vendor had not been sheep farming on the land although he did have some sheep there. The buyers knew all about that and knew what sheep were then on the land. However, the buyers were not expert at sheep farming and they failed to make a success of the farm. The buyers sought rescission for misrepresentation.

Held the statement as to how many sheep the land would support was a mere opinion which could not be a misrepresentation. The buyers should not have relied on it since the vendor had no special knowledge of its truth. The opinion was reasonably held by the vendor. The buyers had not even proved that the vendor's opinion was not a true estimate of the land's capacity if it was properly managed.

Esso Petroleum Ltd v Mardon (1976) CA

In 1961, Esso found a site on a main road in Southport which they thought suitable for a petrol filling station. They estimated that a filling station on that site would be likely to sell about 200,000 gallons of petrol a year. Based on that, Esso bought the site. However, the local authority would only give permission for the entrance to the filling station to be on a side road, instead of on the main road. They therefore built the filling station 'back to front' and it was finished in 1963. Esso then sought a tenant for the filling station and they found Mr Mardon. In negotiations, Esso told Mr Mardon that they estimated the garage would have a throughput of 200,000 gallons a year. On that basis, Mr Mardon made an agreement with Esso to rent the garage from them for three years from April 1963. Despite Mr Mardon's best efforts, the garage sold petrol at less than half the rate estimated by Esso. Esso granted a new lease at a lower rent in September 1964, but the garage still lost money. In December 1966, Esso sued Mr Mardon for rent he had not paid and for petrol supplied. Mr Mardon counter-claimed for damages based on Esso's representation that the garage would sell 200,000 gallons a year.

Held Mr Mardon should be awarded damages either for breach of a collateral warranty or for negligent misstatement. (I) Innocent misrepresentation did not give rise to damages where the misrepresentation took place before the Misrepresentation Act 1967 (see 6.5.1) was passed. (II) Esso had special knowledge of the relevant facts and skill in the making of forecasts about the capacity of a site for selling petrol. In making their forecast of 200,000 gallons Esso were warranting that they had made their forecast with reasonable skill and care. Esso had breached that warranty because it was very careless of them not to revise their forecast after they were refused permission to build the filling station fronting onto the main road. (III) If there was no warranty then Esso were liable for negligent misstatement under the doctrine of *Hedley Byrne & Co v Heller & Partners Ltd*. The tort of negligent misstatement recognised in that case was available as a cause of action even where the parties were also in a contractual relationship.

6.1.4 Silence may be a misrepresentation

With v O'Flanagan (1936) CA

The defendant was a doctor who wished to sell his practice. In January 1934 his agent told the plaintiffs that the practice was 'doing at the rate of £2,000 a year'. This was substantially true of the two years up to 31 December 1933. In April, the plaintiffs were told that the defendant was absent from the practice which was being looked after by a *locum tenens* (temporary doctor). The plaintiffs expressed their concern to the defendant's solicitor who replied 'the present locum is quite efficient and is looking after the practice satisfactorily'. On 1 May, the plaintiffs signed an agreement to buy the practice for £4,000. They took possession that evening but found that there was no practice going on. No customers at all arrived on the next day and the records showed that in the three preceding weeks the practice had taken a total of £15 of which £10 was from a single patient. The plaintiffs had also been unaware that the defendant had been away on and off since January with the practice being handled by several different locums. On 4 May, the plaintiffs commenced this action to rescind the agreement.

Held the failure of the defendant or his agents to correct the statement that the practice had a gross income of £2,000 a year was a misrepresentation which entitled the plaintiffs to rescind the contract. *Per* Lord Wright MR: 'A representation made as a matter of inducement to enter into a contract is to be treated as a continuing representation.' Lord Wright MR also held:

A representation is not like a warranty; it is not necessary that it should be strictly construed or strictly complied with; it is enough if it is substantially true; it is enough if it is substantially complied with.

Wales v Wadham (1976) FD

In 1971, the plaintiff husband left his wife of 26 years for another woman. Later in 1971, the defendant wife said that she would never marry again because of her religious beliefs. In October 1972, the wife became engaged to a Mr Wadham but took steps to keep that fact from the husband. She also hid the engagement from their two children. In February 1973, the husband and wife agreed that the husband would pay the wife a lump sum of £13,000 instead of maintenance. The parties were divorced on 20 August 1973. The wife married Mr Wadham on 7 September 1973. When the husband found out, he brought this action for the rescission of his agreement to pay £13,000 on the grounds that it was induced by the wife's representation that she would not remarry.

Held the husband could not rescind the agreement. Although he had been induced to enter the contract by the wife's statement that she would not marry again, that had been an honest statement of her intention in 1971. Unlike cases where the representation is a matter of fact, the representor is not under a duty to inform the representee if the former's intention changes between making the representation and making the contract. *Per* Tudor Evans J:

> It seems to me that when after a marriage which had lasted for some 26 years the wife told the husband she would never marry again she was not representing to the husband that, she then being barely 50, she would never change her mind.

Q (a) Is there any basis for the principle in this case that a representation of intention never gives rise to a duty to disclose if the intention changes? (b) Could the same result be achieved in this case by holding either that the contractual effect of a representation, at least as to an intention, lapses after a reasonable time in the circumstances, or that a representation is effective only where the representor intended it to be relied upon?

6.2 Reliance on the misrepresentation

Attwood v Small and Others (1838) HL

The defendant seller contracted for the sale of some mines and iron works to the plaintiff buyers. The seller made various representations about the capabilities of the properties which the buyers asked to verify. The buyers sent agents to examine the works and the accounts and then one of the buyers went in person to report on the properties. All of the reports were in agreement with the seller's statements. Six months after the sale, it became apparent that the statements were not correct. The buyers then brought an action based on fraudulent misrepresentation.

Held the buyers had no good cause of action. (I) *Per* Lord Cottenham LC and Lord Brougham, the buyers had failed to prove there was any fraud. (II) *Per* Lord Cottenham LC, at the time of the contract, the buyers knew all the material facts as to which they later claimed to have been misled. (III) *Per* Earl Devon and Lord Brougham, the buyers had not relied on the seller's statements because they had checked them themselves by making their own inspections.

Note ———————————————————————

Argument (III) above is usually taken as being the main *ratio decidendi* of this case, but, as Jessell MR pointed out in *Redgrave v Hurd* (6.2), it is not easy to discern any single ratio of the majority from their three long speeches.

Redgrave v Hurd (1881) CA

The plaintiff was a solicitor who advertised for a partner who would buy the plaintiff's house instead of paying a premium to join the partnership. The advertisement claimed there was a 'moderate practice, with extensive connections in a very populous town'. The defendant went in response to the advertisement to see the plaintiff who told him that the income of the practice was some £300–£400 per year. The defendant then asked to know the amount of income over the previous three years. The plaintiff prepared for the defendant some bills of costs which showed income of about £200 in each of the three years. The plaintiff explained that the other business was evidenced in some other bundles of papers which the defendant could inspect. The defendant did not inspect the other bundles of papers but entered into the contracts for the partnership and the purchase of the plaintiff's house. When the partnership proved to have an income of no more than £200 (which left only £100 profit to be shared between the partners), the defendant refused to complete the purchase of the house. The plaintiff therefore brought this action for specific performance.

Held the defendant was entitled to rescind the contracts and recover the deposit he had paid for the house. The defendant had shown that there was a material misrepresentation by the plaintiff. It was then for the plaintiff to prove that the defendant had not relied on it, which the plaintiff had failed to do. The fact that the defendant had an opportunity to inspect the documents did not mean that he did not rely on the representation.

The defendant did not have a duty to look at the documents and could choose, as he did, to rely on the plaintiff's representation instead.

Edgington v Fitzmaurice and Others (1884) CA

See 6.1.2.

6.3 Damages at common law for the tort of deceit

Derry and Others v Peek (1889) HL

The defendants were directors of a tram company. By a private Act of Parliament, the company was given permission to build some new tramways upon which the trams could be moved by animal power and, with the consent of the Board of Trade, by steam or mechanical power. The defendants believed that they were certain to get the necessary permission to use mechanical power. They issued a prospectus for shares in the company which said:

> One great feature of this undertaking, to which considerable importance should be attached, is, that by the special Act of Parliament obtained, the company has the right to use steam or mechanical motive power, instead of horses, and it is fully expected that by means of this a considerable saving will result in the working expenses of the line as compared with other tramways worked by horses.

Relying on this, the plaintiff bought shares in the company. The Board of Trade refused permission to use steam or mechanical power on most of the routes and the company was wound up. The plaintiff now sought damages for deceit or fraudulent misrepresentation.

Held the plaintiff had not proved fraud so could not obtain damages. Although the defendants were wrong to say that they had permission to use mechanical methods and they had no reasonable grounds for saying so, nonetheless, they believed that the statement in the prospectus was honest and substantially true. *Per* Lord FitzGerald the offending paragraph 'seems on the whole to have been morally true'. *Per* Lord Herschell:

> Fraud is proved when it is shewn that a false representation has been made (1) knowingly, or (2) without belief in its truth, or (3) recklessly, careless whether it be true or false ... To prevent a false statement being fraudulent, there must, I think, always be an honest belief in its truth ... If fraud be proved, the motive of the person guilty of it is immaterial ... Making a false statement through want of care falls far short of, and is a very different thing from, fraud, and the same may be said of a false representation honestly believed though on insufficient grounds.

In a case like this, rescission was no longer possible, so the plaintiff had no remedy for innocent (or negligent) misrepresentation before the passing of the Misrepresentation Act 1967 (see 6.5).

6.4 Rescission at equity for misrepresentation without fraud

6.4.1 Rescission is barred by lapse of time

Leaf v International Galleries (1950) CA

In March 1944, the plaintiff buyer bought from the defendant sellers an oil painting of Salisbury Cathedral for £85. The sellers had represented that the painting was by Constable and they repeated that attribution on the receipt they gave the buyer. Nearly five years later, the buyer took the painting to Christies with a view to selling it. He then discovered that it was not by Constable and was worth little. The buyer sought to rescind the contract. (The buyer did not make a claim for damages for breach of contract, so that was not considered.)

Held it was now too late for the buyer to rescind the contract. (I) (7.1.3) *Per* Denning LJ 'there was a mistake about the quality of the subject matter' of the contract, but no mistake about the subject matter itself which was a specific painting of Salisbury Cathedral. (II) *Per* Denning LJ assuming that the painting being by Constable was a condition of the contract, its breach would give the buyer a right under s 35 of the Sale of Goods Act 1893 (now Sale of Goods Act 1979), to rescind the contract so long as he had not accepted the goods by retaining them beyond a reasonable time. Five years was far too long a time after which to reject the picture for breach of condition. Since 'an innocent misrepresentation is much less potent than a breach of condition', rescission could not be available for the misrepresentation either. (III) *Per* Jennings LJ, since rescission is an equitable remedy, it could not be granted after so long a delay.

Note

In this case, the sellers, but not the buyer, were art dealers. For a similar situation arising between two dealers and raising different points of law, see *Harlingdon and Leinster Enterprises Ltd v Christopher Hull Fine Art Ltd*, 5.6.1.

6.5   Claims under the Misrepresentation Act 1967

6.5.1   The Misrepresentation Act 1967

Section 1   Removal of certain bars to rescission for innocent misrepresentation

Where a person has entered into a contract after a misrepresentation has been made to him, and:

(a)   the misrepresentation has become a term of the contract; or

(b)   the contract has been performed,

or both, then, if otherwise he would be entitled to rescind the contract without alleging fraud, he shall be so entitled, subject to the provisions of this Act, notwithstanding the matters mention in paras (a) and (b) of this section.

Section 2   Damages for misrepresentation

(1)   Where a person has entered into a contract after a misrepresentation has been made to him by another party thereto and as a result thereof he has suffered loss, then if the person making the misrepresentation would be liable to damages in respect thereof had the misrepresentation been made fraudulently, that person shall be so liable notwithstanding that the misrepresentation was not made fraudulently, unless he proves that he had reasonable ground to believe and did believe up to the time the contract was made that the facts represented were true.

(2)   Where a person has entered into a contract after a misrepresentation has been made to him otherwise than fraudulently, and he would be entitled, by reason of the misrepresentation, to rescind the contract, then, if it is claimed, in any proceedings arising out of the contract, that the contract ought to be or has been rescinded the court or arbitrator may declare the contract subsisting and award damages in lieu of rescission, if of opinion that it would be equitable to do so, having regard to the nature of the misrepresentation and the loss that would be caused by it if the contract were upheld, as well as to the loss that rescission would cause to the other party.

(3)   Damages may be awarded against a person under sub-s (2) of this section whether or not he is liable to damages under sub-s (1) thereof, but where he is so liable any award under the said sub-s (2) shall be taken into account in assessing his liability under the said sub-s (1).

Section 3   Avoidance of provision excluding liability for misrepresentation

If a contract contains a term which would exclude or restrict:

(a)   any liability to which a party to a contract may be subject by reason of any misrepresentation made by him before the contract was made; or

(b)   any remedy available to another party to the contract by reason of such a misrepresentation,

the term shall be of no effect except in so far as it satisfies the requirement of reasonableness as stated in s 11(1) of the Unfair Contract Terms Act 1977 and it is for those claiming that the term satisfies that requirement to show that it does.

6.5.2   Section 2(1) – Reasonable grounds for belief

Howard Marine and Dredging Co Ltd v A Ogden & Sons (Excavators) Ltd (1977) CA

The defendants, Ogdens, wanted to submit a tender for some excavation work. They would need to move the earth and clay excavated by barge, so they approached the plaintiffs, Howards, who had some barges to let. The capacity of the barges was very important to Ogdens when they set the price for their tender. One of the factors which limits the capacity of a barge is the weight in tonnes that the barge could carry without falling too low in the water, called the deadweight. During the negotiations over the barges, Mr O'Loughlin of Howards gave the correct capacity in cubic metres, but told Ogdens that the deadweight was about 1,600 tons. Mr O'Loughlin had seen the entry in Lloyd's Register for the barges which gave the deadweight as exceeding 1,600 tons, but he had also seen the documents from the makers of the particular barges owned by Howards which showed that the deadweight was some 1,050 tons. Mr O'Loughlin had remembered the higher figure and forgotten about the lower one. In fact, the lower figure was correct and Lloyd's had made an error in their Register. Ogdens won the tender and hired two barges from Howards. The charterparty included this in clause 1:

> On handing over by the Owners, the vessel shall be tight, staunch and strong, but Charterers' acceptance of handing over the vessel shall be conclusive that they have examined the vessel and found her to be in all respects seaworthy, in good order and condition and in all respects fit for the intended and contemplated use by the Charterers and in every other way satisfactory to them.

When, some six months after the barges were delivered, Ogdens discovered their true deadweight, they refused to pay for the hire. Howards took the barges back and Ogdens hired others. Howards now sued for the hire and Ogdens counter-claimed for damages.

Held Mr O'Loughlin's statement as to the deadweight of the barges was a misrepresentation made innocently but without reasonable grounds. It therefore gave Ogdens a right to damages under the Misrepresentation Act 1967 (see 6.5.1). (I) The statement as to capacity did not appear to be intended as a warranty. (II)(i) The figures as to deadweight in the documents from the barges' makers were obviously more reliable than those in the Lloyd's Register so it was not reasonable for Mr O'Loughlin to give the Lloyd's Register figures. (ii) Lord Denning MR dissented, holding that the Lloyd's Register did give Mr O'Loughlin reasonable grounds for his statement. (III)(i) *Per* Bridge LJ, with whom Shaw LJ agreed on this point, clause 1:

> ... is to be narrowly construed. It can only be relied on as conclusive evidence of the charterers' satisfaction in relation to such attributes of the vessel as would be apparent on an ordinary examination of the vessel. I do not think deadweight capacity is such an attribute.

(ii) Lord Denning MR dissented, holding that it was no longer necessary to construe such clauses strictly since they were now subject to s 3 of the Misrepresentation Act 1967 (see 6.5.1). (IV) (6.5.3) (i) If clause 1 did mean that Ogdens had accepted responsibility for the deadweight when they accepted the barges, then it was of no effect because it failed the reasonableness test imposed by s 3 of the Misrepresentation Act 1967 (see 6.5.1). (ii) Lord Denning MR again dissented, holding that clause 1 was reasonable even if, as he held, it excluded Howard's liability in respect of deadweight. (V)(i) There was no liability for the tort of negligent misstatement under *Hedley Byrne & Co v Heller & Partners Ltd* in this case. (ii) Shaw LJ dissented on this point.

6.5.3 Section 3 – The reasonableness of exclusions of liability for misrepresentation

Howard Marine and Dredging Co Ltd v A Ogden & Sons (Excavators) Ltd (1977) CA

See 6.5.2.

Walker v Boyle (1981) Ch

The buyer was negotiating to buy the vendor's house. The buyer's solicitor made the standard pre-contract inquiries including:

> Is the vendor aware of any disputes regarding the boundaries, easements, covenants or other matters relating to the property or its use?

The vendor's solicitor replied 'Not to the vendor's knowledge'. The replies included in small print these words:

These replies on behalf of the Vendor are believed to be correct but accuracy is not guaranteed and they do not obviate the need to make appropriate searches, inquiries and inspections.

The parties made a contract for the sale of the house which incorporated the National Conditions of Sale, including condition 17 in these terms:

> No error, mis-statement or omission in any preliminary answer concerning the property, or in the sale plan or the Special Conditions, shall annul the sale, nor (save where the error, mis-statement or omission is in a written answer and relates to a matter materially affecting the description or value of the property) shall any damages be payable, or compensation be allowed by either party, in respect thereof.

The buyer paid a deposit but discovered that there was in fact a boundary dispute with a neighbour of the property. The answer to the inquiry had been given because the vendor's husband believed that there was no real dispute because he was in the right over the boundary. The buyer refused to complete the sale and the vendor sold to someone else for a lower figure. The vendor now sought the difference in price and the buyer claimed to recover his deposit.

Held for the buyer the misrepresentation in the replies to preliminary inquiries entitled the buyer to damages. (I) The misrepresentation had not been made fraudulently, but nor was it made upon reasonable grounds. (II) The small print in the replies to inquiries made no difference to the fact that the replies given were representations of fact. (III) Where a vendor has made a material misrepresentation, he cannot rely on condition 17 in any equitable claim because of general equitable principles. (IV) The vendor had not shown that condition 17 was reasonable so it was not effective because of s 3 of the Misrepresentation Act 1967 (see 6.5.1). It did not save the clause that it was a standard form which had evolved through many years of such National Conditions of Sale.

6.5.4 The measure of damages under the Act

Naughton and Another v O'Callaghan (1990) QB

The plaintiffs were seeking a horse to train and race in Ireland. They chose from an auction catalogue a horse called Fondu whose pedigree, as stated in the catalogue, made it likely to succeed on the racecourse. The plaintiffs bought Fondu in September 1981 for 26,000 guineas (£27,300). They spent money training and keeping the horse and entering it in races. Fondu did not do well in races. In June 1983, the plaintiffs discovered that the horse they had was not the one whose pedigree was described in the catalogue. There had been a mix up at the stud farm and Fondu was in fact descended from a line of American dirt track race horses. Although in 1981 the plaintiffs would not have bought Fondu had they known its true pedigree, the horse would still have been valuable to another buyer and might have fetched 23,500 guineas (£24,675). The plaintiffs kept Fondu but wrote to the defendant to complain in June 1984. The plaintiffs obtained judgment in their claim under s 2(1) of the Misrepresentation Act 1967 (6.5.1) and the question was now what damages they should receive. After failing on the race course, Fondu was now worth no more than £1,500.

Held the plaintiffs could recover the difference between 26,000 guineas and £1,500 plus their training costs up to the time when they discovered the truth about Fondu. There was a general rule that the measure of damages in a case about the sale of goods would be the difference between the value which the goods should have had and the value which the goods received actually had at the time of the purchase (in this case, a difference of just 2,500 guineas between 26,000 and 23,500 guineas). In this case, though, Fondu was not a commodity which the buyers would have been expected to sell on but a horse which they would have been expected to train and race. The fall in Fondu's value was not caused by a fall in the market for horses (for which the defendant would not be responsible) but by Fondu's individual failure to win races.

Royscot Trust Ltd v Rogerson and Another (1991) CA

The first defendant customer agreed to buy from the second defendant dealer a used car for £7,600. The customer was to pay a deposit of £1,200 (16%) and pay the remaining £6,400 on hire purchase terms. The plaintiff finance company would only accept transactions where the deposit was at least 20% of the total price. The dealer submitted a proposal to the finance company saying that the price was £8,000 and that £1,600 (20%) had already been paid, leaving £6,400 to pay. The finance company thus lent the required sum of £6,400. As was usual, the form of the transaction was that the finance company bought the car from the dealer and then hired it to the customer. The customer paid some instalments but then wrongfully sold the car and stopped paying. In case they could not recover fully from the customer, the finance company sought damages under s 2(1) of the Misrepresentation Act 1967 (see 6.5.1) from the dealer.

Held the finance company could recover from the dealer the £6,400 they had lent less the amounts received from the customer as instalments or damages. (I) On the construction of s 2(1), the words 'so liable' meant, *per* Balcombe LJ, 'liable as he would be if the misrepresentation had been made fraudulently'. Thus, the measure of damages under the Act was the measure for the tort of deceit, or fraudulent misrepresentation. If a misrepresentation is fraudulent, the innocent party can recover all the losses which it suffered as a result of entering the contract even if they were not foreseeable and this would apply here. In this case, the type of loss was reasonably foreseeable by the dealer and so the customer's default was not a *novus actus interveniens* (an act which breaks the chain of causation). (II) The dealer also argued that the finance company had acquired title to a car worth as much as they had paid so that their loss measured at the date of the contract was nil. This normal rule had not been applied in *Naughton and Another v O'Callaghan* (6.5.4) and would not be applied here because the commercial reality was that the finance company were interested in receiving the customer's repayments, not the car to which they obtained formal title.

Note

In *Smith New Court Securities Ltd v Scrimgeour Vickers (Asset Management) Ltd*, the House of Lords noted that *Royscot Trust v Rogerson* has been the subject of academic criticism and expressly left open the question whether it was correct.

7 Mistake

7.1 Mistake at common law renders the contract void

7.1.1 Where the parties each have a different intention as to what is the subject matter of the contract, the mistake may negative consent

Raffles v Wichelhaus and Another (1864) CE

The parties agreed that the defendants would buy from the plaintiff 125 bales of cotton 'to arrive ex *Peerless* from Bombay'. The defendants were expecting the goods to arrive on a vessel named *Peerless* which was sailing from Bombay in October, but the plaintiff was referring to another ship which was also called *Peerless* expected to sail from Bombay in December.

Held the defendants did not have to accept the goods which were not those for which they intended to contract.

Q   Did the court conclude there was no contract or a contract for cotton ex the October *Peerless*?

Smith v Hughes (1871) CQB

The plaintiff, a farmer, had some oats to sell. He approached the defendant, a racehorse trainer, who said he was always ready to buy good oats. The plaintiff gave the defendant a sample of the oats which the defendant kept until the next day when they agreed a price for the whole quantity of oats. After the oats were delivered, the defendant refused to pay for them on the ground that they were new oats and he only wanted old oats. The defendant said that racehorse trainers only ever bought old oats; the plaintiff denied any knowledge of that. There was also a conflict of evidence between the parties as to whether anything was said in the negotiations about the oats being old. The appeal concerned the questions which the trial judge had left to the jury.

Held there would have to be a new trial. If the oats were described as old in the negotiations, then the defendant would not have to accept them. Their lordships then discussed the principles that would apply if the jury found that the oats being old was not mentioned in the negotiations. (I) *Per* Cockburn CJ there would be judgment for the plaintiff.

> Here, the defendant agreed to buy a specific parcel of oats. The oats were what they were sold as, namely good oats according to the sample. The buyer persuaded himself they were old oats, when they were not so; but the seller neither said nor did anything to contribute to his deception. He has himself to blame ... All that can be said [for the defendant] is, that the two minds were not *ad idem* as to the age of the oats; they certainly were *ad idem* as to the sale and purchase of them.

(II) Blackburn J stated the principle of mistake thus:

> I apprehend that, if one of the parties intends to make a contract on one set of terms, and the other intends to make a contract on another set of terms, or, as it is sometimes expressed, if the parties are not *ad idem*, there is no contract, unless the circumstances are such as to preclude one of the parties from denying that he has agreed to the terms of the other.

In this case, he held that even if the plaintiff knew that the defendant thought the oats were old, he was under no duty to tell the defendant of his mistake. The defendant would lose the case so long as his mistake was only to believe that the oats were old, but he would win if he agreed 'to take the oats under the belief that the plaintiff contracted that they were old'. (III) *Per* Hannen J:

> In order to relieve the defendant, it was necessary that the jury should find not merely that the plaintiff believed the defendant to believe that he was buying old oats, but that he believed the defendant to believe that he, the plaintiff, was contracting to sell old oats.

Note

(a) Blackburn and Hannen JJ both held that there did not appear to be enough evidence to find for the defendant if the oats being old was not mentioned in the negotiations. Only Cockburn CJ held that the plaintiff would definitely succeed. (b) Although the court favoured the plaintiff's view that there was no operative mistake in this case, Blackburn J's *dicta* quoted above about the principle by which mistake can apply are often cited as 'the principle of *Smith v Hughes*'. (c) See, also, Denning LJ's interpretation of this case in *Solle v Butcher*, 7.2.1.

Q Blackburn J appears to set a subjective test of what the defendant actually believed. Should he have said that the matter depends on what it would appear to a reasonable plaintiff that the defendant believed, thus making his test similar to that of Hannen J?

London Holeproof Hosiery Company Ltd v Padmore (1928) CA

The plaintiffs leased a factory from the defendant for a term of three years from 1 August 1925. The agreement contained an option for the plaintiffs to purchase the factory on or before 24 June 1927 for £1,600, having given the defendant six months' notice of the intention to purchase. In November 1926, the factory was almost completely destroyed by fire. Correspondence followed in which the defendant made it clear that he would be rebuilding the factory. On 20 December 1926, the plaintiffs gave the defendant notice that they would be exercising their option to purchase the factory and asked the defendant to repair the factory as soon as possible. The defendant replied that he would not be rebuilding the factory because by exercising their option, the plaintiffs took the property as it then was. The plaintiffs now sought a declaration that they were not bound to continue with the purchase.

Held the plaintiffs were not bound to complete the purchase. The plaintiffs based their exercise of the option on their belief that the defendant would rebuild the factory and the defendant knew that. The case therefore fell under the principle of *Smith v Hughes* (7.1.1): the parties not being *ad idem*, there was no contract.

7.1.2 Where one party takes advantage of the other's wrong belief as to the subject matter of the contract, the mistake may negative consent

Scriven Brothers & Co v Hindley & Co (1913) KB

The plaintiffs sold some Russian hemp and tow at auction. The auction catalogue gave the shipping mark 'SL' and showed two lots of bales: SL 63 to 67 and SL 68 to 79. The catalogue did not mention that the first lot was hemp and the second tow and it was very unusual for Russian hemp and tow to come from the same ship with the same shipping mark. The defendant bid for both lots believing they were both hemp. The second lot was immediately knocked down to the defendant after his first bid, because it was tow, worth much less than hemp. The jury found that the auctioneer knew that the defendant's bid was made under a mistake and that the auctioneer's catalogue and conduct contributed to the mistake.

Held since the auctioneer knew of the defendant's mistake, *per* Lawrence J, 'the parties were never *ad idem* as to the subject matter of the proposed sale; there was therefore in fact no contract of bargain and sale'. Because the plaintiffs' agent, the auctioneer, had contributed to the mistake, the defendant would not be estopped from relying on it. Therefore, the plaintiffs could not enforce the contract to buy the second lot; indeed, there was no such contract.

Hartog v Colin and Shields (1939) KB

The parties discussed the sale by the defendants to the plaintiff of some Argentinean hare skins. They discussed the price in terms of so much per piece as was the practice in that trade. But then, the defendants made an offer priced at so much per pound. These prices worked out at about a third of the right price. The plaintiff realised that the defendants had made a mistake but snapped up the offer on the day upon which it had been made. The defendants refused to complete the contract and the plaintiff sued them, with the defendants counter-claiming for rescission.

Held per Singleton J:

> The plaintiff could not reasonably have supposed that the offer contained the offerers' real intention ... That means there must be judgment for the defendants.

7.1.3 Where the parties both believe the subject matter of their contract is other than it is, the mistake may nullify consent

Couturier and Others v Hastie and Another (1856) HL

The plaintiffs were corn merchants who had a cargo of corn on its way by sea from Salonika to England. They asked the defendants to find a buyer for the corn upon a special kind of commission which made the defendants liable in place of the buyer in the event of a default by the buyer. The defendants found a buyer who agreed to buy the corn and signed a bought note on 15 May 1848 which described the corn as:

> ... free on board, and including freight and insurance, to a safe port in the UK ... payment at two months from this date, or in cash, less discount, at the rate of 5%. per annum for the unexpired time, upon handing shipping documents.

Unknown to any of the parties, the corn was damaged by heat on the voyage and it had therefore been sold at Tunis on 22 April. When he found that out, the buyer withdrew from the contract and the plaintiffs sued the defendants in the buyer's place. The plaintiffs argued (i) that the buyer had contracted to buy all the risks associated with the corn as evidenced by the inclusion of insurance in the agreement and (ii) that his liability to pay arose on the handing over of the shipping documents, which the plaintiffs were willing and able to hand over.

Held the defendants were not liable under the contract. *Per* Lord Cranworth LC:

> ... the whole question turns upon the construction of the contract which was entered into between the parties ... Looking to the contract itself alone, it appears to me clearly that what the parties contemplated, those who bought and those who sold, was that there was an existing something to be sold and

bought, and if sold and bought, then the benefit of insurance should go with it ... The contract plainly imports that there was something which was to be sold at the time of the contract, and something to be purchased. No such thing existing, ... there must be judgment ... for [the defendants].

Note

This case was traditionally classified as one where the contract was void for mistake. However, it was held by the High Court of Australia in *McRae and Another v Commonwealth Disposals Commission and Others* (1951) that this case involved a valid contract which on its true construction required the buyer to pay only for the corn and not simply on the handing over of the shipping documents. This case was thus held to have been decided on the basis that the plaintiffs' consideration failed so that the defendants were not liable to pay. In *Frederick E Rose (London) Ltd v Wm H Pim Jnr & Co Ltd* (see 7.5), Denning LJ adopted the High Court of Australia's view of this case, holding that 'It was not a case where the contract was void for mistake'.

Scott v Coulson (1903) CA

The plaintiffs contracted to sell to the defendants the benefit of a life assurance policy on the life of one AT Death who was assumed to be alive at the time. Before the assignment was completed, the defendants received information which led them to suspect that Death might be dead. They said nothing to the plaintiffs who went ahead with the assignment. They then discovered with certainty that Death had been dead for at least twenty years, so the policy had already matured and was therefore worth more than the defendants had paid for it. The plaintiffs now claimed that the assignment of the policy should be set aside.

Held the contract was void. (I) *Per* Vaughan Williams LJ, the parties contracted under a common mistake about the basis of the contract, rendering the contract void at common law. (II) *Per* Romer LJ, the defendants' knowledge of the correct facts 'rendered it improper to insist upon the completion of the contract'. The defendants ought to have told the plaintiffs of Death's death but they did not. 'Such a transaction cannot be allowed to stand.' (III) Cozens-Hardy LJ combined the reasons of Vaughan Williams and Romer LJJ.

Note

(a) Vaughan Williams LJ's clear opinion that this case was decided on the basis of common mistake is often seen as the *ratio decidendi* of this case.
(b) In *Bell and Another v Lever Brothers Ltd and Others* (7.1.3), this case was cited in support of the dissenting judgment of Lord Warrington of Clyffe, but was also mentioned in one of the majority judgments, where Lord

Thankerton said that it was 'clear that the subject matter of the contract was a policy still current with a surrender value and that, accordingly, the subject matter did not exist at the date of the contract'.

Q (a) Can common mistake really apply in this case after *Bell and Another v Lever Brothers Ltd and Others* (7.1.3)? (b) Romer and Cozens-Hardy LJJ did not hold clearly that common mistake was the whole answer. Is there anything in their apparent view that this decision rested on the fact that the defendants knew the facts before the assignment was completed but after the contract was made?

Galloway v Galloway (1914) KBDC

The defendant married W in 1898. In 1903, W left him. In 1907, the defendant, not being able to trace W, described himself as a widower and married the plaintiff. In 1913, the parties made a deed of separation under which the defendant promised to pay the plaintiff £1 a week for the support of their three children. Then, W reappeared and the defendant fell behind with his payments to the plaintiff who brought this action on the deed of separation. The defendant counter-claimed for rescission.

Held the deed of separation was void. The parties made the deed on the basis of a mistaken belief that they were married to each other. Since W was alive, the defendant's marriage to the plaintiff was void.

Bell and Another v Lever Brothers Ltd and Others (1931) HL

The first plaintiff company, Levers, owned nearly all the shares in the second plaintiff company, Niger, whose business included cocoa trading in West Africa. Niger was not profitable and Levers hired the defendants, Bell and Snelling, to run Niger. The two defendants became directors of Niger. However, their main service contracts were with Levers and commenced in November 1923. The service contracts were extended in July 1926 to last a further five years. Bell and Snelling were successful in turning the fortunes of Niger around and also in negotiating a merger with a competing company the arrangements for which were concluded in March 1929. The merger would make the defendants redundant and so they agreed terms with Levers in March. Levers agreed to pay Bell and Snelling £30,000 and £20,000 respectively in return for the premature ending of their service contracts. The money was paid to the defendants, and they resigned their positions, in May 1929. In July 1929, Levers discovered that the defendants had entered into cocoa transactions on their own account in November and December 1927. Although these transactions did not cause Niger or Levers any loss, they were made secretly by the defendants and were a breach of their duties to both Niger and Levers. In consequence, (i) Bell and Snelling were ordered to pay over their profits on the deals, which totalled £1,360, to the plaintiff companies;

(ii) Levers demanded the repayment of the £50,000 they had paid to end the defendants' service contracts because they were entitled to end them without recompense on the grounds of the defendants' breaches of duty. Levers argued that they entered the contracts to pay the £50,000 under a mistake because they did not realise that the service contracts from which Bell and Snelling were releasing them were voidable by Levers because of the defendants' breaches of duty. The defendants said that the transactions were not before their minds when they negotiated their severance agreements and that at that time they did not realise that Levers could have avoided their service contracts.

Held Levers could not recover the £50,000 because the mistake about the status of the service contracts was not fundamental enough. (I) Their lordships agreed that the plaintiffs' statement of claim (which pleaded only unilateral mistake) would have to be amended if they were to rest their claim on the ground of common mistake. (II) Lord Blanesburgh rested his decision for the defendants on the ground that he would not allow the plaintiffs to amend their statement of claim. He also held that if the plaintiffs were allowed to amend their claim, he would agree with Lord Atkin and Lord Thankerton that their claim would still fail. (III) Lord Atkin and Lord Thankerton rested their decision on the ground that the mistake about the nature of the service agreements, that is the belief that they could not be terminated unilaterally by Levers, was only a mistake as to the quality of the subject matter of the severance contract and did not go to the existence or fundamental substance of the subject matter. *Per* Lord Atkin:

> Mistake as to quality of the thing contracted for raises more difficult questions. In such a case a mistake will not affect assent unless it is the mistake of both parties, and is as to the existence of some quality which makes the thing without the quality essentially different from the thing as it was believed to be ... It would be wrong to decide that an agreement to terminate a definite specified contract is void if it turns out that the agreement had already been broken and could have been terminated otherwise. The contract released is the identical contract in both cases, and the party paying for the release gets exactly what he bargains for. It seems immaterial that he could have got the same result in another way, or that if he had known the true facts he would not have entered into the bargain.

(IV) Lord Warrington of Clyffe, with whom Viscount Hailsham agreed, dissented, holding that the assumption of both parties that the service contracts could only be ended by agreement:

> ... was of such a fundamental character as to constitute an underlying assumption without which the parties would not have made the contract they in fact made.

Leaf v International Galleries (1950) CA

See 6.4.1.

7.1.4 Where one party believes that the contract is with a person other than the other party, the mistake as to identity may negative consent

Boulton v Jones and Others (1857) CE

B owed the defendant some money. The defendant ordered some goods from B intending to set off B's debt to him against their price. The defendant received the goods and used them. He then received an invoice from the plaintiff who had, unknown to the defendant, taken over B's business and supplied the goods to the defendant. The defendant refused to pay for the goods.

Held the defendant did not intend to contract with the plaintiff so there was no contract between them. The plaintiff therefore could not claim any money from the defendant. *Per* Bramwell B:

> ... when anyone makes a contract in which the personality, so to speak, of the particular party contracted with is important, for any reason, whether because it is to write a book or paint a picture, or do any work of personal skill, or whether because there is a set off due from that party, no one else is at liberty to step in and maintain that he is the party contracted with ... Without saying what might have been the effect of the receipt of the invoice before the consumption of the goods, it is sufficient to say that in this case the plaintiff clearly is not entitled to sue and deprive the defendant of his set off.

Q (a) What would have been the effect if the defendant had received the invoice from the plaintiff before consuming the goods? (b) Could the defendant still claim the debt from B after this case?

Cundy and Bevington v Lindsay and Others (1878) HL

A well known and highly respectable firm called W Blenkiron and Son carried on business at 123 Wood Street, Cheapside. One Alfred Blenkarn hired a room in a building on the corner of Wood Street. Blenkarn wrote as from 35 Wood Street, signing his name so that it looked like Blenkiron & Co, to the plaintiffs giving them an order for the cambric handkerchiefs which they manufactured. He did not pay for the handkerchiefs but sold them on to various *bona fide* purchasers, including the defendants who bought 250 dozen. Blenkarn was convicted for his fraud and the plaintiffs brought this action for conversion against the defendants.

Held the plaintiffs intended to sell to Blenkiron and not to Blenkarn. Therefore there was no contract with Blenkarn. Even though Blenkarn took the handkerchiefs which the plaintiffs had intended to send to

Blenkiron, he never had obtained any title to them and therefore he could not pass title on to the defendants. Thus, the defendants were liable for conversion of the plaintiffs' handkerchiefs.

King's Norton Metal Company Ltd v Erridge, Merrett and Company Ltd (1897) CA

The plaintiffs sent a ton of brass rivet wire in response to an order purporting to come from Hallam and Co in Sheffield. Hallam and Co was a name used by one Wallis who sold the wire on to the defendants and failed to pay the plaintiffs for it. The plaintiffs brought this action for conversion to recover the wire.

Held the defendants could keep the wire. The plaintiffs had intended to contract with whoever was writing to them, there being no other Hallam and Co. They therefore made a contract with Wallis which was valid even though it was voidable for fraud. During the time when the plaintiffs had not yet avoided the contract Wallis could give good title to the goods to a purchaser for value like the defendants.

Phillips v Brooks Ltd (1919) KB

A customer entered the plaintiff's jewellery shop and selected some pearls priced at £2,550 and a ring for £450. He wrote out a cheque for £3,000 and said he was Sir George Bullough of St James's Square. The plaintiff, who had heard of Sir George Bullough, checked the address given in the telephone directory and said 'Would you like to take the articles with you?', to which the customer replied 'You had better have the cheque cleared first, but I should like to take the ring as it is my wife's birthday tomorrow'. Next day, the customer took the ring to a pawnbroker, the defendants in this case, who gave him £350 for it. The customer was an impostor and his cheque was dishonoured. He was convicted of obtaining the ring by false pretences. The plaintiff brought this action to recover the ring from the defendants.

Held the plaintiff could not recover the ring because although his contract with the rogue customer was voidable for fraud, it was not void for mistake. Thus, the rogue obtained good title to the ring which he passed on to the defendants. The plaintiff had contracted to sell the ring to the person who was standing in his shop, even though he would not have done so were it not for the fraud as to that person's identity.

Ingram and Others v Little (1960) CA

The three plaintiffs, Miss Elsie Ingram, Miss Hilda Ingram and Miss Badger were joint owners of a Renault Dauphine motor car which they advertised for sale. They negotiated with a potential buyer, the rogue in this case, and agreed a price of £717. The rogue offered a cheque which

Miss Elsie Ingram refused, saying that they would only accept cash. The rogue then said that he was Mr PGM Hutchinson with business interests in Guildford and that he lived at Stanstead House, Stanstead Road, Caterham. Miss Hilda Ingram went out to the post office where she checked in the telephone directory which did have an entry for such a Mr Hutchinson. Thus reassured, the plaintiffs accepted the cheque in return for the car. The rogue had no connection with Mr Hutchinson and was never traced. He sold the car to the defendant and his cheque to the plaintiffs was not honoured. The plaintiffs now sued the defendant for the return of the car or damages for its retention.

Held the defendant was liable to the plaintiffs in respect of the car. (I) Where parties dealt face to face there was a rebuttable presumption that they intended to contract with each other and not with some other person. (II) The plaintiffs made it clear that they would not accept a cheque from the rogue. They offered to accept a cheque from Mr Hutchinson. The rogue knew that they intended only to contract with Mr Hutchinson and therefore there was no offer made to the rogue, the analysis being similar to that of *Cundy and Bevington v Lindsay and Others* (7.1.4). Therefore, the presumption of dealing with the person actually present was rebutted in this case and no contract was formed between the parties. (III) The case was distinguishable from *Phillips v Brooks Ltd* (7.1.4) because there the jeweller dealt with the rogue as a customer and made the main contract before the rogue established his false identity. *Per* Pearce LJ, *Phillips v Brooks Ltd* 'was a borderline case decided on its own particular facts'. Pearce LJ also said that this case was itself 'a borderline case'. (IV) Devlin LJ dissented from argument (II) above and said that he would follow *Phillips v Brooks Ltd*.

Lewis v Averay (1971) CA

The plaintiff wanted to sell his Austin Cooper car and advertised it in a newspaper. A rogue came to buy it who said he was Richard Green. The rogue led the plaintiff to believe that he was the well known actor, Richard Greene. The rogue offered the plaintiff a cheque for the car which he signed 'RA Green'. The plaintiff was unwilling to part with the car in return for the cheque but the rogue insisted. The plaintiff therefore asked him whether he had anything to prove he was Richard Green. The rogue produced a Pinewood Studios pass with the name 'Richard A Green' and a photograph of the rogue. The plaintiff then allowed the rogue to take the car. The rogue's cheque was from a stolen cheque book and was not honoured. The rogue sold the car to the defendant, disappeared and was not traced. The plaintiff brought this action for the return of the car by the defendant.

Held there was a contract between the plaintiff and the rogue, albeit voidable for fraud. Therefore, the rogue passed good title to the defendant who could keep the car. (I) *Per* Lord Denning MR, *Phillips v Brooks Ltd* (7.1.4), *Ingram and Others v Little* (7.1.4) and this case were all indistinguishable from each other. In all these cases, it was the plaintiff sellers who let the rogues take the goods and the defendant buyers could not have acted any more carefully than they did. Therefore, it was right that the seller should bear the loss, so his lordship would not hold that a contract was void because of a mistake as to the identity of a party. (II) *Per* Phillimore LJ, in *Ingram and Others v Little*:

> The Court of Appeal, by a majority and in the very special and unusual facts of that case, decided that it had been sufficiently shown in the particular circumstances that, contrary to the *prima facie* presumption, the lady who was selling the motor car was not dealing with the person actually present. But, in the present case, I am bound to say that I do not think there was anything which could displace the *prima facie* presumption that Mr Lewis was dealing with the gentleman there present in the flat – the rogue.

(III) *Per* Megaw LJ:

> The mistake of Mr Lewis went no further than a mistake as to the attributes of the rogue. It was simply a mistake as to the creditworthiness of the man who was there present and who described himself as Mr Green ... there was not here any evidence that would justify the finding that he, Mr Lewis, regarded the identity of the man who called himself Mr Green as a matter of vital importance.

Q (a) Do the tests applied by Phillimore and Megaw LJJ distinguish this case from *Ingram and Others v Little*, or do you prefer Lord Denning MR's view that *Ingram and Others v Little* is irreconcilable with the other cases? (b) Is there a useful distinction between a mistake as to attributes and a mistake as to identity?

7.2 Mistake in equity

7.2.1 Fundamental mistake renders the contract voidable or liable to be set aside on terms

Cooper v Phibbs and Others (1867) HL

The petitioner made an agreement to lease from the respondent a salmon fishery in Sligo. Neither party realised that the petitioner was himself the tenant for life of the fishery under a family trust. The mistake had arisen owing to complications caused by the diversion of two rivers pursuant to a private Act of Parliament.

Held the agreement would be set aside on terms set by the court. *Per* Lord Westbury 'Private right of ownership is a matter of fact; it may be the result also of a matter of law; but, if parties contract under a mutual mistake and misapprehension as to their relative and respective rights, the result is, that that agreement is liable to be set aside as having proceeded upon a common mistake.'

Solle v Butcher (1949) CA

A certain flat in a house was let in 1938 for £140 a year. During the war, the house was severely damaged by bombing. The defendant landlord then bought the house and carried out substantial repairs in 1946 and 1947. The landlord negotiated with the plaintiff tenant for a new letting of the flat. They agreed that the rent should be £250 a year. However, they were aware that it might be that the rent would be controlled by statute which would keep it at a level linked to its pre-war amount. The question depended upon whether it was substantially the same flat after the repairs as it had been before. The tenant agreed to seek legal advice and did obtain a counsel's opinion. The result was that both parties believed that the rent would not be controlled and they made an agreement that the tenant would take the flat at a rent of £250 a year. Later, the parties fell out and the tenant brought this action to have his rent reduced to £140 and to recover payments he had made in excess of that amount. It was held that the property was indeed subject to a controlled rent based upon the pre-war figure of £140. The remaining question was whether the landlord could obtain any relief for the parties' mistake of believing when they made their agreement that the rent was not controlled.

Held the lease would be set aside with various terms as to the amount the tenant would pay in respect of his occupation of the flat. (I) *Per* Bucknill LJ:

> ... there was a mutual mistake of fact on a matter of fundamental importance ... and the principle laid down by Lord Westbury in *Cooper v Phibbs and Others* [7.2.1] applies.

Per Denning LJ:

> In order to see whether the lease can be avoided for this mistake, it is necessary to remember that mistake is of two kinds: first, mistake which renders the contract void, that is, a nullity from the beginning, which is the kind of mistake which was dealt with by the courts of common law, and, secondly, mistake which renders the contract not void but voidable, that is, liable to be set aside on such terms as the court thinks fit, which is the kind of mistake which was dealt with by the courts of equity. Much of the difficulty which has attended the subject has arisen because, before the fusion of law and equity, the courts of common law, in order to do justice in the case in hand, extended this doctrine

of mistake beyond its proper limits and held contracts to be void which were really only voidable ... Since the fusion of law and equity, there is no reason to continue this process, and it will be found that only those contracts are now held void where the mistake was such as to prevent the formation of any contract at all. [(i) Mistake at law:] ... in the light of *Bell v Lever Bros* [7.1.3] ... once the parties ... have to all outward appearances agreed with sufficient certainty in the same terms on the same subject matter, then ... neither party can rely on his own mistake to say it was a nullity from the beginning, no matter that it was a mistake which to his mind was fundamental, and no matter that the other party knew he was under a mistake ... The cases where goods have perished at the time of the sale, or belong to the buyer, are not really contracts which are void for mistake, but are void by reason of an implied condition to that effect, and even cases like *Smith v Hughes* [7.1.1] turn at law on whether there was a contractual condition or not ... [(ii) Mistake in equity:] It is now clear that a contract will be set aside if the mistake of the one party has been induced by a material misrepresentation of the other, even though it was not fraudulent or fundamental, or if one party, knowing that the other is mistaken about the terms of an offer, or the identity of the person by whom it is made, lets him remain under his delusion and conclude a contract on the mistaken terms instead of pointing out the mistake, which is, I venture to think, the ground on which the defendant in *Smith v Hughes* [7.1.1] would be exempted nowadays ... A contract is also liable in equity to be set aside if the parties were under a common misapprehension either as to facts or as to their relative and respective rights, provided that the misapprehension was fundamental and that the party seeking to set it aside was not himself at fault ... [In this case], as Bucknill LJ has said, there was clearly a mutual mistake, or, as I would prefer to describe it, a common misapprehension, which was fundamental and in no way due to any fault of the landlord, and *Cooper v Phibbs and Others* [7.2.1] affords ample authority for saying that, by reason of the common misapprehension, this lease can be set aside on such terms as the court thinks fit.

(II) Jenkins LJ dissented holding that the mistake was a mistake of law, and not of fact, which did not give rise to a right to rescind. He said that, on the landlord's view, the landlord would be able to rescind the contract even if the tenant had not tried to claim the benefit of the controlled rent, which could not be just.

Q   (a) If the principles enunciated in this case by Denning LJ are correct, why were they not applied, nor even considered, by the House of Lords in *Bell v Lever Bros* (7.1.3)? (b) Do you agree with Denning LJ's view that *Bell v Lever Bros* is authority that a contract once made can never be void for mistake? (See the different view of Steyn J in *Associated Japanese Bank (International) Ltd v Crédit du Nord SA and another* at 7.3.) (c) What are the implications of Denning LJ's sweeping *dicta* about earlier cases classified under the heading of mistake? (d) Does 'voidable' mean the same as 'liable to be set aside on such terms as the court thinks fit'?

Grist v Bailey (1966) Ch

The defendant agreed to sell a certain house in Chelmsford to the plaintiff for £850 'subject to the existing tenancy thereof'. Both parties believed that the tenant of the house held a protected tenancy under the Rent Acts. In fact, there was a new tenant who was not protected, so the freehold of the house was worth about £2,250. The defendant discovered the facts just before completion and refused to complete the sale. The plaintiff brought this action for specific performance and the defendant counter claimed for rescission.

Held rescission would be granted. The difference in value of the house was such as to make the common mistake of the parties fundamental. The defendant was not at fault in any way which prevented her from taking advantage of the mistake. Therefore, following *Solle v Butcher* (above), the contract for sale would be rescinded on terms set by the court.

Note ───────────────────────────────────

See *William Sindall plc v Cambridgeshire County Council* (7.3), argument (III), where this decision is doubted in the Court of Appeal.

Magee v Pennine Insurance Co Ltd (1969) CA

The plaintiff bought a car. An insurance proposal form was completed for him at the garage where he bought the car. The form was completed to say that the plaintiff himself would be the main driver of the car. In fact, the plaintiff did not have any kind of licence to drive and was buying the car for his 18 year old son. Despite this and other errors, the plaintiff signed the proposal form, without any fraudulent intention on his part. The defendant insurance company accepted the form and insured the car. The car was later written off in an accident and the insurance company offered in writing to pay £385 in full settlement of the claim. The offer was accepted orally. But then, the insurance company discovered the true facts which conflicted with those on the proposal form and refused to pay over the £385. Although the insurance company was not bound by the policy to meet the claim because of the mistakes on the form, the question now was whether they could avoid paying under their agreement to pay £385 to settle the claim.

Held the insurance company could avoid payment. (I) *Per* Lord Denning MR, the parties were under a common mistake that the plaintiff was entitled to claim under the policy: 'That common mistake does not make the agreement to pay £385 a nullity, but it makes it liable to be set aside in equity.' *Per* Fenton Atkinson LJ:

In my view, it is the right and equitable result of this case that the insurance company should be entitled to avoid that agreement on the ground of mutual mistake in a fundamental and vital matter.

(II) Winn LJ, dissenting, held that *Bell v Lever Bros* (7.1.3) applied to this case so that the agreement to pay £385 was valid and enforceable.

Q   (a) Can you find any material distinction between the facts of this case and the facts of *Bell v Lever Bros*? (b) What is the distinction between a valid agreement to forbear from suing on a bad legal claim (see 3.6.2) and a voidable agreement to settle a bad claim under an insurance contract (as in this case)?

7.2.2   Relief for a party who makes a mistake without the fault of the other party

Malins v Freeman (1836) CCh

The defendant was employed by one Davies, who was selling some land at auction, to bid on Davies' behalf to ensure that a reserve price was obtained. The defendant arrived at the auction late and bid for the wrong lot. A lot owned by the plaintiff was knocked down to the defendant for £1,400 following some 'hasty and inconsiderate' bidding. The defendant refused to go through with the agreement to buy the land and the plaintiff brought this action for specific performance.

Held specific performance would not be ordered against the defendant who had contracted under a mistake. It could well be that the defendant would have to pay damages at common law for any loss caused to the plaintiff by the breach of contract but it would not be equitable to make an order for specific performance.

Q   In the light of the other decisions in this section, is this case still good law?

Tamplin v James (1880) CA

The plaintiff sellers put up for sale by auction some land which they described as:

> ... all that well accustomed inn, with the brewhouse, outbuildings, and premises known as The Ship, together with the messuage, saddler's shop and premises adjoining thereto, situate at Newerne in the same parish, No 454 and 455 on the said tithe map ...

The lot did not sell at the auction but the defendant agreed afterwards to buy it for £750. The defendant had known the area all his life and he wrongly assumed that some gardens which had been occupied along with The Ship Inn and the saddler's shop were included in the lot. He had not referred to the tithe map which was made available at the auction and which correctly showed the lot without the gardens. The sellers brought this action for specific performance of the contract of sale.

Held the defendant's mistake was made because of his own failure to take reasonable care so it would not nullify the contract. Specific performance would be ordered. The description of the property was not misleading and the defendant should have referred to it and to the map. *Per* Cotton LJ:

> In one sense, he was not bound to look at it [the description], but he cannot abstain from looking at it and then say that he bought under a reasonable belief that he was buying something not included in it.

Riverlate Properties Ltd v Paul (1974) CA

The plaintiff company was a property developer which owned a shop with a two floor maisonette above. The company granted a 99 year lease to the defendant for a price of £6,250. The lease was executed in 1969 and provided that all structural repairs were the responsibility of the lessor. In 1971, the company claimed that this aspect of the lease was a mistake and that the costs of external and structural repairs should be shared equally as were certain other costs under the lease. The company failed to prove that the defendant or her solicitor knew that the lease, which the company had itself prepared, contained a mistake.

Held per Russell LJ, giving the judgment of the court:

> ... since the defendant neither directly nor through her solicitor ... knew of the plaintiff's mistake, and was not guilty of anything approaching sharp practice in relation thereto, it is a case of mere unilateral mistake which cannot entitle the plaintiff to rescission of the lease either with or without the option to the defendant to accept rectification to cure the plaintiff's mistake.

Centrovincial Estates plc v Merchant Investors Assurance Company Ltd (1983) CA

The plaintiffs let part of an office building to the defendants at a rent of £68,320 a year subject to review from 25 December 1982. According to the lease, the review could only be upwards and would take the rent to the current market rate as agreed between the parties or assessed by an independent surveyor if they could not agree. On 22 June 1982, the plaintiffs' solicitors wrote to the defendants asking them to agree that the market rent was now £65,000. On 23 June, the defendants replied giving their agreement. The plaintiffs' solicitors immediately explained that their letter contained an error and that they had meant to suggest £126,000 but the defendants said they would hold the plaintiffs to the agreement they had reached. The plaintiffs now sought a declaration that no binding agreement had been made. The plaintiffs obtained summary judgment and the appeal was against that summary judgment.

Held per Slade LJ, giving the judgment of the court:

> In the absence of any proof, as yet [that is, at the summary judgment stage], that the defendants either knew or ought reasonably to have known of the plaintiffs' error at the time when they purported to accept the plaintiffs' offer, why should the plaintiffs now be allowed to resile from that offer? It is a well established principle of the English law of contract that an offer falls to be interpreted not subjectively by reference to what has actually passed through the mind of the offeror, but objectively, by reference to the interpretation which a reasonable man in the shoes of the offeree would place on the offer. It is an equally well established principle that ordinarily an offer, when unequivocally accepted according to its precise terms, will give rise to a legally binding agreement as soon as acceptance is communicated to the offeror in the manner contemplated by the offer, and cannot thereafter be revoked without the consent of the other party.

It was irrelevant that the defendants had not done anything to change their position in reliance on the plaintiffs' offer; their promise to accept the valuation was sufficient consideration for the plaintiffs' offer, even though it was of little or no commercial value to the plaintiffs.

7.3 The relationship between equitable and common law mistake

Solle v Butcher (1949) CA

See 7.2.1.

Associated Japanese Bank (International) Ltd v Crédit du Nord SA and Another (1988) QB

Mr Bennett wanted to borrow money. He negotiated with the plaintiffs, AJB, a sale and leaseback arrangement. This meant that AJB bought four machines from Mr Bennett for about £1,000,000 and then leased them back to him in return for rental payments calculated by reference to the interest rate. Such a transaction is in substance a loan, but its leaseback form brings tax benefits to both parties. For a fee, the defendants, CDN, guaranteed Mr Bennett's obligations under the lease agreement. The agreements were made in February 1984, but in May, Mr Bennett was arrested for fraud and in July he was adjudged bankrupt. It transpired that the machines which were the subject of the sale and leaseback did not exist, and had never existed. Since Mr Bennett had not paid the instalments, AJB claimed them from CDN under the guarantee. CDN argued that the common mistake made by both parties that the machines existed excused them from paying.

Held, by Steyn J, CDN did not have to pay. (I) The guarantee was subject to an express condition precedent that the machines existed, so that, if they did not, CDN were entitled to treat the agreement as repudiated. (II) If that construction of the guarantee was wrong, there was an implied condition precedent that the machines existed. (III) In case the first two arguments were wrong, mistake must be considered. (i) *Bell and Another v Lever Brothers Ltd and Others* (7.1.3) showed that common mistake at common law was restricted to, in Lord Atkin's words, mistakes as to 'the existence of some quality which makes the thing without the quality essentially different from the thing as it was believed to be'. Denning LJ's view in *Solle v Butcher* (see 7.2.1) that *Bell and Another v Lever Brothers Ltd and Others* decided that common mistake never makes a contract void at common law was 'an individual opinion' which 'does not do justice to the speeches of the majority', (ii):

> Logically, before one can turn to the rules as to mistake, whether at common law or in equity, one must first determine whether the contract itself, by express or implied condition precedent or otherwise, provides who bears the risk of the relevant mistake. It is at this hurdle that many pleas of mistake will either fail or prove to have been unnecessary. Only if the contract is silent on the point is there scope for invoking mistake. That brings me to the relationship between common law mistake and mistake in equity. Where common law mistake has been pleaded, the court must first consider this plea. If the contract is held to be void, no question of mistake in equity arises. But, if the contract is held to be valid, a plea of mistake in equity may have to be considered.

(iii) For a mistake to be operative at common law, it:

> ... must render the subject matter of the contract essentially and radically different from the subject matter which the parties believed to exist.

This test was satisfied here, so the guarantee was void *ab initio* for common law mistake. (IV) Finally, his lordship said:

> If I had not decided in favour of CDN on construction and common law mistake, I would have held that the guarantee must be set aside on equitable principles.

William Sindall plc v Cambridgeshire County Council (1993) CA

The defendant council offered for sale by tender some playing fields for which they had registered outline planning consent for residential development. The plaintiff company, Sindall, bought the playing fields for over £5,000,000 in December 1988 for the purpose of a residential development. The contract of sale included National Conditions of Sale (20th edn) condition 14:

Without prejudice to the duty of the vendor to disclose all latent easements and latent liabilities known to the vendor to affect the property, the property is sold subject to any rights of way and water, rights of common and other rights, easements, quasi-easements, liabilities and public rights affecting the same.

The council said in answer to a pre-contract inquiry that it was not aware of any rights or easements affecting the property. It took until October 1990 for Sindall to obtain the necessary detailed planning permission for the development. In the meantime, the property market had collapsed and the site was worth less than half what Sindall had paid for it. Sindall were not sure whether to continue with the development or to try to sell the site. On 30 October 1990, it was discovered that the land was crossed diagonally by a sewer underground. The planned development could not be implemented while the sewer remained. Sindall therefore wrote to the Council rescinding the purchase of the land for misrepresentation and mistake. It was later found that the sewer could have been diverted to enable the development to go ahead, but Sindall did not explore that possibility because they preferred to rescind the contract if they could.

Held Sindall could not rescind the contract. (I) When it said that it was not aware of any rights affecting the property, the council represented that it had taken reasonable steps to find out about any such rights. Even though such a right, the sewer, did exist, the representations that the council did not know about it and had taken reasonable steps to find out were true so there was no misrepresentation. (II) Condition 14 was not subject to s 3 of the Misrepresentation Act 1967 because it did not exclude liability for misrepresentation, but instead went to the question of whether there was a misrepresentation. (III) Turning to mistake, Hoffman LJ adopted the *dicta* of Steyn J in *Associated Japanese Bank (International) Ltd v Crédit du Nord SA and Another* (7.3) to the effect that any contractual allocation of risk must be considered before mistake. His lordship added:

I should say that neither in *Grist v Bailey* [see 7.2.1] nor in *Laurence v Lexcourt Holdings Ltd* did the judges who decided those cases at first instance advert to the question of contractual allocation of risk. I am not sure that the decisions would have been the same if they had. In this case, the contract says in express terms that it is subject to all easements other than those of which the vendor knows or has the means of knowledge. This allocates the risk of such incumbrances to the buyer and leaves no room for rescission on the grounds of mistake.

(IV) *Per* Evans LJ:

It must be assumed, I think, that there is a category of mistake which is 'fundamental', so as to permit the equitable remedy of rescission, which is wider than the kind of 'serious and radical' mistake which means that the agreement is void and of no effect in law ... The difference may be that the common law rule is limited to mistakes with regard to the subject matter of the contract, whilst equity can have regard to a wider and perhaps unlimited category of 'fundamental' mistake ... [In this case] Given the breadth of the contract terms, in particular condition number 14 which on its face was intended to cover precisely such a situation as this, and the relatively minor consequences of the discovery of the sewer, even if some period of delay as well as additional cost was involved, it is impossible to hold, in my judgment, that there is scope for rescission here.

Note

In relation to arguments (I) and (II), contrast this case with *Walker v Boyle* at 6.5.3.

7.4 *Non est factum*

Saunders v Anglia Building Society: Gallie v Lee (1970) HL

In 1962, the plaintiff aunt was 78 years old. She owned a long lease of a house. Her nephew, who was about 40, needed money for his business. The aunt wanted to help him and was prepared to give the nephew the house so that he could raise a mortgage on it, provided that she could live there for her life. The nephew was afraid to own the house in case it would allow his wife to force him to pay maintenance for her and their children. The nephew had a friend, Mr Lee, who needed money. The nephew and Mr Lee therefore planned that Mr Lee would buy the house from the aunt and raise a mortgage on it. He would then pay the purchase price by instalments to the nephew's mistress, so that the nephew would have the benefit of the money but the nephew's wife could not gain access to it. The nephew and Mr Lee went to see the aunt. They put before her a deed which transferred the house to Mr Lee for £3,000 (which Mr Lee did not actually intend to pay, but which would make the transaction more acceptable to a mortgage lender). Having broken her spectacles, the aunt could not read. Mr Lee told her that the deed was to do with the gift of the house to the nephew. The nephew said nothing and the aunt signed the deed. The defendant building society, seeing only the documents, then lent £2,000 to Mr Lee secured on the house. Mr Lee used the money to pay existing debts and never made any payments to the nephew. When the building society claimed the house because Mr Lee had not kept up payments on the mortgage, the aunt claimed that the assignment of the house to Mr Lee was void, pleading *non est factum*.

Held the aunt was not entitled to the plea *non est factum*, and the building society could rely on the assignment. The following principles were enunciated in different words by all of their lordships. (I) One who seeks to invoke *non est factum* must discharge a heavy burden of proof. (II)

That includes proving that he took reasonable care and was not too lazy or too busy to read what he signed. (III) *Per* Lord Reid:

> There must, I think, be a radical difference between what he signed and what he thought he was signing – or one could use the words 'fundamental' or 'serious' or 'very substantial'. But, what amounts to a radical difference will depend on all the circumstances. If he thinks he is giving property to A whereas the document gives it to B, the difference may often by of vital importance, but, in the circumstances of the present case, I do not think that it is.

Per Lord Hodson:

> The difference ... must be in a particular which goes to the substance of the whole consideration or to the root of the matter.

In this case, the document was broadly for the object which the plaintiff understood it to be for – enabling the nephew to raise money – and her misunderstanding of its full detail was not fundamental enough to enable her to plead *non est factum*.

Note ────────────────────────────────

As against Mr Lee, who was not a party to the final appeal, the assignment was avoided by the plaintiff for fraud. It was only as against the building society that the plaintiff had no effective remedy.

United Dominions Trust v Western and Another (1975) CA

The defendant wanted to buy a second hand Ford Corsair car from the third party dealer. They agreed a price of £550 with a deposit of £34. The defendant asked for a hire purchase arrangement and signed a form with the spaces left blank which the dealer gave him for that purpose. The form was the plaintiff's standard form for a loan application, not for hire purchase. The dealer filled in the blanks on the form with the car's price as £730 and the deposit as £185. Later, the defendant asked the plaintiff for a copy of the agreement which they sent him. The defendant made no complaint then that the terms of the agreement were wrong. The car was stolen and written off and the defendant paid no instalments under the agreement. The plaintiff brought an action for the loan repayments and the defendant argued that the fraudulent completion of the form by the dealer enabled him to plead *non est factum*.

Held the principles of *Saunders v Anglia Building Society: Gallie v Lee* (7.4) applied to a form signed in blank. Therefore, the defendant had the onus of showing that he had acted carefully, which he had failed to do. One who allows another to fill in blanks in a document he has signed must bear the risk of fraudulent or mistaken completion of the document and cannot plead *non est factum*.

Note ———————————————————————————

The facts of this case are similar to those of *Royscot Trust Ltd v Rogerson and Another* (at 6.5.4).

Lloyds Bank plc v Waterhouse (1990) CA

The defendant father was a farmer, who was illiterate. His son wanted to buy his own farm and the father signed a guarantee of a loan to the son from the plaintiff bank. The father thought that he was guaranteeing only a loan for the farm and that the farm would be sold before his guarantee would be called in. In discussions before he signed, the bank had reinforced his impression that the guarantee was for the purpose of the loan for the land. In fact, the document was a guarantee for all the son's indebtedness to the bank. Eventually, the bank took action to recover from the father over £193,000 which they had lent to the son.

Held the father was not bound to pay under the guarantee. Their lordships gave various reasons. (I) *Per* Purchas LJ, the father was under a disability (illiteracy), had shown that he had taken reasonable care over what he was signing and that the document was fundamentally different from that which he thought it was. He was therefore entitled to the plea of *non est factum*. His lordship held that the father also had a defence of negligent misrepresentation by the bank. (II) Woolf LJ was not satisfied either that the guarantee was sufficiently different from that which the father thought it was, or that the father had taken sufficient care as to the contents of the document he signed to establish *non est factum*. He preferred to find for the father on the basis of misrepresentation. (III) In the circumstances, the bank ought to have known that the father would not have been willing to guarantee such a great liability. Therefore, the father was acting under a mistake which was induced by the bank, as in *Scriven Brothers & Co v Hindley & Co* (see 7.1.2).

7.5   Rectification

Frederick E Rose (London) Ltd v Wm H Pim Jnr & Co Ltd (1953) CA

The buyers' Egyptian associates sent them a cable asking for '500 tons Moroccan horsebeans described here as feveroles'. The buyers did not know what feveroles were, but they asked the sellers. The sellers considered the matter and then said that feveroles were simply horsebeans from Algeria, Tunisia or Morocco. The sellers obtained some Tunisian horsebeans and sold them to the buyers for £32 a ton. The contract for sale was contained in a number of letters and cables which all referred to horsebeans and did not mention feveroles. In fact, 'horsebeans' was a generic term and feveroles were the most valuable kind. The buyers were unable to sell on the horsebeans in Egypt because they were not feveroles. Since the buyers had accepted the beans before they realised the mistake, it was too late to claim rescission of the contract. The buyers brought this action seeking rectification of the contract by the insertion of the word 'feveroles'.

Held this was not a suitable case for rectification. There was a contract for the sale of horsebeans even though that was based on the mistaken belief of both parties that horsebeans were the same as feveroles. Since the written agreement correctly expressed the intentions displayed by the parties to contract to buy and sell horsebeans, it could not be rectified. *Per* Denning LJ:

Rectification is concerned with contracts and documents, not with intentions. In order to get rectification, it is necessary to show that the parties were in complete agreement on the terms of their contract, but by an error wrote them down wrongly.

Denning LJ also held that this contract was not void for mistake at common law, but could have been voidable in equity were it not too late for rescission.

A Roberts & Co Ltd and Another v Leicestershire County Council (1961) Ch

The defendant council wanted a school to be built and sought tenders for the construction work. The plaintiffs submitted a tender, which the council decided to accept, with the contract to last for 18 months. During the negotiations, the council changed the written contract so that it would last for 30 months. The council did nothing to draw the plaintiffs' attention to the change, which the plaintiffs would not have accepted without charging a higher price. However, the plaintiffs eventually signed the contract without noticing the change.

Held there was no common mistake, as the parties were not at one on the contract period. However, it had been shown that the council knew that the plaintiffs believed the contract period was 18 months at the time the contract was made. Since they knew that, the council could not be heard to say that it was not mistaken in the contract period itself. Therefore, rectification could be made to amend the contract period to 18 months, the figure which the council knew that the plaintiffs believed they were contracting for.

Joscelyne v Nissen and Another (1969) CA

The daughter agreed to take over the father's car hire business and to pay the father a pension. Their negotiations were concluded by the signature of a written contract. Throughout the negotiations, it was understood by both parties that the daughter would pay the father's household bills, but this understanding was not properly included in the written contract. For some time, the agreement was carried out by the parties, but, when a dispute arose between them, the daughter stopped paying the father's household bills. The father now sought rectification of the written contract to reflect the agreement for the payment of his household bills.

Held rectification would be granted in this case. Russell LJ, delivering the judgment of the court, considered the principles which applied to rectification. His lordship held that it was not necessary to find that a concluded binding contract existed before a written document was executed in order to rectify the document. It was sufficient to find (in the words of Simmonds J in another case, adopted by the court) 'a common continuing intention in regard to a particular provision or aspect of the agreement'. Convincing proof of the common intention would be required.

Commission for the New Towns v Cooper (GB) Limited (1995) CA

The plaintiff was the successor in title to the Milton Keynes Development Corporation ('MK'). MK was a large commercial landlord in Milton Keynes. EHL occupied Unit 3A Michigan Drive as a tenant of MK. On 15 August 1986, MK made a number of agreements with EHL: (i) MK agreed to carry out certain works on the property to be paid for by EHL; (ii) EHL was to have an option to surrender the lease if it chose to do so on each fifth anniversary of the date of the deed (the 'put option'); (iii) EHL was given an option to take a larger premises from MK instead of Unit 3A; and (iv) EHL was to have an option to acquire a lease over a plot of land adjoining Unit 3A (the 'side land option'). The side land option was to expire in August 1989. The options were personal to EHL and could not be assigned. In November 1987, EHL sold its business and assets to the defendant. The defendant failed to make the business profitable and by the end of 1990 the defendant's American parent company had decided that the business must be sold or closed. The defendant therefore wanted to acquire the put option to allow it to surrender the lease, but it did not believe that MK would be likely to grant it to them. In January 1991, the defendant arranged a meeting with MK to discuss some disputes which had arisen over works carried out by MK and over rent payments. At the meeting, the defendant offered a generous payment to settle the disputes and said that it might be interested in the side land option and would therefore like to be granted the rights which EHL had previously enjoyed including a renewed side land option. The defendant raised the side land option as a smokescreen to distract MK's attention from its real goal, the put option. After the meeting, the defendant wrote to MK confirming that the defendant would now pay for the works done by MK. The letter also said:

> You confirmed at our meeting that you will treat [the defendant] in all respects as having the same rights and benefits under the original documentation as [EHL]. This is important as, for example, the right to require completion of the remedial works and the obligation to pay for extras, otherwise remains with [EHL].

The letter went on to give considerable detail about the renewal of the side land option. MK's representatives at the meeting gave written confirmation of the content of the letter without ever considering the put option. The defendant immediately gave notice that it intended to exercise the put option and leave Milton Keynes altogether. MK applied, *inter alia*, to have the agreement rectified so that it did not include the put option. It was not disputed that the confirmation by MK's representatives of the defendant's letter constituted a valid acceptance.

Held the defendant had not obtained the put option. (I) The letter had to be construed in the context of the discussions between the parties. As a matter of construction, the letter did not refer to the put option, but only to the payment for work done by MK and the side land option. (II) If argument (I) was wrong, rectification would be granted. It was unusual to grant rectification in a case of unilateral mistake, but not impossible. *Per* Stuart-Smith LJ with whom Farquharson LJ agreed:

> ... were it necessary to do so in this case, I would hold that where A intends B to be mistaken as to the construction of the agreement, so conducts himself that he diverts B's attention from discovering the mistake by making false and misleading statements, and B in fact makes the very mistake that A intends, then notwithstanding that A does not actually know, but merely suspects that B is mistaken, and it cannot be shown that the mistake was induced by any misrepresentation, rectification may be granted. A's conduct is unconscionable and he cannot insist on performance in accordance to the strict letter of the contract; that is sufficient for rescission. But, it may also not be unjust or inequitable to insist that the contract be performed according to B's understanding, where that was the meaning that A intended that B should put upon it.

(III) MK's representatives did not have authority to issue the put option to the defendant and the agreement was not valid for this reason also. (IV) The exchange of letters was not sufficient to satisfy the requirements of formality in contracts for the disposition of land made by s 2 of the Law of Property (Miscellaneous Provisions) Act 1989. This was another reason why the put option could not have been transferred to the defendant.

8 Frustration

8.1 The original rule: contractual obligations are binding

Paradine v Jane (1647)

The defendant was the plaintiff's tenant. The defendant was kept out of the land for three years by Prince Rupert's army and he did not pay the rent for that period.

Held the defendant must pay the rent for the period. The reasons, according to the report of the case, were: (I) 'when the party by his own contract creates a duty or charge upon himself, he is bound to make it good, if he may, notwithstanding any accident by inevitable necessity, because he might have provided against it by his contract'; and (II) 'as the lessee is to have the advantage of casual profits, so he must run the hazard of casual losses'.

8.2 The development of the doctrine of frustration

8.2.1 There may be an implied term that certain events will relieve the parties of their obligations under the contract

Taylor and Another v Caldwell and Another (1863) CQB

The plaintiffs and the defendants agreed that the plaintiffs would use the defendants' 'Surrey Gardens and Music Hall' for four concerts for a fee of £100 for each concert. Before the date of the first concert, the Hall was destroyed by fire, without the fault of either party. The agreement contained no express stipulation for such a situation.

Held both parties were excused from carrying out their obligations under the contract. *Per* Blackburn J, giving the judgment of the court:

> The principle seems to us to be that, in contracts in which the performance depends on the continued existence of a given person or thing, a condition is implied that the impossibility of performance arising from the perishing of the person or thing shall excuse the performance ... that excuse is by law implied,

because from the nature of the contract it is apparent that the parties contracted on the basis of the continued existence of the particular person or chattel.

Jackson v The Union Marine Insurance Company Ltd (1874) EC

The plaintiff owned a ship, *Spirit of the Dawn*, which was chartered to a third party charterer to go from Liverpool to Newport where it would pick up some iron rails which it would take to San Francisco. The charter provided that the ship would sail to Newport with all possible dispatch, perils of the sea excepted. The plaintiff insured the freight (fee) he would earn from the voyage with the defendant insurers. The *Spirit of the Dawn* left Liverpool on 2 January, but ran aground in Caernarvon Bay the next day. On 16 February, with the *Spirit of the Dawn* still not removed from the rocks, the charterers chartered another ship. The repairs of the *Spirit of the Dawn* continued until the end of August. The plaintiff now claimed from the insurers for his loss of freight.

Held the charterer had a right to withdraw from the charter so the plaintiff had a good claim on the insurers. Because the ship failed to arrive within a reasonable time for the charterer's voyage, an implied condition of the charter was not complied with. Since the failure arose from a peril of the sea, which was excepted, there was no breach of contract by the plaintiff, and the charterer had no cause of action against the plaintiff. However, the charterer still had a right to withdraw from the contract because of the implied condition not being performed. *Per* Bramwell B, delivering the judgment of the majority, 'though non-performance of a condition may be excused, it does not take away the right to rescind from him for whose benefit the condition was introduced'.

Krell v Henry (1903) CA

The plaintiff owned a flat in Pall Mall and he advertised that he would let it out for the purpose of viewing the coronation procession of Edward VII. The defendant agreed to take the rooms for two days for £75. The coronation was postponed and the defendant refused to pay the unpaid balance of the £75.

Held the parties were excused from further performance of the contract, so the plaintiff could not recover the remaining price. Although the letters between the parties did not mention the coronation, the use of the rooms to view the coronation procession was the foundation of the contract. The performance of the contract became impossible in a way which could not have been contemplated by the parties when they made their agreement. *Per* Vaughan Williams LJ:

> It is not essential to the application of the principle of *Taylor v Caldwell* [8.2.1] that the direct subject of the contract should perish or fail to be in existence at the date of performance of the contract. It is sufficient if a state of things or

condition expressed in the contract and essential to its performance perishes or fails to be in existence at the time.

Note

In *Maritime National Fish Ltd v Ocean Trawlers Ltd* (see 8.2.6), the Privy Council expressed doubts about this case. *Per* Lord Wright, giving the judgment of the Board, 'The authority is certainly not one to be extended'.

8.2.2 The implied term may be excluded by an express term

F A Tamplin Steamship Company Ltd v Anglo-Mexican Petroleum Products Company Ltd (1916) HL

The owners and charterers agreed a time charter to last from 4 December 1912 until 4 December 1917. The charterparty contained exceptions (in condition number 20) for restraints of princes, rulers and peoples. In December 1914, the ship was requisitioned by the British Government for use in the war. The requisition remained in force at the time the case was heard. The owners contended that the charter had been frustrated by the requisitioning but the charterers wished it to continue, since they were being paid for the ship by the government.

Held the contract did continue. The doctrine of frustration was based on the principle that a term could be implied into a contract that in certain circumstances the parties would be excused from further performance. There could be no such term in this case. (I) *Per* Earl Loreburn:

Taking into account ... all that has happened, I cannot infer that the interruption either has been or will be in this case such as makes it unreasonable to require the parties to go on. There may be many months during which this ship will be available for commercial purposes before the five years have expired. It might be a valuable right for the charterer during those months to have the use of this ship at the stipulated freight. Why should he be deprived of it?

(II) *Per* Lord Parker of Waddington (with whom Lord Buckmaster LC agreed):

This principle is one of contract law, depending on some term or condition to be implied in the contract itself and not on something entirely dehors [outside] the contract which brings the contract to an end. It is, of course, impossible to imply in a contract any term or condition inconsistent with its express provisions, or with the intention of the parties as gathered from those provisions ... My Lords, I entertain no doubt that the requisitioning of the steamship by His Majesty's Government in the present case is a 'restraint of princes' within the 20th condition. The parties therefore have expressly contracted that for the period during which by reason of such restraint the owners are unable to keep the ship at the disposition of the charterers the freight is to continue payable, and the owners are to be free from liability ... Moreover (and this seems to me the vital point), the charterparty does not contemplate any definite adventure or object to be performed or carried out within reasonable limits of time so as to justify a distinction being drawn between delays which may render such an adventure or object impossible and delays which may not.

Q (a) If it had been the charterer who had sought to end the contract, would Earl Loreburn have reached a different conclusion? (b) Did the fact that the government paid compensation make any difference? (Lord Parker of Waddington said that it did not, but Lord Dunedin, in his speech in *Metropolitan Water Board v Dick, Kerr and Company Ltd* (see below), said that, if the government had not paid any compensation, frustration would have applied to excuse the charterer from paying the hire had the owner demanded it.)

Metropolitan Water Board v Dick, Kerr and Company Ltd (1917) HL

The company agreed in 1914 to construct a reservoir for the Board in a period not exceeding six years. The contract contained as condition 32, the following clause allowing the six years to be extended.

Provided always that if by reason of any additional works or enlargement of the works ..., or for any other just cause arising with the Board or with the engineer, or in consequence of any unusual inclemency of the weather, or general or local strikes, or combination of workmen, or for want or deficiency of any orders, drawings or directions, or by reason of any difficulties, impediments, obstructions, oppositions, doubts, disputes, or differences, whatsoever and howsoever occasioned, the contractor shall, in the opinion of the engineer (whose decision shall be final), have been unduly delayed or impeded in the completion of this contract, it shall be lawful for the engineer, if he shall so think fit, to grant from time to time, and at any time or times ... such extension of time either prospectively or retrospectively, and to assign such other day or days for or as for completion, as to him may seem reasonable, without thereby prejudicing or in any manner affecting the validity of the contract, or the adequacy of the contract price, or the adequacy of the sums or prices mentioned in the third schedule ...

In February 1916, the company was ordered to stop work on the reservoir by the Ministry of Works which also seized the plant being used in the construction for use in war work. The Board insisted that the contract remained in force while the company argued that it had been frustrated.

Held the contract was frustrated so the company need not complete the work. *Per* Lord Finlay LC: 'Condition 32 does not cover the case in which the interruption is of such a character and duration that it vitally and fundamentally changes the conditions of the contract, and could not possibly have been in the contemplation of the parties to the contract when it was made.' *Per* Lord Parmoor:

> This language [of condition 32] is no doubt wide, and the general words may be large enough to include the contingency of legislative interference stopping the works or postponing their erection for an indefinite time. I think, however, that the language was used *alio intuitu*, and that it is not reasonable to hold that it had any reference to such a contingency, or that such a contingency was in the contemplation of the parties when framing the terms of the section. A mere extension of time at the discretion of the engineer is not in any sense an appropriate remedy for the contingency which has occurred. In my opinion, neither party intended to leave the decision as to what should be done in such a contingency to the discretion of the engineer, under an ordinary extension of time clause in a works contract.

Q (a) Are their lordships in danger of crossing the line between construction of the contract and correction of it? (b) If the war had ended in March 1916, would this contract still have been frustrated? If not, when did the frustration occur?

8.2.3 A contract will not be frustrated by an event which does not make performance radically different or the risk of which is borne by one of the parties

Herne Bay Steam Boat Company v Hutton (1903) CA

The plaintiffs owned the steamboat *Cynthia*. The defendant wanted to charter the steamboat to take paying customers to see the naval review at Spithead, which was to take place in connection with the coronation of Edward VII, and to see the fleet there. The parties made an agreement on 23 May 1902:

> The *Cynthia* to be at Mr Hutton's disposal at an approved pier or berth at Southampton on the morning of 28 June, perils of the sea, &c, permitting, to take out a party, not exceeding the number for which the vessel is licensed, to the position assigned by the Admiralty, for the purpose of viewing the naval review and for a day's cruise round the fleet; also on Sunday 29 June, for similar purposes ...

On 25 June, it was announced that the review was cancelled because of the postponement of the coronation. Although the fleet itself remained at Spithead, the defendant did not go ahead with the use of the *Cynthia* and refused to pay the balance of the hire charges due to the plaintiffs under their contract.

Held there was no frustration here so the defendant must pay the loss caused by his repudiation of the contract. This was a contract to place the vessel at the disposal of the defendant for two certain days, not a contract for the viewing of the naval review. The purposes for which the defendant wished to hire the boat was a matter which concerned only the defendant, and not the plaintiffs. The risk that the objects of the voyage might become limited was one which the defendant had taken. Romer LJ further noted that there was not here a total failure of consideration.

Note

Compare this case with the similar facts of *Krell v Henry* (see 8.2.1).

Davis Contractors Ltd v Fareham Urban District Council (1956) HL

In July 1946, the parties agreed that the contractors would build for the council 78 houses in eight months for £85,836. The work was delayed, chiefly by a shortage of skilled labour, and was only completed after 22 months. This left the contractors facing a loss on the contract and they now claimed that the delay had frustrated the original contract and they were entitled to be paid on a *quantum meruit* basis, in place of the payment under the contract.

Held this was clearly not a case of frustration. The contractors' obligations turned out to be more onerous than they had expected but they remained essentially the same as at the time of the contract. The risk of a delay like the one which occurred was one which the contractors must be taken to have accepted when they made the contract. Their lordships also considered the basis of the doctrine of frustration. *Per* Lord Reid:

It appears to me that frustration depends, at least in most cases, not on adding any implied term but on the true construction of the terms which are, in the contract, read in the light of the nature of the contract and of the relevant surrounding circumstances when the contract was made ... The question is whether the contract which they did make is, on its true construction, wide enough to apply to the new situation: if it is not, then it is at an end.

Per Lord Radcliffe, who also criticised the implied term approach:

So, perhaps, it would be simpler to say at the outset that frustration occurs whenever the law recognises that, without default of either party, a contractual obligation has become incapable of being performed because the circumstances in which performance is called for would render it a thing radically different from that which was undertaken by the contract. *Non haec in foedera veni*. It was not this that I promised to do.

Tsakiroglou & Co Ltd v Noblee Thorl GmbH (1961) HL

The sellers agreed in October 1956 to sell 300 tons of Sudanese groundnuts to the buyers to be delivered by the sellers to Hamburg. Shipment was to be in November or December 1956. Both parties expected that the nuts would be shipped by the usual route from Sudan to Hamburg which was through the Suez Canal. The sellers booked space in a suitable ship sailing that way. However, the Suez Canal was closed due to an international dispute from 2 November 1956 and remained closed until April 1957. The sellers could still have delivered the groundnuts to Hamburg by way of the Cape of Good Hope for about twice the price of the voyage through the Canal. However, they chose instead to repudiate the contract and argued that it was frustrated.

Held the contract was not frustrated. (I) There was no implied term in the contract that the groundnuts must be transported by the usual route at the time of the contract being made. (II) The sellers' obligation was to deliver the groundnuts by any reasonable route and they could fulfil that obligation even after the closure of the Canal. *Per* Lord Radcliffe:

A man may habitually leave his house by the front door to keep his appointments; but, if the front door is stuck, he would hardly be excused for not leaving by the back.

Amalgamated Investment and Property Co Ltd v John Walker & Sons Ltd (1976) CA

On 25 September 1973, the parties exchanged contracts for the sale of a warehouse in East London by the defendants to the plaintiffs for £1,710,000. Both parties knew that the plaintiffs intended to redevelop the warehouse. The plaintiffs had made inquiries and believed that they were likely to be able to obtain the necessary planning permission. On 26 September, the Department of the Environment wrote to the defendants telling them that the property had been listed as being of special architectural or historical interest. The listing had been decided on 22 August and took legal effect from 27 September. The effect of the listing was that planning permission would be much harder to obtain and consequently the value of the property was reduced to about £200,000. The plaintiffs now sought to avoid completing the contract and the defendants counter-claimed for specific performance.

Held the contract had to be completed by the plaintiffs. (I) Since, at the date of the contract, the listing had not happened yet, there was no operative mistake. (II) Frustration did not apply because the plaintiffs took the risk of obtaining planning permission and the risk that the building might be listed in the future when they signed the contract. The risk of listing was one which every property purchaser had to take. The contract could be carried out by the plaintiffs completing the purchase and it would be substantially the same contract as was originally agreed. A further point was that the plaintiffs had not shown that in fact they would not eventually obtain planning permission.

8.2.4 A contract for personal services may be frustrated if the person cannot perform

Morgan v Manser (1947) KB

Under a contract of February 1938, the plaintiff manager agreed to act as manager for the defendant, the variety artiste, Charlie Chester, for 10 years and to obtain for the latter engagements and fees. In June 1940, the artiste was called up to military service. After 18 months' training, the artiste was transferred to the Entertainments Pool of the forces, where he served until he was demobilised in February 1946. The manager continued to try to keep the artiste's name before the public during the period of the latter's war service, but after the war the artiste claimed to be released from the contract and engaged his services to other managers and theatre proprietors. The manager claimed damages for breach of contract.

Held the contract was frustrated and the work done by the manager after June 1940 was not done under the contract. *Per* Streatfield J:

> I have come to the conclusion that there was here such a change of circumstances and for such a duration that the original contract, looked at as a whole, was so fundamentally invaded by the calling up of the artiste that it must be held to have been frustrated by reason of that event.

Condor v The Barron Knights Ltd (1965) Ass

The plaintiff, who was 16 years old, joined the defendant group as a drummer on 8 December 1962 under a contract for five years. He went from his mother's home in Darlington to live on his own in a caravan in Leighton Buzzard. The group worked seven nights a week, sometimes performing twice in one evening. On 16 January 1963, the plaintiff collapsed and was treated in hospital. The doctor said that he could not continue to live under such strain and must only go back to work for three or four nights a week. On 1 February, the group terminated his contract, despite the plaintiff's insistence that he was fit to rejoin the group as before. The plaintiff sought damages for breach of contract.

Held there was no wrongful dismissal of the plaintiff because he was unable to continue to perform the contract in the way it was intended.

8.2.5 Frustration may, but will only very rarely, apply to a lease

Cricklewood Property and Investment Trust Ltd and Others v Leightons Investment Trust Ltd (1945) HL

The defendant tenants took a 99 year lease of some land at Potters Bar from the plaintiff landlords' predecessors in 1936. The lessors were building a residential estate and the defendants were to build a shopping centre. The defendants' obligation to start building had not arisen when war broke out in 1939 and they had not in fact started to build. The building work was prohibited by war regulations. The defendants stopped paying rent and claimed that the lease had been frustrated.

Held the defendants were not excused from paying rent. (I) Their lordships were unanimous in holding that even if a lease was capable of being frustrated, this one was not frustrated on these facts. It was clear that there was no frustration because the lease was for 99 years, most of which would be unaffected by the war and because the lease itself made clear that the defendants should continue to pay rent even if the building of shops was delayed. *Per* Viscount Simon LC:

> Frustration may be defined as the premature determination of an agreement between parties, lawfully entered into and in course of operation at the time of its premature determination, owing to the occurrence of an intervening event or change of circumstances so fundamental as to be regarded by the law both as striking at the root of the agreement, and as entirely beyond what was contemplated by the parties when they entered into the agreement. If therefore the intervening circumstance is one which the law would not regard as so fundamental as to destroy the basis of the agreement there is no frustration. Equally, if the terms of the agreement show that the parties contemplated the possibility of such an intervening circumstance arising, frustration does not occur.

(II) Lord Russell of Killowen and Lord Goddard held that a lease could never be frustrated because it was an interest in land and not merely a contract. Viscount Simon LC and Lord Wright held that a lease could, in rare circumstances, be frustrated. Lord Porter did not express an opinion on this question.

National Carriers Ltd v Panalpina (Northern) Ltd (1980) HL

In 1974, the defendants agreed to lease for 10 years from the plaintiffs a triangular warehouse in Hull. In May 1979, the street the warehouse was in was closed to vehicles because another warehouse there had become dangerous owing to disrepair. When the appeal was heard in October 1980, it seemed likely that the road would be re-opened in January 1981. The defendants refused to pay rent, claiming that the lease had been frustrated.

Held there was no frustration here. (I) The loss of use for two years out of 10 was not sufficient for frustration. (II) Four of their lordships held that the doctrine of frustration could apply to leases, though it would only do so in very rare circumstances. Lord Russell of Killowen dissented, holding that the doctrine should never be applied to leases. (III) There was some discussion of the basis of the doctrine of frustration. Lord Hailsham LC said that there were five theories: (i) the implied term theory of *Taylor v*

Caldwell (see 8.2.1); (ii) the total failure of consideration theory, which could not explain many of the cases where the contract had been partly executed; (iii) that the doctrine was a special exception to the rules of contract to do justice, which did not provide a basis at all; (iv) the 'theory of "frustration of the adventure" or "foundation of the contract" formulation, said to have originated with *Jackson v Union Marine Insurance Co Ltd* [see 8.2.1]'; and (v) the construction theory that the doctrine is based on finding the true meaning of the contract. Lord Hailsham LC preferred the last mentioned theory and Lord Radcliffe's expression of it in *Davis Contractors Ltd v Fareham Urban District Council* (see 8.2.3). Lord Simon of Glaisdale criticised the implied term theory and said that the 'theory of a radical change in obligation' or 'construction theory' was the one 'which appears to be most generally accepted today'. Lord Roskill, like Lord Hailsham LC, expressed his preference for Lord Radcliffe's formulation in *Davis Contractors Ltd v Fareham Urban District Council*.

8.2.6   A party is not excused by self-induced frustration

Maritime National Fish Ltd v Ocean Trawlers Ltd (1935) PC

The charterers chartered from the owners a trawler, the *St Cuthbert*, to be employed in the fishing industry only, by a charter that was renewed from year to year. The *St Cuthbert* operated, and could only operate, with an otter trawl. When the parties agreed to renew the charter for a year from 25 October 1932, they knew of a (Canadian) statute which made it necessary to obtain a licence to fish using an otter trawl. In March 1933, the charterers applied for a licence for each of its five trawlers. In April, they were informed that they would be awarded only three licences and would have to choose three of their five trawlers. The charterers chose three which did not include the *St Cuthbert*, and they then sought to return the vessel to the owners from 1 May, after which they had no use for her. The owners sued for the hire charges from May to October.

Held there was no frustration of this contract. (I) *Per* Lord Wright, giving the judgment of the Board:

> ... it was the act and election of [the charterers] which prevented the *St Cuthbert* from being licensed for fishing with an otter trawl ... The essence of 'frustration' is that it should not be due to the act or election of the party.

(II) Since their lordships were content to rest their decision on that ground, they did not state a conclusion on an argument which was raised that the contract could not have been frustrated by an event which the parties must have contemplated at the making of the contract, because they knew of the requirement to obtain a licence.

J Lauritzen AS v Wijsmuller BV: *The Super Servant Two* **(1989) CA**

The plaintiffs, Lauritzen, owned a large drilling rig. The defendants, Wijsmuller, agreed to transport the rig from the Japanese shipyard where it was being built to Rotterdam. By the contract dated 7 July 1980, the rig was to be transported by '*Super Servant One* or *Super Servant Two* in Wijsmuller's option'. The rig was to be delivered between 20 June 1981 and 20 August 1981. Wijsmuller decided to use *Super Servant Two* to carry the rig; *Super Servant One* was booked for use in other contracts. On 29 January 1981 *Super Servant Two* was lost in the Zaire river. On 16 February 1981, Wijsmuller told Lauritzen that they could not use either *Super Servant* to transport the rig.

Held the additional costs of transporting the rig by another means would be borne by Wijsmuller who could not rely on frustration. (I) Discussing the doctrine in general, Bingham LJ said that the classical statement of the modern law of frustration was that of Lord Radcliffe in *Davis Contractors Ltd v Fareham Urban District Council* (see 8.2.3). *Per* Bingham LJ:

> Certain propositions, established by the highest authority, are not open to question: (1) The doctrine of frustration was evolved to mitigate the rigour of the common law's insistence on literal performance of absolute promises ... (2) Since the effect of frustration is to kill the contract and discharge the parties from further liability under it, the doctrine is not to be lightly invoked, must be kept within very narrow limits and ought not to be extended ... (3) Frustration brings the contract to an end forthwith, without more and automatically ... (4) The essence of frustration is that it should not be due to the act or election of the party seeking to rely on it ... A frustrating event must be some outside event or extraneous change of situation ... (5) A frustrating event must take place without blame or fault on the side of the party seeking to rely on it.

(II) In this case, the fact that Wijsmuller had a choice of two vessels meant that the loss of one could not frustrate the contract, following the decision in *Maritime National Fish Ltd v Ocean Trawlers Ltd* (8.2.6). Since frustration ends a contract forthwith and, without more, the loss of the *Super Servant Two* could not frustrate the contract because the contract would have continued if Wijsmuller had not afterwards decided that they would not use *Super Servant One*.

8.2.7 Even an event contemplated by the parties may be a frustrating event

Ocean Tramp Tankers Corporation v V/O Sovfracht: *The Eugenia* **(1963) CA**

During the Suez crisis, but before the Canal was closed, the parties negotiated the charter of the vessel, *The Eugenia*, to carry iron and steel from the Black Sea to India. They tried to specify what would happen if the Suez Canal closed, but failed to agree. They therefore made the charterparty with the standard war clause which prohibited the charterers from ordering the vessel into any war zone. The vessel was sent by the charterers on the normal route which took it through the Suez Canal. While it was in the Canal, on 31 October 1956, the Canal was closed, trapping *The Eugenia*. On 4 January 1957, the charterers claimed that the charterparty had been frustrated by the closing of the Canal. In early January, the vessel was able to move out of the Canal, but only to the north, where it had come in from. The owners, treating the charterers' actions as repudiation, made a new charterparty with the sub-charterers whose iron and steel was on *The Eugenia*. The vessel finally reached India via the Cape of Good Hope in April and in the same month the southern exit from the Canal was opened. The owners now claimed payment from the charterers for the time spent in the Canal.

Held the charterers must pay the outstanding hire fees. (I) The charterers were in breach of the war clause by ordering *The Eugenia* into the Canal. (II)(i) The charterers could not say that the trapping of the vessel in the Canal excused them, for that was their own fault as they sent the vessel there in breach of the war clause. (ii) The fact that the parties had considered the possibility of the Canal being closed did not mean that that event could not be one which frustrated the contract. Frustration was not based on an implied term, which could not be found when the parties had failed to agree on the matter, but on Lord Radcliffe's test from *Davis Contractors Ltd v Fareham Urban District Council* (see 8.2.3). (iii) The closing of the Canal made the voyage to India longer and more expensive, but it did not make it a fundamentally different voyage. Therefore, the contract was not frustrated by the closure of the Canal.

8.3　The consequences of frustration

8.3.1　Consequences of frustration at common law

Fibrosa Spolka Akcyjna v Fairbairn Lawson Combe Barbour Ltd (1943) HL

In July 1939, the parties made a written contract for the sale of some flax-hackling machines which the sellers were to deliver to the buyers in Poland. The buyers would pay £1,600 with the order and £3,200 when they received the shipping documents. The buyers paid £1,000 on account of the first £1,600. Then Germany invaded Poland and Great Britain declared war on Germany. Since delivery of the machines was impossible, the buyers sought the return of their £1,000.

Held the £1,000 should be returned to the buyers. The decision is an application of the rule that money is recoverable where there is a total failure of the consideration for which it had been paid. If the true construction of the contract is that a payment was intended to be final or absolute, then it would not be recoverable under this rule. But, where, as here, money is paid provisionally in the expectation of some consideration to come, it may be recovered if the consideration fails totally.

Note

There were seven speeches in the House of Lords in this case, and all proceeded on similar lines. Their lordships unanimously overruled *Chandler v Webster* (1904) in which the Court of Appeal had refused to apply the doctrine of failure of consideration to frustration cases.

8.3.2 Sale of Goods Act 1979

Section 6 Goods which have perished

Where there is a contract for the sale of specific goods, and the goods without the knowledge of the seller have perished at the time when the contract is made, the contract is void.

Section 7 Goods perishing before sale but after agreement to sell

Where there is an agreement to sell specific goods and subsequently the goods, without any fault on the part of the seller or buyer, perish before the risk passes to the buyer, the agreement is avoided.

8.3.3 Law Reform (Frustrated Contracts) Act 1943

Section 1 Adjustments of rights and liabilities of parties to frustrated contracts

(1) Where a contract governed by English law has become impossible of performance or been otherwise frustrated, and the parties thereto have for that reason been discharged from the further performance of the contract, the following provisions of this section shall, subject to the provisions of s 2 of this Act, have effect in relation thereto.

(2) All sums paid or payable to any party in pursuance of the contract before the time when the parties were so discharged (in this Act referred to as 'the time of discharge') shall, in the case of sums so paid, be recoverable from him as money received by him for the use of the party by whom the sums were paid, and, in the case of sums so payable, cease to be so payable:

Provided that, if the party to whom the sums were so paid or payable incurred expenses at the time of discharge in, or for the purpose of, the performance of the contract, the court may, if it considers it just to do so having regard to all the circumstances of the case, allow him to retain or, as the case may be, recover the whole or any part of the sums so paid or payable, not being an amount in excess of the expenses so incurred.

(3) Where any party to the contract has, by reason of anything done by any other party thereto in, or for the purpose of, the performance of the contract, obtained a valuable benefit (other than a payment of money to which the last foregoing subsection applies) before the time of discharge there shall be recoverable from him by the said other party such sum (if any), not exceeding the value of the said benefit to the party obtaining it, as the court considers just, having regard to all the circumstances of the case and, in particular:

    (a) the amount of any expenses incurred before the time of the discharge by the benefited party in, or for the purpose of, the performance of the contract, including any sums paid or payable by him to any other party in pursuance of the contract and retained or recoverable by that party under the last foregoing subsection; and

    (b) the effect, in relation to the said benefit, of the circumstances giving rise to the frustration of the contract.

(4) In estimating, for the purposes of the foregoing provisions of this section, the amount of any expenses incurred by any party to the contract, the court may, without prejudice to the generality of the said provisions, include such sum as appears to be reasonable in respect of overhead expenses and in respect of any work or services performed personally by the said party.

(5) In considering whether any sum ought to be recovered or retained under the foregoing provisions of this section by any party to the contract, the court shall not take into account any sums which have, by reason of the circumstances giving rise to the frustration of the contract, become payable to that party under any contract of insurance unless there was an obligation to insure imposed by an express term of the frustrated contract or by or under any enactment.

(6) Where any person has assumed obligations under the contract in consideration of the conferring of a benefit by any other party to the contract upon any other person, whether a party to the contract or not, the court may, if in all the circumstances of the case it considers it just to do so, treat for the purpose of sub-s (3) of this section any benefit so conferred as a benefit obtained by the person who has assumed the obligations aforesaid.

Section 2   Provision as to application of this Act

(1)   This Act shall apply to contracts, whether made before or after the commencement of this Act, as respects which the time of discharge is on or after the 1 July 1943, but not to contracts as respects which the time of discharge is before the said date.

(2)   This Act shall apply to contracts to which the Crown is a party in like manner as to contracts between subjects.

(3)   Where any contract to which this Act applies contains any provision which, upon the true construction of the contract, is intended to have effect in the event of circumstances arising which operate, or would but for the said provision operate, to frustrate the contract, or is intended to have effect whether such circumstances arise or not, the court shall give effect to the said provision and shall only give effect to the foregoing section of this Act to such extent, if any, as appears to the court to be consistent with the said provision.

(4)   Where it appears to the court that a part of any contract to which this Act applies can properly be severed from the remainder of the contract, being a part wholly performed before the time of discharge, or so performed except for the payment in respect of that part of the contract of sums which are or can be ascertained under the contract, the court shall treat that part of the contract as if it were a separate contract and had not been frustrated and shall treat the foregoing section of this Act as only applicable to the remainder of that contract.

(5)   This Act shall not apply:

(a)   to any charterparty, except a time charterparty or a charterparty by way of demise, or to any contract (other than a charterparty) for the carriage of goods be sea; or

(b)   to any contract of insurance save as is provided by sub-s (5) of the foregoing section; or

(c)   to any contract to which s 7 of the Sale of Goods Act 1979 (which avoids contracts for the sale of specific goods which perish before the risk has passed to the buyer) applies, or to any other contract for the sale, or for the sale and delivery, of specific goods, where the contract is frustrated by reason of the fact that the goods have perished.

Section 3   Short title and interpretation

(1)   This Act may be cited as the Law Reform (Frustrated Contracts) Act 1943.

(2)   In this Act, the expression 'court' means, in relation to any matter, the court or arbitrator by or before whom the matter falls to be determined.

9 Illegality

9.1 Contracts to oust the jurisdiction of the courts

9.1.1 An arbitration clause may be binding

Scott v Avery (1855) HL

In a contract for the insurance of ships, there was a clause which provided that if there was a dispute about a claim it must first be submitted to arbitration in a form specified in the contract. The clause continued:

> And the obtaining the decision of such arbitrators on the matters and claims in dispute, is hereby declared to be a condition precedent to the right of any member to maintain any such action or suit.

The plaintiff made a claim under the contract but refused to go to arbitration when he did not agree with the insurance company's proposed settlement.

Held the arbitration clause was binding. (I) Although the jurisdiction of the courts over breaches of contract could not be ousted, no action was maintainable until an arbitration award had been obtained. (II) The rule that the court's jurisdiction could not be ousted is a rule of public policy. *Per* Lord Campbell:

> I can see not the slightest ill consequences that can flow from such an agreement, and I see great advantage that may arise from it. Public policy, therefore, seems to me to require that effect should be given to the contract.

9.2 Immoral contracts

9.2.1 A contract for a known immoral purpose may be void

Pearce and Another v Brooks (1866) CE

The plaintiffs sold a new miniature brougham to the defendant which was to be paid for by instalments. The defendant was a prostitute and wanted the brougham for use in attracting trade. The jury found that these facts were known to the plaintiffs at the time of the contract. When the defendant did not pay the second instalment and returned the brougham damaged, the plaintiffs sued for the remaining payment or the cost of the damage.

Held the plaintiffs could not recover anything on a contract for an immoral purpose. *Per* Pollock CB:

> ... any person who contributes to the performance of an illegal act by supplying a thing with the knowledge that it is going to be used for that purpose, cannot recover the price of the thing so supplied ... Nor can any distinction be made between an illegal and an immoral purpose; the rule which is applicable to the matter is *ex turpi causa non oritur actio*, and whether it is an immoral or an illegal purpose in which the plaintiff has participated, it comes equally within the terms of that maxim, and the effect is the same; no cause of action can arise out of either one or the other.

Armhouse Lee Ltd v Chappell (1996) CA

The defendants were pornographers. Their business included the operation of telephone sex lines at premium rates. The plaintiffs acted as advertising agents for the defendants. In this action, the plaintiffs sued for the sums outstanding for their advertising services, payment of which was resisted by the defendants on the grounds that the advertising contracts were vitiated by illegality.

Held the advertising contracts were enforceable and the pornographers must pay for their advertisements. *Per* Simon Brown LJ:

> On any view of the law, public policy still precludes the enforcement of contracts for the promotion of an undoubtedly immoral purpose such as prostitution. *Pearce v Brooks* [9.2.1] remains good law.

However, his lordship held that 'lewd discussion over the telephone offering sexual excitement in return for payment' was not tantamount to prostitution. His lordship continued as follows:

> I readily accept that contracts for a sexually immoral purpose are contrary to public policy and that contracts tending to promote sexual immorality are illegal and unenforceable ... Necessarily, however, for that principle to apply, the court cannot avoid the question: what for this purpose is sexual immorality? Clearly it encompasses prostitution. That, as stated, is settled law. No less clearly ... , it would include, for example, bestiality or paedophilia. But does it include sexual arousal over the telephone, even accepting that the premium rates charged make that a service for reward? ... In my judgment, it is plain that no generally accepted moral code condemns these telephone sex lines. On the contrary, society appears not merely to have accepted their existence but to have placed them under the express control of an independent body, ICSTIS, who publish a detailed code of practice governing both the services themselves and all associated promotional material ... Returning then to the essential question

raised on this part of the case – is a contract for the advertising telephonic sexual arousal for reward contrary to public policy? I would answer firmly in the negative. Tempting though it is, I do not do so on the broad basis that the courts are courts of law and not of morals and leave it at that. That, I am persuaded, would be an impermissibly simplistic response to this appeal. There are occasions when perforce the court must grapple with concepts of morality.

Q Is it, and should it be, the task of the court to take account of immorality as well as illegality?

9.3 Contracts for illegal purposes

9.3.1 Certain contracts relating to marriage are illegal

Hermann v Charlesworth (1905) CA

The defendant advertised that he would arrange introductions with a view to marriage. The plaintiff paid the defendant £52 to arrange introductions for her. She was to pay a further £250 if the introductions resulted in her marriage, but if she was not engaged within nine months, the defendant would return £47 of the £52 to her. After four months, the plaintiff asked for the return of her money.

Held the plaintiff was entitled to her money back because the contract was for an illegal purpose. *Per* Collins MR:

Many elements have no doubt entered into the judgements in different cases, but at the root of the question of the illegality of a marriage brokerage contract is the introduction of the consideration of a money payment into that which should be free from any such taint.

Per Mathew LJ:

The object of the courts in discountenancing marriage brokerage contracts and pronouncing them to be illegal has been to prevent reckless and unsuitable marriages. The real nature of the contract is that it is nudum pactum, and the law declares that it imports no consideration, and that no rights arise under it ... There was an executory contract, no legal consideration, and consequently the plaintiff was entitled to rescind and to recover the money that she had paid.

Brodie v Brodie (1917) P

The petitioner was pregnant by the respondent and asked him to marry her. He agreed on condition that she signed an agreement to separate after the marriage and not to take any proceedings either for the restitution of conjugal rights or to obtain a judicial separation. The petitioner signed and then, after the marriage, brought this action for the restitution of conjugal rights.

Held the agreement was void and against public policy. It was therefore no defence to the petition which was granted.

9.3.2 Contracts contrary to statute are void

Anderson Ltd v Daniel (1923) CA

The sweepings from the holds of vessels which had carried certain substances were collected up and sold as 'salvage' for use as artificial fertiliser. The plaintiffs sold 10 tons of this salvage to the defendant. When the plaintiffs sued the defendant for the price of the salvage supplied, the defendant argued that the contract was illegal and therefore void. Section 1 of the Fertilisers and Feeding Stuffs Act 1906 provided that:

> Every person who sells for use as a fertiliser of the soil any article ... which has been imported from abroad, shall give to the purchaser an invoice stating the name of the article and what are the respective percentages, if any, of nitrogen, soluble phosphates, insoluble phosphates, and potash contained in the article.

Section 6 of the Act made it an offence to fail:

> ... without reasonable excuse to give, on or before or as soon as possible after the delivery of the article, the invoice required by the Act.

Held the contract was illegal and could not be enforced by the plaintiffs. (I) The fact that the contract was not illegal when it was made because it was perfectly possible for the invoice to be provided under the contract, did not prevent the contract from becoming illegal later. *Per* Atkin LJ:

> The question of illegality in a contract generally arises in connection with its formation, but it may also arise, as it does here, in connection with its performance. In the former case, where the parties have agreed to something which is prohibited by Act of Parliament, it is indisputable that the contract is unenforceable by either party. And I think that it is equally unenforceable by the offending party where the illegality arises from the fact that the mode of performance adopted by the party performing it is in violation of some statute, even though the contract as agreed upon between the parties was capable of being performed in a perfectly legal manner.

(II) The impracticability of making the necessary analysis of the salvage was not a 'reasonable excuse' under the Act.

Q Would this contract have been enforceable by the defendant?

St John Shipping Corporation v Joseph Rank Ltd (1956) QB

The Merchant Shipping (Safety and Load Line Conventions) Act 1932 made it an offence to load a ship so that her load line was submerged. However, the maximum fine under the Act was fixed in 1932 and by 1955 it was smaller than the additional profit which a ship owner could make by carrying excess freight. The plaintiffs' ship was found to have been overloaded and the defendants, who were among the owners of goods carried on the ship withheld some of the freight payment due to the plaintiffs. The plaintiffs now sued to recover the payment.

Held the payment could be recovered as the contract was not illegal. *Per* Devlin J:

> There are two general principles. The first is that a contract which is entered into with the object of committing an illegal act is unenforceable ... The second principle is that the court will not enforce a contract which is expressly or impliedly prohibited by statute. If the contract is of this class, it does not matter what the intention of the parties is; if the statute prohibits the contract, it is unenforceable whether the parties meant to break the law or not.

The statute in this case impliedly prohibited contracts for the improper loading of ships:

> But, an implied prohibition of contracts of loading does not necessarily extend to contracts for the carriage of goods by improperly loaded vessels. Of course, if the parties knowingly agree to ship goods by an overloaded vessel, such a contract would be illegal; but its illegality does not depend on whether it is impliedly prohibited by the statute, since it falls within the first of the two general heads of illegality I noted above where there is an intent to break the law. The way to test the question whether a particular class of contract is prohibited by the statute is to test it in relation to a contract made in ignorance of its effect. In my judgment, contracts for the carriage of goods are not within the ambit of this statute at all. A court should not hold that any contract or class of contracts is prohibited by statute unless there is a clear implication, or 'necessary inference', as Parke B put it, that the statute so intended.

Archbolds (Freightage) Ltd v S Spanglett Ltd (1960) CA

The defendants carried a van load of whisky for the plaintiffs from Leeds to London. The whisky was lost because of the negligence of the defendants' driver and the plaintiffs now sought damages for the loss. Under the Road and Rail Traffic Act 1933 an 'A' licence was required by anyone whose vehicle carried goods for reward. Since the defendants did not have such a licence, they argued that the contract of carriage was illegal so that the plaintiffs could not recover under it. It was shown that the plaintiffs had no reason to know that the defendants lacked the 'A' licence.

Held in the absence of knowledge of the lack of the licence, the contract was enforceable. *Per* Pearce LJ:

> If a contract is expressly or by necessary implication forbidden by statute, or if it is *ex facie* illegal, or if both parties know that, though *ex facie* legal, it can only be performed by illegality or is intended to be performed illegally, the law will

not help the plaintiffs in any way that is a direct or indirect enforcement of rights under the contract; and, for this purpose, both parties are presumed to know the law.

This statute did not prohibit the contract of carriage either expressly or impliedly. It was only an offence for the defendants, not for the plaintiffs, when the whisky was carried without a licence. The court should not be quick to find that a contract is impliedly forbidden by statute. Devlin LJ suggested that there might have been an implied warranty in the contract that the van was licensed, but the point had not been argued and was not decided.

9.3.3 Contracts tainted by an illegal purpose are unenforceable

Taylor v Bhail (1995) CA

The defendant was headmaster of a school which suffered damage as a result of gales. He agreed with the plaintiff building contractor that the plaintiff would provide an estimate for repair work which would be inflated by £1,000 so that the school could claim an additional £1,000 from its insurers as well as the sums necessary for the works to be carried out. The plaintiff provided a quote in the sum of £13,480 and did the necessary repair work. The defendant paid £7,400 and this was an action by the plaintiff to recover the remainder of the actual price of the work of £12,480.

Held the entire contract between the parties was vitiated by the intended fraud on the insurance company. Therefore, the plaintiff could not recover the balance of the price. An additional consequence was that the defendant would not be permitted to claim on his insurance or to retain any money already claimed. *Per* Sir Stephen Brown P:

> I believe this to be a very clear case, and the message should be sent out loud and clear that, if parties conspire to defraud an insurance company, as in this case, they cannot expect the courts to assist them in implementing their agreement. It is a remarkable feature of this case that the evidence was disclosed, not in the course of cross-examination, but as part of the case for the plaintiff himself. It would further appear that he could see nothing wrong in this.

9.3.4 An innocent party to an illegal contract may claim in restitution

Mohamed v Alaga & Co (1999) CA

The plaintiff was a leading member of the UK Somali community and a professional translator between English, Somali and Arabic. He alleged that he had made an agreement with the defendant firm of solicitors that he would introduce to the defendants Somalis who wished to apply for asylum in the UK. The defendants were to apply for legal aid on behalf of the applicants for asylum and the plaintiff would assist the defendants in making the applications by interpreting for the applicants, filling out forms, writing letters, etc. In consideration for all of this, the plaintiff alleged that he was to receive 50% of the fees received by the defendants from the Legal Aid Board. After introducing 242 such clients, the plaintiff sued for his share of the legal aid fees received by the defendants. The defendants applied to strike out the Statement of Claim on the ground that, if the agreement had been made (which the defendants denied), it was in breach of the Solicitors' Practice Rules made by The Law Society under the Solicitors Act 1974.

Held as a matter of construction of the Solicitors' Practice Rules, which had the force of law, the contract was illegal and therefore unenforceable. However, because in this case the plaintiff may have been ignorant of the rules which rendered the contract illegal whereas the defendants did know, or should have known, about them, the plaintiff could claim a reasonable sum by way of remuneration for the professional services he had rendered to the defendants. This would be a claim in quasi-contract or restitution. The plaintiff's innocence distinguished this case from *Taylor v Bhail* (9.3.3). It was also arguable that the plaintiff had a claim in the tort of negligence against the defendants for failing to point out the unlawfulness of the alleged contract.

9.3.5 Illegality only vitiates an equitable interest in property where it must be relied on to prove a claim

Tinsley v Milligan (1993) HL

The parties both contributed to the purchase price of a house in which they were to live together as lovers. The house was bought in the sole name of the plaintiff to facilitate a fraud which the parties were committing against the Department of Social Security. The parties fell out and the plaintiff brought a claim for possession of the house. The defendant counter claimed for a declaration that the plaintiff held the house on trust for the two of them.

Held the right of the defendant to half of the house must be recognised. (I) In the older cases, equity would give no relief to either side where a transaction was tainted with illegality, thus leaving the house in the hands of its owner at common law, the plaintiff in this case. Lord Goff of Chieveley, with whom Lord Keith of Kinkel agreed, found these older cases decisive and therefore dissented in the final result. (II) The purchase of a house with contributions from both parties gave rise to a presumption that the house was held on trust for both of them. Unless rebutted, this gave the defendant an equitable interest in the house. She already had that interest which the court only had to recognise. This was not the same as enforcing the performance of an illegal agreement which was only partly executed, which the court would not do. (III) The defendant did not have to rely on evidence of the illegality to establish her counter claim (which depended on the contributions made to the purchase price). The illegality was raised by the plaintiff as a defence to the defendant's counter claim. *Per* Lord Lowry:

> For A to take proceedings in order to vindicate his equitable rights as sole or joint beneficial owner is not an example of the maxim *ex turpi causa non oritur actio* because his equitable title and his cause of action do not arise out of his illegal or immoral act. It is B who must rely on the *turpis causa* as a defence. The foregoing considerations render me all the more convinced that the right view is that a party cannot *rely* on his own illegality in order to prove his equitable right, and *not* that a party cannot recover if his illegality is proved as a defence to his claim.

Note and Q

This case is based on a claim under a trust rather than a contract. Does the reasoning in arguments (II) and (III) apply also to equitable interests which pass under contracts for illegal purposes?

9.4 Contracts in restraint of trade

9.4.1 A restraint given for the purchase of goodwill may be valid

Nordenfelt v The Maxim Nordenfelt Guns and Ammunition Company Ltd (1894) HL

The defendant was an inventor and manufacturer of guns and ammunition. In 1886, the defendant sold his business to a new company, the Nordenfelt Guns and Ammunition Company, of which he became managing director. In 1888, the company merged with the Maxim Gun Company, to form the plaintiff company. As part of the merger agreement, the defendant agreed not to trade, unless for the new company, as a manufacturer of guns and so on, or in any competing business, for a period of 25 years. When the defendant made an agreement to work with a competing company, the plaintiff company brought this action for an injunction to enforce the agreement not to compete.

Held the covenant was enforceable. *Per* Lord Macnaghten:

> The true view at the present time, I think, is this: The public have an interest in every person's carrying on his trade freely: so has the individual. All interference with individual liberty of action in trading, and all restraints of

trade of themselves, if there is nothing more, are contrary to public policy, and therefore void. That is the general rule. But, there are exceptions: restraints of trade and interference with individual liberty of action may be justified by the special circumstances of a particular case. It is a sufficient justification, and indeed it is the only justification, if the restriction is reasonable – reasonable, that is, in reference to the interests of the parties concerned and reasonable in reference to the interests of the public, so framed and so guarded as to afford adequate protection to the party in whose favour it is imposed, while at the same time it is in no way injurious to the public.

This restraint was reasonable because it was given in return for the purchase of the defendant's goodwill (this was the substance of the transaction, even though in form the goodwill belonged to the Nordenfelt company, and not to the defendant). If such restraints were not upheld, it would be much harder for businesses to be bought and sold.

9.4.2 A restraint on employees will often not be valid

Attwood v Lamont (1920) CA

The plaintiff traded as a general outfitter in a shop with a number of departments. The defendant was employed by the plaintiff as head of the tailoring department. When the defendant joined the plaintiff's firm in 1909, he made an agreement by which he promised:

> ... that he will not at any time hereafter either on his own account or that of any wife of his or in partnership with or as assistant servant or agent to any other person persons or company carry on or be in any way directly or indirectly concerned in any of the following trades or businesses, that is to say, the trade or business of a tailor, dressmaker, general draper, milliner, hatter, haberdasher, gentlemen's ladies' or children's outfitter at any place within a radius of 10 miles of the employers' place of business at Regent House Kidderminster.

In 1919, the defendant set up on his own account at Worcester, which is more than 10 miles from Kidderminster. However, he did business with several of the plaintiff's customers and also took orders from them and fitted and supplied them with clothes within 10 miles of Kidderminster. The plaintiff brought this action for an injunction to prevent the defendant breaching his agreement.

Held the agreement could not be enforced. (I) Covenants between master and servant are treated differently from those between buyer and seller of goodwill. *Per* Younger LJ, with whom Atkin LJ agreed:

> An employer is not entitled by a covenant taken from his employee to protect himself after the employment has ceased against his servant's competition *per se* ...

The only restraints which are valid between master and servant are for the protection of proprietary rights of the employer such as 'trade connection' or 'trade secrets'. (II) *Per* Younger LJ:

> It is the covenantee ... who has to show that the restriction sought to be imposed upon the covenantor goes no further than is reasonable for the protection of his business.

(III) The extension of the covenant in this case to trades with which the defendant was not connected in his employment with the plaintiff meant that the covenant was too wide to be reasonable. (IV) (9.4.5) *Per* Younger LJ:

> The doctrine of severance has not, I think, gone further than to make it permissible in a case where the covenant is not really a single covenant but is in effect a combination of several distinct covenants. In that case and where the severance can be carried out without the addition or alteration of a word, it is permissible. But, in that case only.

In this case, there was one covenant to protect the one business of the plaintiff. Severance was therefore not possible. (V) *Per* Younger LJ, the agreement would not have been enforceable even if severed so that it only applied to tailoring, because it would still be covenant against competition *per se*. Lord Sterndale MR did not express an opinion on this point.

Q   Is there any conflict between the reasoning in (III), which relies on analysing the plaintiff's business into several trades, and the reasoning in (IV), which relies on the plaintiff only having one business protected by the covenant?

Wyatt v Kreglinger and Fernau (1933) CA

The plaintiff was employed by the defendants until, in 1923, the defendants gave him notice under his contract. The defendants were not obliged to make any payment to the plaintiff, but they wrote to him saying:

> Upon your retirement on 31 July next, we have decided to grant you a pension of £200 per annum, payable by monthly instalments. You are at liberty to undertake any other employment, or enter into any business on your own account, except in the wool trade, and the only other stipulation we attach to the continuance of this pension is that you do nothing at any time to our detriment (fair business competition excepted).

In a later letter, the defendants referred to the pension as 'remuneration'. In 1932, the defendants were cutting costs and stopped paying the plaintiff's pension. The plaintiff brought this action to enforce the agreement to pay him £200 per year.

Held the defendants were not obliged to keep up the payments. (I) *Per* Scrutton LJ, there was no contract here, but only a promise of a gratuitous payment. (II) On the assumption that there was a contract, it was void as being a restraint of trade contrary to the public interest. *Per* Slesser LJ:

> It seems to me that to say to a man that he should be deprived of a benefit if he fails to restrain himself from entering into a particular trade, when such restraint would be a general restraint, is just as much contrary to public policy and deprives the public of his services as much as if he made an express covenant not to enter that trade.

Q Did the defendants' letter offer a contract by requesting that the plaintiff keep out of the wool trade, or was it a promise of future conditional gifts?

Kores Manufacturing Co Ltd v Kolok Manufacturing Co Ltd (1958) CA

The parties were both manufacturers of carbon paper, typewriter ribbons and similar products. The defendants' factory was at Tottenham. In 1934, the plaintiffs were moving their factory to a site adjoining the defendants' factory in Tottenham. The parties made an agreement that neither would employ anyone who had been an employee of the other within the five years before the employment. In 1955, the plaintiffs moved their premises to Harlow, some 20 miles from Tottenham. In 1957, one of the plaintiffs' employees wanted to leave and join the defendants. The plaintiffs now sought a declaration that the agreement of 1934 remained valid between the parties.

Held the restraint was not valid. (I) It would be assumed in the plaintiffs' favour that the agreement contained an implied term making it terminable on six months' notice. (II) The restraint was far in excess of what was required to protect the plaintiffs' business. It was not limited to the time during which the parties' factories were adjacent to each other. It did not distinguish between employees who might have trade secrets and those who could not have any such secrets. *Per* Jenkins LJ, giving the judgment of the court:

> But, an employer has no legitimate interest in preventing an employee, after leaving his service, from entering the service of a competitor merely on the ground that the new employer is a competitor.

The agreement was therefore unreasonable as between the parties and it was not necessary to consider whether it or not it was also unreasonable in the public interest.

Note

Eastham v Newcastle United Football Club Ltd and Others (1963) Ch

The plaintiff was an inside forward with the defendant football club, Newcastle. He decided that he wished to move from Newcastle, but they declined to release him and they put him on a list of retained players. The system of retained players was supported by the Football Association and the Football League and by FIFA. This meant that while Newcastle did not want to release him, the plaintiff could not play professional football for any other club almost anywhere in the world. Although the plaintiff was finally transferred during this case, he still sought declarations that the rules were invalid.

Held declarations would be granted against Newcastle, the Football Association and the Football League. There were here no trade secrets to protect, nor any danger of the canvassing of the employer's customers. None of the defendants had any legitimate interest which was protected by the rules on retained players. These rules were therefore illegal and declarations to that effect should be granted.

A Schroeder Music Publishing Co Ltd v Macaulay (1974) HL

The plaintiff was an unknown songwriter. The defendants were music publishers. In July 1966, the plaintiff signed up to the defendants' standard contract by which he agreed to offer all his compositions to the defendants for the next five years which was extendible to 10 years if the royalties for the first five years reached a total of £5,000. The contract contained no safeguard for the plaintiff in the event of the defendants choosing not to publish or promote his work. He was stuck with them for five or 10 years in any event. The plaintiff received an initial £50 for making the agreement, but no other payment unless his work was published. The plaintiff now sought a declaration that the agreement was void.

Held the declaration would be granted that the contract was void. In the absence of any safeguard for the plaintiff, it was unreasonable to tie him for such a long period. *Per* Lord Diplock:

> If one looks at the reasoning of 19th century judges in cases about contracts in restraint of trade, one finds lip service paid to current economic theories but, if one looks at what they said in the light of what they did, one finds that they struck down a bargain if they thought it was unconscionable as between the

parties to it, and upheld it if they thought that it was not. So, I would hold that the question to be answered as respects a contract in restraint of trade of the kind with which this appeal is concerned is: was the bargain fair? The test of fairness is, no doubt, whether the restrictions are both reasonably necessary for the protection of the legitimate interests of the promisee and commensurate with the benefits secured to the promisor under the contract. For the purpose of this test, all the provisions of the contract must be taken into consideration.

9.4.3 A restraint given as part of a scheme to regulate a market may be valid

English Hop Growers Ltd v Dering (1928) CA

The plaintiff company was formed by hop growers to act as their buying agent to keep up the price of hops and to prevent undue competition. The members of the company, including the defendant, agreed not to dispose of any hops other than to the company for a period of five years. The defendant broke the agreement and the company sought damages. The defendant argued that the agreement was unreasonable as between the parties but did not argue that it was unreasonable in the public interest.

Held the restraint was valid. *Per* Scrutton LJ:

In view of the fluctuating character of the yearly supply of hops, I see nothing unreasonable in hop growers combining to secure a steady and profitable price, by eliminating competition amongst themselves, and putting the marketing in the hands of one agent, with full power to fix prices and hold up supplies, the benefit and loss being divided amongst the members.

9.4.4 Solus agreements are subject to the rules on restraint of trade

Esso Petroleum Co Ltd v Harper's Garage (Stourport) Ltd (1967) HL

The defendant company owned two garages: Corner Garage and Mustow Green. They made separate agreements in respect of each garage with the plaintiff company, Esso, to the effect that they would buy petrol only from Esso in return for Esso selling them petrol at a discounted price. The Mustow Green agreement was for a period of four years and five months, whereas the Corner Garage agreement was for a period of 21 years and also included a mortgage loan by Esso to the defendants. When the defendants began to buy petrol from another supplier, Esso sought to enforce the solus agreements.

Held the agreement for four years and five months was enforceable, but the agreement for 21 years was void. Esso had legitimate interests in making solus agreements of this kind which would make distribution more economical and give a more certain future income to allow long term investments to be made. Longer ties were more economical for Esso than shorter ones because the process of renegotiation and renewal was disruptive to their business. A tie of up to five years would be reasonable. However, *per* Lord Reid:

A tie for 21 years stretches far beyond any period for which developments are reasonably foreseeable. Restrictions on the garage owner which might seem tolerable and reasonable in reasonably foreseeable conditions might come to have a very different effect in quite different conditions: the public interest comes in here more strongly.

Per Lord Morris of Borth-y-Gest:

In regard to the period of 21 years, I consider that [Esso] have failed to show that a period of that length was reasonable in the interests of the parties.

Lord Hodson said of the unreasonableness of the Corner Garage agreement:

I would rest my decision on the public interest rather than that of the parties, public interest being a surer foundation than the interest of private persons or corporations when widespread commercial activities such as these are concerned.

9.4.5 An unreasonable contract in restraint of trade may be severed to leave a reasonable part

Goldsoll v Goldman (1914) CA

The parties were competitors in the imitation jewellery business. For good consideration, the defendant agreed that:

... he will not ... for a period of 10 years from 31 of October 1912 ... carry on ... the business of a vendor of or dealer in *real or* imitation jewellery in the county of London, England, Scotland, Ireland, Wales, or any part of the UK and Ireland and the Isle of Man *or in France, the US, Russia, or Spain, or within 25 miles of Potsdamerstrasse, Berlin, or St Stefans Kirche, Vienna.*

The defendant took part in a business identical to that of the plaintiffs in the same street and the plaintiffs sought to enforce his covenant.

Held the covenant could be enforced in a modified form. It was unreasonable to allow it to extend overseas and it was also unreasonable to include real jewellery which was not the plaintiffs' business. Therefore, the covenant would be severed by taking out the words italicised above and an injunction to enforce the severed covenant would be granted. The period of 10 years was not too long to be reasonable.

Attwood v Lamont (1920) CA

See 9.4.2.

10 Duress and Undue Influence

10.1 Duress

D and C Builders Ltd v Rees (1965) CA

See 3.8.2.

Q Should duress have been considered in this case?

North Ocean Shipping Co Ltd v Hyundai Construction Co Ltd and Another: *The Atlantic Baron* (1978) QB

See 3.7.4.

Pao On and Others v Lau Yiu Long and Another (1979) PC

See 3.5.2.

Universe Tankships Inc of Monrovia v International Transport Workers Federation and Others: *The Universe Sentinel* (1982) HL

The defendant trade union, ITF, demanded that the plaintiff ship owner make certain agreements with ITF in order to obtain a certificate that the ship, *The Universe Sentinel*, was not on ITF's blacking list. Without this certificate, the ship would have been stranded in port because of blacking by ITF. The agreements included terms that the owner would pay certain sums to the crew of the ship and would pay union dues to ITF on behalf of the crew members. The appeal concerned a payment made under the agreements to 'Seafarers' International Welfare Protection and Assistance Fund'. The payment was calculated by reference to the number of crew members on the ship and was expressed to be made on their behalf. However, it was found that in fact the Fund was under the control of ITF who could spend it as they wished. The owner now sought the return of the money paid to the 'Welfare Fund' on the ground that the agreement to pay it was made under duress.

Held the payment was recoverable. *Per* Lord Diplock, with whom Lord Russell of Killowen agreed:

> The rationale [of economic duress] is that his apparent consent was induced by pressure exercised upon him by that other party which the law does not regard

as legitimate, with the consequence that the consent is treated in law as revocable unless approbated either expressly or by implication after the illegitimate pressure has ceased to operate on his mind ... The remedy to which economic duress gives rise is not an action for damages but an action for restitution of property or money exacted under such duress and the avoidance of any contract that had been induced by it; but where the particular form taken by the economic duress used is itself a tort, the restitutional remedy for money had and received by the defendant to the plaintiff's use is one which the plaintiff is entitled to pursue as an alternative remedy to an action for damages in tort.

Per Lord Scarman, who dissented in the final result:

The authorities ... reveal two elements in the wrong of duress: (1) pressure amounting to compulsion of the will of the victim; and (2) the illegitimacy of the pressure exerted.

Atlas Express Ltd v Kafco (Importers and Distributors) Ltd (1989) QB

The defendants made basketware. In October 1986, they made an agreement with Woolworth to supply basketware for Woolworth's shops. Later that month, the defendants agreed with the plaintiffs that the plaintiffs would deliver the defendants' goods for them. The price was to be £1.10 per carton of basketware, but the agreement was silent as to the size of the cartons and the number of cartons per load. When the plaintiffs saw the first load of cartons, they found that they were larger than expected, so that there were also fewer than the plaintiffs had expected. The plaintiffs now demanded a minimum price per load and the defendants reluctantly accepted. The defendants had no choice because they could not have found another contractor to make deliveries at that time of year. The plaintiffs made deliveries under the revised agreement until the end of 1986. In February 1987, the defendants sent a payment on account to the plaintiffs. In March 1987, the defendants wrote saying that they had only accepted the revised terms under duress and this action was commenced three months later.

Held by Tucker J:

I find that the defendants' apparent consent to the agreement was induced by pressure which was illegitimate and I find that it was not approbated. In my judgment, that pressure can properly be described as economic duress, which is a concept recognised by English law, and which in the circumstances of the present case vitiates the defendants' apparent consent to the agreement. In any event, I find that there was no consideration for the new agreement. The plaintiffs were already obliged to deliver the defendants' goods at the rates agreed under the terms of the original agreement. There was no consideration for the increased minimum charge ... per trailer.

Williams v Roffey Bros and Nicholls (Contractors) Ltd (1989) CA

See 3.7.4.

CTN Cash and Carry Ltd v Gallaher Ltd (1993) CA

The defendants were sole distributors in the UK of a certain popular brand of cigarettes. The plaintiffs, a wholesaler, received from the defendants a consignment of cigarettes that was later stolen from the plaintiffs' warehouse. In the *bona fide* belief that property in the cigarettes had passed to the plaintiffs by the time of the theft, the defendants insisted on payment for them. The plaintiffs, who believed that they had never in law received the cigarettes before their theft, refused to pay. The defendants threatened to withdraw credit facilities from the plaintiffs if the latter did not pay and the plaintiffs then paid the price of the cigarettes. It was held at trial that property had not passed and the defendants had no right to claim the price of the stolen consignment from the plaintiffs. The plaintiffs now sought the return of the money they had paid on the basis that they had agreed to pay as a result of economic duress.

Held the doctrine of economic duress did not apply to this case. Steyn LJ, giving the leading judgment in the Court of Appeal, noted the following factors:

[I]... the common law does not recognise the doctrine of inequality of bargaining power in commercial dealings [see *National Westminster Bank plc v Morgan* (10.2)]. The fact that the defendants were in a monopoly position cannot therefore by itself convert what is not otherwise duress into duress.

(II) The defendants were under no obligation to offer credit facilities to the plaintiffs or indeed to contract with them at all. (III) The defendants' *bona fide* belief that the money was due to them was 'critically important'.

10.2 Undue influence

Allcard v Skinner (1887) CA

The plaintiff was introduced by her vicar to the anglican sisterhood of St Mary at the Cross, the lady superior of which was the defendant. The plaintiff joined the sisterhood in 1871, going to live there and submitting herself to its strict rules. The rules included implicit obedience to the lady superior, poverty and a prohibition on seeking advice from anyone outside the sisterhood without permission. The plaintiff made a will leaving her whole estate to the sisterhood which was placed on the altar. The plaintiff had substantial property in the form of stocks and securities which she handed over to the lady superior in pursuance of her vow of poverty. The money was mostly used to build an hospital. In 1879, the plaintiff left the sisterhood and was received into the Roman Catholic Church. She asked for and received her will back from the sisterhood in 1880, but she said nothing about the property she had already given. In 1885, the plaintiff started this action for the return of the property she had given to the sisterhood amounting to nearly £8,500.

Held the gifts of property had been voidable for undue influence, but could no longer be avoided because of the plaintiff's long delay. (I) The cases of undue influence fell into two groups. The first group consisted of those where, *per* Lindley LJ:

> ... there has been some unfair and improper conduct, some coercion from outside, some overreaching, some form of cheating, and generally, though not always, some personal advantage obtained by a donee placed in some close and confidential relation to the donor ... The second group consists of cases in which the position of the donor to the donee has been such that it has been the duty of the donee to advise the donor, or even to manage his property for him. In such cases, the court throws upon the donee the burden of proving that the gift made to him has not been brought about by any undue influence on his part. In this class of cases, it has been considered necessary to shew that the donor had independent advice, and was removed from the influence of the donee when the gift to him was made.

This case was in the second group. The influence of the lady superior over the plaintiff, especially given the rule against consulting outsiders, was such that the gifts to the lady superior were voidable. (II) The plaintiff did not ask for her property to be returned for some five years after leaving the sisterhood. She had also asked for her will to be returned without mentioning the other property. In those circumstances, it would have been reasonable for the sisterhood to suppose that the plaintiff had decided to let them keep the gifts, and, therefore, it was now too late for the gifts to be avoided.

Lloyds Bank v Bundy (1974) CA

The defendant father was a farmer who had one son. The son had a limited company which traded as a hirer of plant. The father, son and company all banked at the same branch of the plaintiff bank. The father's only substantial asset was his farm which was worth about £10,000. The company ran up an overdraft which was partly covered by a guarantee of £6,500 from the father and a charge on his farm of £7,500. When the overdraft reached about £10,000, the bank demanded more security. At a meeting between the bank's assistant manager, the son and his wife and the father and his wife, the bank demanded that the father increase his guarantee and the charge on his farm to £11,000. The father trusted the bank assistant manager and signed the papers in order to support his son.

Five months later, the bank stopped all overdraft facilities for the company and eventually sought possession of the farm.

Held the bank could not enforce the charge on the farm. (I) *Per* Lord Denning MR:

> ... there is a principle of 'inequality of bargaining power'. By virtue of it, the English law gives relief to one who, without independent advice, enters into a contract upon terms which are very unfair or transfers property for a consideration which is grossly inadequate, when his bargaining power is grievously impaired by reason of his own needs or desires, or by his own ignorance or infirmity, coupled with undue influences or pressures brought to bear on him by or for the benefit of the other.

In this case, the bank gave only a brief respite in return for the extended charge; the father trusted the bank to advise him; the father was influenced by his natural affection for his son; the bank did not advise the father to seek independent advice despite the conflict of interest between the bank and the father. (II) *Per* Sir Eric Sachs, with whom Cairns LJ agreed, this was a case of undue influence. The father relied on the bank for advice in this transaction and the bank failed in their duty to advise him properly.

Q Do you agree with Lord Denning MR's view that undue influence should be subsumed into a wider category of inequality of bargaining power, which was disapproved in *National Westminster Bank plc v Morgan* (below, argument (III))?

National Westminster Bank plc v Morgan (1985) HL

Mr and Mrs Morgan ran into difficulties in making mortgage payments to Abbey National. This was because of Mr Morgan's business problems. Mr Morgan sought a loan from the plaintiff bank which was to be a bridging loan for five weeks which Mr Morgan would use to pay off the existing mortgage. The bank agreed subject to Mr and Mrs Morgan executing an unlimited mortgage over their home. Mrs Morgan told the bank manager that she would only sign the charge on the house if it was limited to the bridging loan to pay off the mortgage. The manager told Mrs Morgan that it was so limited. In fact the charge signed by Mrs Morgan covered all of Mr Morgan's indebtedness to the bank without limit. However, the bank never intended, or tried, to use the charge to recover any other borrowings than the bridging loan. When the loan was not repaid, the bank sought possession of the house and Mrs Morgan argued that the charge had been obtained from her by the undue influence of the bank.

Held this was not a case of undue influence and the charge could be enforced. The main judgment in the House was delivered by Lord Scarman with whom the other Lords all agreed. (I) The relationship between the bank and Mrs Morgan was not one in which the bank had any special duties to advise Mrs Morgan, but was an ordinary business relationship between banker and customer. (II) The charge was not to the manifest disadvantage of Mrs Morgan and the transaction was not wrongful. (III) Considering the case of *Lloyds Bank v Bundy* (10.2), the reasoning of Sir Eric Sachs was to be preferred to that of Lord Denning MR. There was no need for the principle of undue influence to be supported by a wider principle of inequality of bargaining power.

Note ───

Argument (II) was qualified in *CIBC Mortgages plc v Pitt and Another* (10.2).

Barclays Bank plc v O'Brien and Another (1993) HL

Mr O'Brien had an interest in a company which had an increasing overdraft with the plaintiff bank. The bank asked for a charge over Mr O'Brien's home in return for continuing and further increasing the company's overdraft. The charge had to be given by Mr and Mrs O'Brien since the home was owned by them jointly. Mrs O'Brien was presented with the documents by the bank along with a side letter for her signature which included a statement that the bank had recommended that the O'Briens should obtain independent legal advice before signing the letter. Mrs O'Brien did not read the documents or the letter and no one suggested she should obtain advice before signing them. When the bank sought to enforce their security against the matrimonial home to recover some £154,000 owed to them by the company, Mrs O'Brien resisted them on the ground that her signature to the charge had been obtained by the misrepresentation of her husband, who had told her that the charge was only for £60,000 and that it was temporary.

Held the bank could not enforce the charge against Mrs O'Brien because they had constructive notice of the equity raised in her favour by Mr O'Brien's misrepresentation. The main judgment was delivered by Lord Browne-Wilkinson, with whom the other Lords all agreed. Even though this was a case of misrepresentation his lordship considered the rules relating to undue influence. (I) Undue influence falls into the following three categories:

Class 1: actual undue influence. In these cases it is necessary for the claimant to prove affirmatively that the wrongdoer exerted undue influence on the complainant to enter into the particular transaction which is impugned ... Class 2A: Certain relationships (for example solicitor and client, medical advisor and patient) as a matter of law raise the presumption that undue influence has been exercised. Class 2B: Even if there is no relationship falling within Class 2A, if the complainant proves the *de facto* existence of a relationship under which the complainant generally reposed trust and confidence in the wrongdoer, the existence of such relationship raises the presumption of undue influence.

Once a presumption is raised under Class 2A or 2B, 'the burden shifts to the wrongdoer to prove that the complainant entered into the impugned transaction freely'. (II) The relationship of spouses does not fall within Class 2A, but in all cases of an emotional relationship between cohabitees there may well be influence in Class 2B. (III) If there is undue influence, it gives the complainant an equity to set aside the transaction as against the wrongdoer. If a creditor has notice of the undue influence, then the creditor's rights are subject to that equity. Notice may be actual or constructive. Constructive notice is present when the creditor knows facts which put him on inquiry as to the possible existence of the complainant's rights but he fails to make reasonable inquiries to find out about them. (IV):

> Therefore, in my judgment, a creditor is put on inquiry when a wife offers to stand surety for her husband's debts by the combination of two factors: (a) the transaction is on its face not to the financial advantage of the wife; and (b) there is a substantial risk in transactions of that kind that, in procuring the wife to act as surety, the husband has committed a legal or equitable wrong that entitles the wife the set aside the transaction.

(V) A creditor must therefore take reasonable steps to avoid being fixed with constructive notice of the wife's rights in this situation. The creditor must see the wife without the presence of the husband and tell her of the risk she is running and urge her to take independent legal advice. If the creditor has knowledge of further facts which make undue influence not just possible but probable, then the creditor may have to *insist* on the wife having independent advice. (VI) In this case, the bank were put on inquiry as described in argument (IV) but failed to take the steps in argument (V). Mrs O'Brien was therefore entitled to set aside the charge because of misrepresentation.

CIBC Mortgages plc v Pitt and Another (1993) HL

Mr Pitt told Mrs Pitt that he wanted to borrow money to invest in shares. Mrs Pitt was reluctant to agree, but did so after Mr Pitt used what was shown to have been actual undue influence over her. Mr Pitt told the plaintiff bank that the money was for the purchase of a holiday home. The bank lent money to Mr and Mrs Pitt jointly, secured by a charge on their house. Mrs Pitt signed the various documents without reading them. Mr Pitt lost the money when the stock market crashed in October 1987 and eventually the bank brought proceedings for the possession of the house.

Held the bank could enforce the charge because they had no notice of the undue influence used to procure Mrs Pitt's agreement to the loan. The appeal was heard along with that in *Barclays Bank plc v O'Brien and Another* and, as in that case, the only considered judgment was given by Lord Browne-Wilkinson:

[I] Whatever the merits of requiring a complainant to show manifest disadvantage in order to raise a class 2 presumption of undue influence, in my judgment, there is no logic in imposing such a requirement where actual undue influence has been exercised and proved ... I should add that the exact limits of the decision in *Morgan* [10.2] may have to be considered in the future.

The general principle is that those owing fiduciary duties have to show the fairness of any transactions they enter into with those to whom they owe those duties:

This principle is in sharp contrast with the view of this House in *Morgan* that in cases of presumed undue influence ... it is for the claimant to prove that the transaction was disadvantageous rather than for the fiduciary to prove that it was not disadvantageous. Unfortunately, the attention of this House in *Morgan* was not drawn to the abuse of confidence cases and therefore the interaction between the two principles (if indeed they are two separate principles) remains obscure.

(II) In this case, so far as the bank knew, they were making a joint loan to husband and wife to buy a holiday home. There was nothing to indicate that the loan was only for the benefit of one party. The bank therefore had no duty to make inquiries.

Dunbar Bank plc v Nadeem (1998) CA

Mrs Nadeem left financial matters to her husband. She habitually signed whatever documents Mr Nadeem asked her to sign without seeking or receiving any explanation for them. Until 1991, Mrs Nadeem had no proprietary interest in the marital home. In 1991, Mr Nadeem had the opportunity to purchase an extended lease over the matrimonial home. The extended lease would cost £210,000 but was valued at £400,000. The plaintiff bank lent Mr and Mrs Nadeem £260,000 of which £210,000 was to be used for the purchase of the extended lease by Mr and Mrs Nadeem jointly, and £50,000 was to be used to pay outstanding interest owed by Mr Nadeem alone on another account with the bank. The loan was to be secured by a charge on the property. Mrs Nadeem signed the charge at her husband's request. The loan was not repaid and the bank sought possession of the property. Mrs Nadeem asked for the charge to be set aside as against her on the ground that it was procured by her husband's undue influence of which the bank had notice.

Held the bank was entitled to possession against Mrs Nadeem. (1) On the facts, Mrs Nadeem had established a relationship of trust and confidence within class 2B of the *Barclays Bank plc v O'Brien and Another* classification. (2) The transaction gave Mrs Nadeem an interest in the property for the first time. Viewed objectively, Mr Nadeem did not take unfair advantage of his position and did not act unconscionably. Accordingly, there was no actual undue influence in this case. (3) In a case of presumed but not actual undue influence, it is necessary for the influenced party to show that the transaction was manifestly disadvantageous to her. Mrs Nadeem had not established manifest disadvantage. In fact, because she obtained an interest in the property for the first time, the transaction was not disadvantageous to Mrs Nadeem even though she became jointly liable for an advance part of which (the £50,000) was to be used for her husband's sole benefit.

11 Capacity

11.1 Minors

11.1.1 Family Law Reform Act 1969

Section 1   Reduction of age of majority from 21 to 18

(1)   As from the date on which this section comes into force, a person shall attain full age on attaining the age of 18 instead of on attaining the age of 21; and a person shall attain full age on that date if he has then already attained the age of 18 but not the age of 21.

11.1.2 Sale of Goods Act 1979

Section 3   Capacity to buy and sell

(1)   Capacity to buy and sell is regulated by the general law concerning capacity to contract and to transfer and acquire property.

(2)   Where necessaries are sold and delivered to a minor or to a person who by reason of mental incapacity or drunkenness is incompetent to contract, he must pay a reasonable price for them.

(3)   In sub-s (2) above, 'necessaries' means goods suitable to the condition in life of the minor or other person concerned and to his actual requirements at the time of the sale and delivery.

11.1.3 Minors' Contracts Act 1987

Section 2   Guarantees

Where:

(a)   a guarantee is given in respect of an obligation of a party to a contract made after the commencement of this Act; and

(b)   the obligation is unenforceable against him (or he repudiates the contract) because he was a minor when the contract was made, the guarantee shall not for that reason alone be unenforceable against the guarantor.

Section 3   *Restitution*

Where:

(a)   a person ('the plaintiff') has after the commencement of this Act entered into a contract with another ('the defendant'); and

(b)   the contract is unenforceable against the defendant (or he repudiates it) because he was a minor when the contract was made, the court may, if it is just and equitable to do so, require the defendant to transfer to the plaintiff any property acquired by the defendant under the contract, or any property representing it.

(2)   Nothing in this section shall be taken to prejudice any other remedy available to the plaintiff.

11.1.4 Minors must pay a reasonable price for necessaries but not for other goods

Nash v Inman (1908) CA

The plaintiff was a tailor of Saville Row. He had sold to an undergraduate at Cambridge University 'clothing of an extravagant and ridiculous style having regard to the position of the boy' (*per* Buckley LJ), 'including an extravagant number of waistcoats' (*per* Fletcher Moulton LJ). The plaintiff now sued for the price of the clothes, £145. The undergraduate's father gave evidence that his son had been supplied with sufficient clothes on going up to Cambridge.

Held the extravagant clothing could not be classified as 'necessary'. Accordingly, the plaintiff could not claim the price of the goods supplied.

Leslie v Shiell (1914) CA

The plaintiff was a money lender, who had lent two sums of £200 each to the defendant. The defendant was a minor, but had lied to the plaintiff about his age. The plaintiff was deceived and believed the defendant to have been of full age. The defendant resisted repaying the loan and interest, a total of £475, on the ground that he was a minor at the time the contract was made.

Held the money lender could not obtain repayment of the loan. There was no exception to the general principle that a minor is not liable on such a contract, even where, as in this case, the minor had deceived the other contracting party as to his age. The plaintiff's action for damages for the tort of deceit and for the restitution to him of the loans as monies had and received would also fail because they were in effect attempts to enforce the void contract.

Steinberg v Scala (Leeds) Ltd (1923) CA

The plaintiff, one Miss Tulip Steinberg, subscribed for shares in the defendant company. While still a minor, the plaintiff sought to rescind the contract to buy the shares and to recover the money which she had paid to the company.

Held the plaintiff was entitled to rescind the contract on the grounds of her minority, and her name would be removed from the company's register of shareholders. However, the plaintiff could not recover the money which she had paid to the company unless she could show that there had been a total failure of consideration. There was no total failure of consideration in this case because the shares were of significant value when they were issued. Accordingly, the plaintiff's claim for the return of the money she had paid failed.

Note ───

In other cases where a party is entitled to rescind a contract, that party may recover monies paid pursuant to the contract. The explanation for the different principle in the case of minors appears to be that in general a minor's contract is not truly voidable, but is unenforceable against the minor.

──

11.1.5 Minors are bound by contracts of employment and similar contracts for their benefit

Clements v London and North Western Railway Company (1894) CA

The plaintiff, while under age, became a porter employed by the defendant railway company. While at work, he suffered an injury for which he now claimed damages. The company's defence was that under the plaintiff's employment contract he was entitled to certain payments in the event of injury but not to any further damages.

Held this was a contract for the employment of the minor. Taking the contract as a whole, it was for the minor's benefit. In those circumstances, the contract was enforceable and the plaintiff's claim failed.

Roberts v Gray (1912) CA

The defendant minor made a contract to accompany a professional billiards player on a tour of the world for 18 months. Following disputes about the kind of billiards balls to be used, the defendant repudiated the contract and refused to go on the tour. The plaintiff sought damages for breach of contract and the defendant counter-claimed for rescission.

Held the contract was a contract for necessaries, primarily because the plaintiff was a distinguished billiards player from whom the defendant would receive considerable instruction which would be of value to the defendant in his chosen career as a professional billiards player. Furthermore, the contract was for the defendant's advantage.

Chaplin v Leslie Frewin (Publishers) Limited (1965) CA

The plaintiff was the son of Charlie Chaplin. While a minor, he agreed with the defendant publishers that, with the help of ghost writers, he would be the author of an autobiography which the defendants would publish. When the book, entitled *I Couldn't Smoke the Grass on my Father's Lawn*, was at the proof stage, the plaintiff apparently realised that it showed him as 'a depraved creature content to broadcast my failings to the world and for gain', it contained many factual inaccuracies, indicated 'a debased, cynical and irresponsible approach to life' and was libellous of a number of people. The plaintiff sought to repudiate the contract and asked for an injunction to restrain the defendants from publishing the book.

Held the plaintiff was bound by the publishing contract and the injunction would not be granted. (I) The plaintiff had already transferred or assigned copyright in the book to the defendants. Even if the plaintiff was entitled to rescind the contract, he could not now recover the copyright which had already passed to the defendants. (II) A publishing contract fell within the class of contracts which were binding on a minor if they were for his advantage. The time for judging whether the contract was beneficial to the minor was the time when it was made. In this case, *per* Danckwerts LJ the contract 'would enable the plaintiff to make a start as an author and thus earn money to keep himself and his wife'.

11.2 Mental incapacity and drunkenness

11.2.1 A lunatic or an intoxicated person may avoid a contract only where his insanity or intoxication was known to the other party

Hart v O'Connor (1985) PC

The late Jack O'Connor had been sole trustee of the O'Connor estate in New Zealand. He was a person of unsound mind and he agreed to sell the land (for the market price) to the appellant, Mr Hart. The beneficiaries of the trust were unhappy with the sale and claimed that it should be set aside because of the late Jack O'Connor's incapacity. It was found at trial that the appellant did not know of the incapacity at the time the contract was made.

Held the contract was valid. *Per* Lord Brightman (giving the judgment of the Board):

To sum the matter up, in the opinion of their Lordships, the validity of a contract entered into by a lunatic who is ostensibly sane is to be judged by the same standards as a contract by a person of sound mind, and is not voidable by the lunatic or his representatives by reason of unfairness unless such unfairness amounts to equitable fraud which would have enabled the complaining party to avoid the contract even if he had been sane.

11.3 Illiteracy is no incapacity

Barclays Bank plc v Schwartz (1995) CA

The defendant was born in Romania and was educated in a Talmudic College in the United States and in a Rabbinical College in London and had a very poor understanding of the English language. The defendant controlled a group of property companies and gave personal guarantees of their debts. When the plaintiff bank sought to enforce the guarantees, the defendant argued that his poor English gave him a defence of incapacity.

Held the defence failed. *Per* Millet LJ:

Illiteracy and unfamiliarity with the English language were not to be equated with disabilities like mental incapacity or drunkenness. All four conditions were disabilities which might prevent the sufferer from possessing a full understanding of a transaction into which he entered. Mental capacity and drunkenness might not only deprive the sufferer of understanding the transaction, but also deprive him of the awareness that he did not understand it. An illiterate knew that he could not read. A man who was unfamiliar with English was aware of that fact. If he signed a document which he did not understand, he had only himself to blame. A man who signed a document in a language with which he was insufficiently familiar to understand could be in no better position than the man who signed a document which he did not read because he was too busy. Accordingly, mental incapacity and drunkenness provided defences to a claim in contract if the other party was aware of the defendant's condition but illiteracy and unfamiliarity with the English language did not.

12 Exclusion Clauses

12.1 The *contra proferentem* rule

12.1.1 Exclusion clauses will be construed strictly against the party seeking to rely on them

Wallis, Son and Wells v Pratt and Haynes (1911) HL

See 5.7.2.

Andrews Brothers (Bournemouth) Ltd v Singer and Company Ltd (1933) CA

By a 'Main Dealers' Agreement', the defendants appointed the plaintiffs to be their sole dealers within a certain area 'for the sale of new Singer cars' and the plaintiffs agreed to buy a certain number of the cars. Clause 5 of the agreement said:

> All cars sold by [the defendants] are subject to the terms of the warranty set out in Sched No 3 of this agreement, and all conditions, warranties and liabilities implied by statute, common law or otherwise are excluded.

In pursuance of the agreement, the plaintiffs ordered a car which the defendants delivered. However, the car had already travelled some 550 miles when it reached the plaintiffs, because the defendants had previously sent it to Darlington to be tested by a potential purchaser. The defendants argued that they were protected by clause 5 from any condition or warranty that the car would be new.

Held the defendants had to compensate the plaintiffs for their loss. *Per* Scrutton LJ:

> In my opinion, this was a contract for the sale of a new Singer car. The contract continually uses the phrase 'new Singer cars' ... Where goods are expressly described in the contract and do not comply with that description, it is quite inaccurate to say that there is an implied term; the term is expressed in the contract.

The defendants were thus liable for having breached an express term from which clause 5 did not exempt them.

12.1.2 Clauses which merely limit liability will not be construed as strictly as those which exclude liability

Ailsa Craig Fishing Co Ltd v Malvern Fishing Co Ltd and Another (1981) HL

By an agreement with the owners of a number of vessels, Securicor were bound to provide security cover in Aberdeen harbour. As a result of Securicor's negligence in carrying out their obligations under the contract, a fishing boat owned by the plaintiffs sank and was lost in the harbour. Securicor sought to rely on a clause of their contract which limited their liability for any loss or damage to £1,000 per claim and a maximum of £10,000 for the claims arising from any one incident.

Held Securicor could rely on their limitation clause. *Per* Lord Wilberforce:

Clauses of limitation are not regarded by the courts with the same hostility as clauses of exclusion; this is because they must be related to other contractual terms, in particular to the risks to which the defending party may be exposed, the remuneration which he receives, and possibly also the opportunity of the other party to insure.

Per Lord Fraser of Tullybelton:

Such clauses [limitation clauses] will of course be read *contra proferentem* and must be clearly expressed, but there is no reason why they should be judged by the specially exacting standards which are applied to exclusion and indemnity clauses.

12.2 Excluding liability for negligence

12.2.1 Liability for negligence will not normally be excluded unless clear words are used

Olley v Marlborough Court Ltd (1948) CA

See 5.3.2.

White v John Warwick & Co Ltd (1953) CA

The plaintiff was a newsagent. He made an agreement with the defendants that they would supply him with a cycle with a basket in front for delivering newspapers. The contract was on the defendants' standard form and it committed the defendants to supply a replacement cycle when the main one needed repairs. Clause 11 of the contract was:

Nothing in this agreement shall render the owners liable for any personal injuries to the riders of the machines hired nor for any third party claims, nor loss of any goods, belonging to the hirer, in the machines.

One of the replacement cycles lent to the plaintiff under the agreement had a loose saddle as a result of which the plaintiff was thrown off and injured. The plaintiff argued that although clause 11 excluded the defendants' liability for claims for breach of contract, it did not defeat the plaintiff's action for the tort of negligence.

Held the clause was truly construed as exempting the defendants from liability for breach of contract, but not from liability for negligence. There was no reason why the same facts could not give rise to claims under both heads. Since it was not clear whether or not the accident was caused by the defendants' negligence, there would have to be a new trial.

Hollier v Rambler Motors (AMC) Ltd (1971) CA

See 5.3.3.

12.2.2 Liability for negligence may be excluded if negligence is the only potential liability

Rutter v Palmer (1922) CA

The plaintiff owned a Le Gui motor car which he asked the defendant, a motor dealer, to sell for him. Their agreement contained a clause that 'Customers' cars are driven by your [the defendant's] staff at customers' sole risk'. When in the care of one of the defendant's drivers, who was showing the car to a potential buyer, the car was damaged due to the driver's negligence.

Held the defendant was protected by the exclusion clause and need not pay for the damage. (I) Where one who seeks to rely on an exclusion clause could be liable for the damage excluded in a number of ways, the clause will have to use plain words to cover negligence. However, a motor dealer is a bailee and therefore is liable for damage to the car only if he is negligent. Since negligence was the only source of the defendant's potential liability, the exclusion clause had to be taken to refer to damage caused by the defendant's negligence as that was the only application it could have. (II) Car owners could insure themselves for all risks. The purpose of the clause might have been to ensure that owners insured themselves for accidents while the car was in the defendant's custody.

Alderslade v Hendon Laundry Ltd (1945) CA

The defendant laundry company accepted some handkerchiefs for laundering from the plaintiff customer on terms including this clause:

The maximum amount allowed for lost or damaged articles is 20 times the charge made for laundering.

The handkerchiefs were not returned to the customer and they could not be found. The question on the appeal was whether or not the clause noted above was effective to limit the company's liability for the loss.

Held since the only way in which the company was likely to become liable for the loss of laundry was through its own negligence, the limitation clause must be taken to apply to such situations. The case was thus similar to *Rutter v Palmer* (above).

12.3 Fraud or misrepresentation will defeat an exclusion clause

Curtis v Chemical Cleaning and Dyeing Co (1951) CA

The plaintiff took a white satin wedding dress to the defendants for cleaning. The plaintiff was asked to sign a document headed 'Receipt'. The plaintiff asked the assistant why she had to sign and was told that the defendants would not accept liability for any damage to beads or sequins. The plaintiff then signed the document which in fact included this exclusion clause: 'This or these articles is accepted on condition that the company is not liable for any damage howsoever arising, or delay.' The dress came back to the plaintiff with a stain which had not been there before and which was found to have been caused by the defendants' negligence. The defendants argued that they had no liability for the damage caused.

Held the defendants were liable. They could not rely on the exclusion clause because the plaintiff had been induced to sign it by a misrepresentation, albeit innocent. Their lordships based their opinions on the *dicta* of Scrutton LJ in *L'Estrange v F Graucob Ltd*, in 5.1.

Q Why should a misrepresentation enable the representee to avoid one particular clause of the contract while the rest of it remains binding on both sides?

12.4 An exclusion clause may be effective despite a fundamental breach of contract

Suisse Atlantique Société d'Armement Maritime SA v NV Rotterdamsche Kolen Centrale (1966) HL

The charterers chartered a vessel from the owners for two years consecutive voyages to carry coal from the US to Europe. The vessel was to proceed and be loaded 'with all possible dispatch'. In the event of delays, the owners were to pay the charterers $1,000 a day demurrage. There were considerable delays which the charterers claimed caused them losses well in excess of $1,000 a day. The charterers argued that since the delays amounted to a serious enough breach of contract to justify them in treating the contract as repudiated, that is, they were a fundamental breach, they should operate to prevent the owners from relying on the demurrage clause to limit their liability.

Held there was no rule of law that an exemption or limitation clause could never be effective in respect of liabilities arising from fundamental breaches of contract. There was a rule of construction that such a clause should normally be presumed not to apply to cases where the party relying on the clause had breached the contract in a fundamental way, but the presumption could be rebutted or excluded by the parties. In this case, if the charterers had acquired a right to elect to treat the contract as repudiated, they had actually affirmed the contract instead by continuing with it. They therefore remained bound by the demurrage clause which limited the owners' liability for delay to $1,000 a day. Note that, in Lord Upjohn's opinion, the question did not really arise because the demurrage clause was one which estimated damages rather than one which limited liability. There was thus, in Lord Upjohn's view, no need to construe it with any special strictness at all.

Q Would their lordships have looked on the clause in this case differently if it had excluded altogether liability for delay?

Mendelssohn v Normand Ltd (1969) CA

The plaintiff drove a car into the defendants' garage in central London. An attendant told the plaintiff that he could not lock his car. The plaintiff protested that the luggage in the car was valuable and that he would not be long, but the attendant insisted. Therefore, the plaintiff gave the attendant the key and the attendant agreed to lock the car after he had moved it. The attendant gave the plaintiff a ticket which the plaintiff put in his pocket without reading. The ticket included these conditions:

> (1) The [defendants] will not accept responsibility for any loss or damage sustained by the vehicle its accessories or contents however caused ... (6) No variation of these conditions will bind the [defendants] unless made in writing signed by their duly authorised manager.

When the plaintiff returned, he found the car had been moved a few yards and was still unlocked, but was otherwise undisturbed. Later, he realised that the valuable luggage was missing. It was found by the trial judge that the luggage was taken by one of the attendants at the garage.

Held the defendants could not rely on their conditions to exempt them from liability for the plaintiff's loss. (I) The conditions on the ticket were incorporated into the contract because the plaintiff accepted the ticket in circumstances where it was likely to contain contractual terms. (II) The attendant's oral representation overrode the conditions on the ticket. *Per* Lord Denning MR, who referred to *Couchman v Hill* (see 5.2.3); *Harling v Eddy* (see 5.2.3); and *Curtis v Chemical Cleaning and Dyeing Co* (see 12.3):

The reason is because the oral promise or representation has a decisive influence on the transaction – it is the very thing which induces the other to contract – and it would be most unjust to allow the maker to go back on it.

Phillimore LJ based his decision on the authority of *Curtis v Chemical Cleaning and Dyeing Co*, and the view that printed clauses must fail in so far as they are repugnant to an express undertaking. (III) The doctrine of fundamental breach applied. *Per* Lord Denning MR:

> Those cases [of fundamental breach] still stand and are in no way diminished in authority by *Suisse Atlantique Société d'Armement Maritime SA v NV Rotterdamsche Kolen Centrale* [12.4]. It was there said to be all a matter of construction. So here, the defendants agreed to keep this Rolls Royce car locked up; instead they left it unlocked and whilst unlocked their servant stole the suitcase. This was so entirely different a way of carrying out the contract that the exemption clause cannot be construed as extending to it.

Q Was there any inconsistency between the undertaking to lock the car and the exemption clause in this case (as Phillimore LJ implied)? If not, do the earlier cases cited by Lord Denning MR have any bearing on this one?

Photo Production Ltd v Securicor Transport Ltd (1980) HL

The defendants, Securicor, were a security company. In 1968, they agreed to provide security services for the plaintiffs, Photo Productions, for a weekly charge. The contract included this condition:

> In no circumstances shall the Company [Securicor] be responsible for any injurious act or default by any employee of the Company unless such act or default could have been foreseen and avoided by the exercise of due diligence on the part of the Company as his employer; nor, in any event, shall the Company be held responsible for; (a) Any loss suffered by the customer through burglary, theft, fire or any other cause, except insofar as such loss is solely attributable to the negligence of the Company's employees acting within the course of their employment ...

One Sunday night, Securicor's duty employee visited Photo Productions' factory at the time he was meant to. When inside, he deliberately started a fire by throwing a match onto some cartons. It was not established what the employee's intention was in starting the fire, but the result was to burn down most of the factory. The Court of Appeal held that, since Securicor's breach of contract in, through their employee, starting the fire was fundamental, they could not rely on their exclusion clause.

Held Securicor could rely on their exclusion clause to avoid liability for the fire. (I) It was wrong for the Court of Appeal to hold that an exclusion clause had no effect to exclude liability for fundamental breaches of contract, as that was to apply the principle which the House of Lords had denied in *Suisse Atlantique Société d'Armement Maritime SA v NV Rotterdamsche Kolen Centrale* (12.4). The earlier case where the Court of Appeal had sought to resurrect the doctrine of fundamental breach, *Harbutt's Plasticine Ltd v Wayne Tank and Pump Co Ltd*, must be overruled. (II) Although clear words must be used to excuse a party from the consequences of his own wrongdoing, the words of the condition in this case were clear. (III) Although the contract in this case was made before the passing of the Unfair Contract Terms Act 1977 (see 12.5), Lord Wilberforce, with whom Lord Keith of Kinkel and Lord Scarman agreed, commented:

> After this Act, in commercial matters generally, when the parties are not of unequal bargaining power, and when risks are normally borne by insurance, not only is the case for judicial intervention undemonstrated, but there is everything to be said, and this seems to have been Parliament's intention, for leaving the parties free to apportion the risks as they think fit and for respecting their decisions.

Lord Diplock made a similar point.

12.5 The Unfair Contract Terms Act 1977

12.5.1 The Act

Part I

Section 1   Scope of Pt I

(1)   For the purposes of this Part of this Act, 'negligence' means the breach:

    (a)   of any obligation, arising from the express or implied terms of a contract, to take reasonable care or exercise reasonable skill in the performance of the contract;

    (b)   of any common law duty to take reasonable care or exercise reasonable skill (but not any stricter duty);

    (c)   of the common duty of care imposed by the Occupiers' Liability Act 1957 ...

(2)   This Part of this Act is subject to Pt III; and in relation to contracts, the operation of ss 2 to 4 and 7 is subject to the exceptions made by Sched 1.

(3)   In the case of both contract and tort, ss 2 to 7 apply (except where the contrary is stated in s 6(4)) only to business liability, that is liability for breach of obligations or duty arising:

(a) from things done or to be done by a person in the course of a business (whether his own business or another's); or

(b) from the occupation of premises used for business purposes of the occupier; ...

(4) In relation to any breach of duty or obligation, it is immaterial for any purpose of this Part of this Act whether the breach was inadvertent or unintentional, or whether liability for it arises directly or vicariously.

Section 2   Negligence liability

(1) A person cannot by reference to any contract term or to a notice given to persons generally or to particular persons exclude or restrict his liability for death or personal injury resulting from negligence.

(2) In the case of other loss or damage, a person cannot so exclude or restrict his liability for negligence except in so far as the term or notice satisfies the requirement of reasonableness.

(3) Where a contract term or notice purports to exclude or restrict liability for negligence, a person's agreement to or awareness of it is not of itself to be taken as indicating his voluntary acceptance of any risk.

Section 3   Liability arising in contract

(1) This section applies as between contracting parties where one of them deals as consumer or on the other's written standard terms of business.

(2) As against that party, the other cannot by reference to any contract term:

(a) when himself in breach of contract, exclude or restrict any liability of his in respect of the breach; or

(b) claim to be entitled:

(i) to render a contractual performance substantially different from that which was reasonably expected of him; or

(ii) in respect of the whole or any part of his contractual obligation, to render no performance at all,

except in so far as (in any of the cases mentioned above in this subsection) the contract term satisfies the requirement of reasonableness.

Section 4   Unreasonable indemnity clauses

(1)   A person dealing as consumer cannot by reference to any contract term be made to indemnify another person (whether a party to the contract or not) in respect of liability that may be incurred by the other for negligence or breach of contract, except in so far as the contract term satisfies the requirement of reasonableness.

(2)   This section applies whether the liability in question:

(a)   is directly that of the person to be indemnified or is incurred by him vicariously;

(b)   is to the person dealing as consumer or to someone else.

Section 5   'Guarantee' of consumer goods

(1)   In the case of goods of a type ordinarily supplied for private use or consumption, where loss or damage:

(a)   arises from the goods proving defective while in consumer use; and

(b)   results from the negligence of a person concerned in the manufacture or distribution of the goods,

liability for the loss or damage cannot be excluded or restricted by reference to any contract term or notice contained in or operating by reference to a guarantee of the goods.

(2)   For these purposes:

(a)   goods are to be regarded as 'in consumer use' when a person is using them, or has them in his possession for use, otherwise than exclusively for the purposes of a business; and

(b)   anything in writing is a guarantee if it contains or purports to contain some promise or assurance (however worded or presented) that defects will be made good by complete or partial replacement, or by repair, monetary compensation or otherwise.

(3)   This section does not apply as between the parties to a contract under or in pursuance of which possession or ownership of the goods passed.

Section 6   Sale or hire purchase

(1)   Liability for breach of the obligations arising from:

(a)   s 12 of the Sale of Goods Act 1979 (seller's implied undertakings as to title, etc) [see 5.6.1];

(b) s 8 of the Supply of Goods (Implied Terms) Act 1973 (the corresponding thing in relation to hire purchase),

cannot be excluded or restricted by reference to any contract term.

(2) As against a person dealing as consumer, liability for breach of the obligations arising from:

(a) ss 13, 14, and 15 of the 1979 Act (seller's implied undertakings as to conformity of the goods with description or sample, or as to their quality or fitness for a particular purpose) [see 5.6.1];

(b) ss 9, 10 or 11 of the 1973 Act (the corresponding things in relation to hire purchase),

cannot be excluded or restricted by reference to any contract term.

(3) As against a person dealing otherwise than as consumer, the liability specified in sub-s (2) above can be excluded or restricted by reference to a contract term, but only in so far as the term satisfies the requirement of reasonableness.

(4) The liabilities referred to in this section are not only the business liabilities defined by s 1(3), but include those arising under any contract of sale of goods or hire purchase agreement.

Section 7   Miscellaneous contracts under which goods pass

(1) Where the possession or ownership of goods passes under or in pursuance of a contract not governed by the law of sale of goods or hire purchase, sub-ss (2) to (4) below apply as regards the effect (if any) to be given to contract terms excluding or restricting liability for breach of obligation arising by implication of law from the nature of the contract.

(2) As against a person dealing as consumer, liability in respect of the goods' correspondence with description or sample, or their quality or fitness for any particular purpose, cannot be excluded or restricted by reference to any such term.

(3) As against a person dealing otherwise than as consumer, that liability can be excluded or restricted by reference to such a term, but only in so far as the term satisfies the requirement of reasonableness.

(3A) Liability for breach of the obligations arising under s 2 of the Supply of Goods and Services Act 1982 (implied terms about title, etc, in certain contracts for the transfer of the property in goods) cannot be excluded or restricted by references to any such term.

(4) Liability in respect of:

(a) the right to transfer ownership of the goods, or give possession; or

(b)   the assurance of quiet possession to a person taking goods in pursuance of the contract,

cannot (in a case to which sub-s (3A) above does not apply) be excluded or restricted by reference to any such term except in so far as the term satisfies the requirement of reasonableness.

(5)   This section does not apply in the case of goods passing on a redemption of trading stamps within the Trading Stamps Act 1964 or the Trading Stamps Act (Northern Ireland) 1965.

Section 8   (Amends the Misrepresentation Act 1967.)

Section 9   Effect of breach

(1)   Where for reliance upon it a contract term has to satisfy the requirement of reasonableness, it may be found to do so and be given effect accordingly notwithstanding that the contract has been terminated either by breach or by a party electing to treat it as repudiated.

(2)   Where on a breach the contract is nevertheless affirmed by a party entitled to treat it as repudiated, this does not of itself exclude the requirement of reasonableness in relation to any contract term.

Section 10   Evasion by means of secondary contract

A person is not bound by any contract term prejudicing or taking away rights of his which arise under, or in connection with the performance of, another contract, so far as those rights extend to the enforcement of another's liability which this Part of this Act prevents that other from excluding or restricting.

Section 11   The 'reasonableness' test

(1)   In relation to a contract term, the requirement of reasonableness for the purposes of this Part of this Act, s 3 of the Misrepresentation Act 1967 (see 6.5.1) and s 3 of the Misrepresentation Act (Northern Ireland) 1967 is that the term shall have been a fair and reasonable one to be included having regard to the circumstances which were, or ought reasonably to have been, known to or in the contemplation of the parties when the contract was made.

(2)   In determining for the purposes of s 6 or s 7 above whether a contract term satisfies the requirement of reasonableness, regard shall be had in particular to the matters specified in Sched 2 to this Act; but this sub-section does not prevent the court or arbitrator from holding, in accordance with any rule of law, that a term which purports to exclude or restrict any relevant liability is not a term of the contract.

(3)   In relation to a notice (not being a notice having contractual effect), the requirement of reasonableness under this Act is that it should be fair and reasonable to allow reliance on it, having regard to all the circumstances obtaining when the liability arose or (but for the notice) would have arisen.

(4)   Where by reference to a contract term or notice a person seeks to restrict liability to a specified sum of money, and the question arises (under this or any other Act) whether the term or notice satisfies the requirement of reasonableness, regard shall be had in particular (but without prejudice to sub-s (2) above in the case of contract terms) to:

(a)   the resources which he could expect to be available to him for the purpose of meeting the liability should it arise; and

(b)   how far it was open to him to cover himself by insurance.

(5)   It is for those claiming that a contract term or notice satisfies the requirement of reasonableness to show that it does.

Section 12 'Dealing as consumer'

(1)   A party to a contract 'deals as consumer' in relation to another party if:

(a)   he neither makes the contract in the course of a business nor holds himself as doing so; and

(b)   the other party does make the contract in the course of a business; and

(c)   in the case of a contract governed by the law of sale of goods or hire- purchase, or by s 7 of this Act, the goods passing under or in pursuance of the contract are of a type ordinarily supplied for private use or consumption.

(2)   But on a sale by auction or by competitive tender, the buyer is not in any circumstances to be regarded as dealing as consumer.

(3)   Subject to this, it is for those claiming that a party does not deal as consumer to show that he does not.

Section 3   Varieties of exemption clause

(1)   To the extent that this Part of this Act prevents the exclusion or restriction of any liability, it also prevents:

(a)   making the liability or its enforcement subject to restrictive or onerous conditions;

(b)   excluding or restricting any right or remedy in respect of the liability, or subjecting a person to any prejudice in consequence of his pursuing any such right or remedy;

(c) excluding or restricting rules of evidence or procedure; and (to that extent) ss 2 and 5 to 7 also prevent excluding or restricting liability by reference to terms and notices which exclude or restrict the relevant obligation or duty.

(2) But an agreement in writing to submit present or future differences to arbitration is not to be treated under this Part of this Act as excluding or restricting any liability.

Part II
(Amends Scottish law.)

Part III
(Contains miscellaneous provisions.)

Schedule I Scope of ss 2 to 4 and 7

(1) Sections 2 to 4 and 7 of this Act do not extend to:

(a) any contract of insurance (including a contract to pay an annuity on human life);

(b) any contract so far as it relates to the creation or transfer of an interest in land, or to the termination of such an interest, whether by extinction, merger, surrender, forfeiture or otherwise;

(c) any contract so far as it relates to the creation or transfer of a right or interest in any patent, trade mark, copyright or design right, registered design, technical or commercial information or other intellectual property, or relates to the termination of any such right or interest;

(d) any contract so far as it relates:

(i) to the formation or dissolution of a company (which means any body corporate or unincorporated association and includes a partnership); or

(ii) to its constitution or the rights or obligations of its corporators or members;

(e) any contract so far as it relates to the creation or transfer of securities or of any right or interest in securities.

(2) Section 2(1) extends to:

(a) any contract of marine salvage or towage;

(b) any charterparty of a ship or hovercraft; and

(c) any contract for the carriage of goods by ship or hovercraft,

but, subject to this, ss 2 to 4 and 7 do not extend to any such contract except in favour of a person dealing as consumer.

(3)   Where goods are carried by ship or hovercraft in pursuance of a contract which either:

(a)   specifies that as the means of carriage over part of the journey to be covered; or

(b)   makes no provision as to the means of carriage and does not exclude that means,

then ss 2(2), 3 and 4 do not, except in favour of a person dealing as consumer, extend to the contract as it operates for and in relation to the carriage of goods by that means.

(4)   Section 2(1) and (2) do not extend to a contract of employment, except in favour of the employee.

(5)   ...

Schedule 2 'Guidelines' for application of reasonableness test

The matters to which regard is to be had in particular for the purposes of ss 6(3), 7(3) and (4) ..., are any of the following which appear to be relevant:

(a)   the strength of the bargaining positions of the parties relative to each other, taking into account (among other things) alternative means by which the customer's requirements could have been met;

(b)   whether the customer received an inducement to agree to the term, or in accepting it had an opportunity of entering into a similar contract with other persons, but without having to accept a similar term;

(c)   whether the customer knew or ought reasonably to have known of the existence and extent of the term (having regard, among other things, to any custom of the trade and any previous course of dealing between the parties);

(d)   where the term excludes or restricts any relevant liability if some condition is not complied with, whether it was reasonable at the time of the contract to expect that compliance with that condition would be practicable;

(e)   whether the goods were manufactured, processed or adapted to the special order of the customer.

12.5.2 When is it fair and reasonable to rely on an exclusion clause?

George Mitchell (Chesterhall) Ltd v Finney Lock Seeds Ltd (1983) HL

The plaintiffs, who were farmers, ordered 30 lb of Dutch winter white cabbage seeds, costing £201.60, from the defendants, who were seed merchants. The defendants sent some inferior autumn cabbage seeds which the plaintiffs planted on 63 acres of their land. The crop failed because the seeds were wrong and the plaintiffs sought recompense from the defendants. The defendants relied on the wide exclusions in their conditions of sale which included:

> We hereby exclude all liability for any loss or damage arising from the use of any seeds or plants supplied by us and for any consequential loss or damage arising out of such use or any failure in the performance of or defect in any seeds or plants supplied by us or for any other loss or damage whatsoever save for, at our option, liability for any such replacement or refund as aforesaid. In accordance with the established custom of the seed trade any express or implied condition, statement or warranty, statutory or otherwise, not stated in these Conditions is hereby excluded.

Held the defendants could not rely on the exclusion clause. (I) Bearing in mind the comments of the House of Lords in *Photo Production Ltd v Securicor Transport Ltd* (see 12.4), it was no longer right to adopt a strained construction of exclusion clauses. Reversing the Court of Appeal on this point, the exclusion clause did cover the situation which occurred. (II) It must then be considered whether 'it would not be fair and reasonable to allow reliance on the term' under s 55(4) of the Sale of Goods Act 1979 (which applied to contracts made before the Unfair Contract Terms Act 1977 came into force). It was not reasonable in all the circumstances. A telling point was that in similar situations seed companies usually negotiated a payment of damages in excess of the price of the seeds. This showed that those in the industry did not think it reasonable to rely on their exclusion clauses. Also, seed merchants could obtain insurance against this kind of loss without materially increasing the price of seeds.

Note

Compare the requirement of reasonableness discussed in this case which assesses reliance on the term with the requirement of reasonableness in s 11(1) of the Unfair Contract Terms Act 1977 which assesses the inclusion of the term.

Smith v Eric S Bush (A Firm), Harris and Another v Wyre Forest District Council and Another (1989) HL

In each of these two cases, the plaintiff had bought a house relying on the survey obtained by the prospective mortgage lender from the defendant surveyor. The plaintiffs had accepted terms from the mortgagees which excluded any liability of the surveyor to the plaintiffs. The surveys were stated to be for the mortgagees' purposes only. In the event, the houses were defective in ways which the surveyors should have detected. One of the claims succeeded and the other failed before differently constituted

Courts of Appeal. The two cases were now heard together by the House of Lords.

Held the surveyors would have to pay damages to the plaintiffs. (I) In the law of tort, the surveyors did owe a duty of care to the purchasers. (II) The exclusions did come within the Unfair Contract Terms Act 1977. (III) It was not fair and reasonable for the surveyors to rely on their exclusion clauses in all the circumstances. *Per* Lord Templeman:

> The valuer is a professional man who offers his services for reward. He is paid for those services. The valuer knows that 90% of purchasers in fact rely on a mortgage valuation and do not commission their own survey ... Many purchasers cannot afford a second valuation. If a purchaser obtains a second valuation the sale may go off and then both valuation fees will be wasted. Moreover, he knows that mortgagees ... are trustworthy and that they appoint careful and competent valuers and he trusts the professional man so appointed. Finally, the valuer knows full well that failure on his part to exercise reasonable skill and care may be disastrous to the purchaser.

Per Lord Griffiths, the outcome might be different in the case of commercial property or even a very expensive domestic house, when it might be reasonable to expect the purchaser to obtain his own survey.

12.5.3 When is it fair and reasonable to include an exclusion clause (s 11(1))?

Edmund Murray Ltd v BSP International Foundations Ltd (1992) CA

EML were pile driving contractors employing about 20 people. BSP were manufacturers of pile driving plant and equipment. BSP were the only manufacturers of drilling rigs in the UK. EML asked BSP for a drilling rig with certain specifications. An agreement was made on BSP's standard terms for the supply of a rig to certain specifications for £45,000 less a 10% discount and the rig was delivered in July 1984. The rig did not function properly and after the parties failed to reach a negotiated agreement EML sued for damages in July 1987. BSP's standard conditions included a partial guarantee for six months which was stated, in condition 12.5, to be:

> ... in lieu of and excludes any other conditions, guarantees, liabilities or warranties expressed or implied statutory or otherwise and in no event shall the Sellers be liable for any loss, injury or damage howsoever caused or arising EXCEPT for death or personal injury arising from the proven negligence of the Sellers ...

Since the six months were passed, BSP denied liability for the rig's failings.

Held it was not fair and reasonable for BSP to rely on their exclusion clause to exclude liability for their failure to meet the specifications required by EML. (I) Although the parties were of equal bargaining power and EML knew about the terms in the contract, it could still not be reasonable for BSP to avoid liability for failing to meet the particular specifications which EML had ordered. Neill LJ said that, if a bystander at the time the contract was made had pointed out that EML would have no remedy if the rig failed to meet its specifications, the parties would have rejected that idea. (II) *Per* Ralph Gibson LJ, the unfairness of condition 12.5 could have been avoided by words in the contract where the specifications are given stating that the specifications had no contractual effect. (III) Their lordships also held that the 'circumstances ... known to ... the parties ...'. referred to in s 11(1) of the Act (see 12.5.1) only meant circumstances known etc to both parties, not just to one of them. (IV) (12.5.5) Their lordships discussed the possibility of severing a part of one of the exclusion clauses in this contract to leave a reasonable remainder. They assumed that such a severance was possible at least in some circumstances.

Q (a) Do their lordships' reasons for finding this clause to be unfair amount to a reintroduction of the doctrine of fundamental breach? (b) Would BSP have reacted to Neill LJ's bystander in the way Neill LJ suggests?

12.5.4 A business may deal as consumer

R and B Customs Brokers Co Ltd v United Dominions Trust Ltd (1987) CA

The plaintiffs were a company with only two directors, Mr Bell and his wife. The company owned a Volvo motor car which was used by Mr Bell for both business and private purposes. Mr Bell decided to trade in the Volvo for a different car and consequently the plaintiffs bought a Colt Shogun car from the third party car dealer. The purchase was financed by the defendants, a finance company. The form of the transaction was that the plaintiffs' only contract was with the defendants who bought the car from the dealer and then passed it to the plaintiffs by a conditional sale arrangement. Therefore, when the car proved to be unsuitable for driving because of a persistently leaking roof, the plaintiffs sued the finance company for breach of the implied terms that the car would be suitable for its purpose and of merchantable quality. The finance company relied on its exclusion of all warranties or conditions in the case of a buyer who did not deal as consumer within the meaning of s 12 of the Unfair Contract Terms Act 1977 (see 12.5.1).

Held the finance company could not rely on its exclusion clause in this case because the plaintiffs did deal as consumer. Although in one sense a company must always act in the course of its business, the test in s 12 was not to be interpreted in that broad sense. For transactions which are only incidental to the company's business, like buying a company car for an employee, *per* Dillon LJ:

... a degree of regularity is required before it can be said that they are an integral part of the business carried on and so entered into in the course of that business.

This being the second or third vehicle acquired by the company on credit terms, the required regularity was not present, so the company did not transact in the course of its business.

12.5.5 The reasonableness test applies to the whole term, not to the particular reliance placed on it

Stewart Gill Ltd v Horatio Myer & Co Ltd (1992) CA

The defendants were manufacturers of beds. They bought an overhead conveyor system from the plaintiffs for £266,400. The price was payable by instalments and the plaintiffs' claim was for the last 10% which the defendants had not paid on time. The defendants argued that they could withhold payment because of certain breaches of contract on the part of the plaintiffs. However, the plaintiffs sought to rely on clause 12.4 of the contract of sale which said:

The Customer shall not be entitled to withhold payment of any amount due to the Company under the Contract by reason of any payment credit set off counter-claim allegation of incorrect or defective Goods or for any other reason whatsoever which the Customer may allege excuses him from performing his obligations hereunder.

Held the clause was not fair and reasonable and so the plaintiffs could not rely upon it. It was the whole term which the plaintiffs had to show was reasonable and not just the part of it which they wanted to rely upon in the case. Their lordships gave the following four reasons for their conclusion. (I) The Act constantly refers to a, the or any 'contract term', which must mean a whole term. (II) The parties must be able to judge at the time the contract is made whether a term is reasonable or not. (III) Some of the considerations given in Sched 2 of the Act (see above at 12.5.1) could only be applied to whole terms. (IV) It would not, *per* Stuart-Smith LJ:

... be consistent with the policy and purpose of the Act to permit a contractor to impose a contractual term, which taken as a whole is completely unreasonable, to put a blue pencil through the most offensive parts and say that what is left is reasonable and sufficient to exclude or restrict his liability in a manner relied upon.

Q How is a single term to be defined – by its grammatical form or by its conceptual content?

Edmund Murray Ltd v BSP International Foundations Ltd (1992) CA

See 12.5.3.

Q Are the *dicta* on severance in this case consistent with the *dicta* against blue pencilling in *Stewart Gill Ltd v Horatio Myer & Co Ltd* (above)?

12.6 The Unfair Terms in Consumer Contracts Regulations 1999

*Citation and commencement**

1 These Regulations may be cited as the Unfair Terms in Consumer Contracts Regulations 1999 and shall come into force on 1 October 1999.

Revocation

2 The Unfair Terms in Consumer Contracts Regulations 1994 are hereby revoked.

Interpretation

3(1) In these Regulations:

'the Community' means the European Community;

'consumer' means any natural person who, in contracts covered by these Regulations, is acting for purposes which are outside his trade, business or profession;

'court' in relation to England and Wales and Northern Ireland means a county court or the High Court, and in relation to Scotland, the Sheriff or the Court of Session;

'Director' means the Director General of Fair Trading;

'EEA Agreement' means the Agreement on the European Economic Area signed at Oporto on 2 May 1992 as adjusted by the protocol signed at Brussels on 17 March 1993[4];

'Member State' means a State which is a contracting party to the EEA Agreement;

'notified' means notified in writing;

'qualifying body' means a person specified in Sched 1;

---

* Crown copyright 1999; with the permission of the Controller of Her Majesty's Stationery Office.

'seller or supplier' means any natural or legal person who, in contracts covered by these Regulations, is acting for purposes relating to his trade, business or profession, whether publicly owned or privately owned;

'unfair terms' means the contractual terms referred to in reg 5.

(2)   In the application of these Regulations to Scotland for references to an 'injunction' or an 'interim injunction', there shall be substituted references to an 'interdict' or 'interim interdict' respectively.

Terms to which these Regulations apply

4(1)   These Regulations apply in relation to unfair terms in contracts concluded between a seller or a supplier and a consumer.

(2)   These Regulations do not apply to contractual terms which reflect:

(a)   mandatory statutory or regulatory provisions (including such provisions under the law of any Member State or in Community legislation having effect in the United Kingdom without further enactment);

(b)   the provisions or principles of international conventions to which the Member States or the Community are party.

Unfair terms

5(1)   A contractual term which has not been individually negotiated shall be regarded as unfair if, contrary to the requirement of good faith, it causes a significant imbalance in the parties' rights and obligations arising under the contract, to the detriment of the consumer.

(2)   A term shall always be regarded as not having been individually negotiated where it has been drafted in advance and the consumer has therefore not been able to influence the substance of the term.

(3)   Notwithstanding that a specific term or certain aspects of it in a contract has been individually negotiated, these Regulations shall apply to the rest of a contract if an overall assessment of it indicates that it is a pre-formulated standard contract.

(4)   It shall be for any seller or supplier who claims that a term was individually negotiated to show that it was.

(5)   Schedule 2 to these Regulations contains an indicative and non-exhaustive list of the terms which may be regarded as unfair.

Assessment of unfair terms

6(1)   Without prejudice to reg 12, the unfairness of a contractual term shall be assessed, taking into account the nature of the goods or services for which the contract was concluded and by referring, at the time of conclusion of the contract, to all the circumstances attending the conclusion of the contract and to all the other terms of the contract or of another contract on which it is dependent.

(2)   In so far as it is in plain intelligible language, the assessment of fairness of a term shall not relate:

(a)   to the definition of the main subject matter of the contract; or

(b)   to the adequacy of the price or remuneration, as against the goods or services supplied in exchange.

Written contracts

7(1) A seller or supplier shall ensure that any written term of a contract is expressed in plain, intelligible language.

(2)   If there is doubt about the meaning of a written term, the interpretation which is most favourable to the consumer shall prevail but this rule shall not apply in proceedings brought under reg 12.

Effect of unfair term

8(1) An unfair term in a contract concluded with a consumer by a seller or supplier shall not be binding on the consumer.

(2)   The contract shall continue to bind the parties if it is capable of continuing in existence without the unfair term.

Choice of law clauses

9   These Regulations shall apply notwithstanding any contract term which applies or purports to apply the law of a non-Member State, if the contract has a close connection with the territory of the Member States.

Complaints – consideration by Director

10(1) It shall be the duty of the Director to consider any complaint made to him that any contract term drawn up for general use is unfair, unless:

(a)   the complaint appears to the Director to be frivolous or vexatious; or

(b)   a qualifying body has notified the Director that it agrees to consider the complaint.

(2)   The Director shall give reasons for his decision to apply or not to apply, as the case may be, for an injunction under reg 12 in relation to any complaint which these Regulations require him to consider.

(3)   In deciding whether or not to apply for an injunction in respect of a term which the Director considers to be unfair, he may, if he considers it appropriate to do so, have regard to any undertakings

given to him by or on behalf of any person as to the continued use of such a term in contracts concluded with consumers.

Complaints – consideration by qualifying bodies

11(1) If a qualifying body specified in Part One of Sched 1 notifies the Director that it agrees to consider a complaint that any contract term drawn up for general use is unfair, it shall be under a duty to consider that complaint.

(2) Regulation 10(2) and (3) shall apply to a qualifying body which is under a duty to consider a complaint as they apply to the Director. Injunctions to prevent continued use of unfair terms.

12(1) The Director or, subject to para (2), any qualifying body may apply for an injunction (including an interim injunction) against any person appearing to the Director or that body to be using, or recommending use of, an unfair term drawn up for general use in contracts concluded with consumers.

(2) A qualifying body may apply for an injunction only where:

(a) it has notified the Director of its intention to apply at least 14 days before the date on which the application is made, beginning with the date on which the notification was given; or

(b) the Director consents to the application being made within a shorter period.

(3) The court on an application under this regulation may grant an injunction on such terms as it thinks fit.

(4) An injunction may relate not only to use of a particular contract term drawn up for general use but to any similar term, or a term having like effect, used or recommended for use by any person.

Powers of the Director and qualifying bodies to obtain documents and information

13(1) The Director may exercise the power conferred by this regulation for the purpose of:

(a) facilitating his consideration of a complaint that a contract term drawn up for general use is unfair; or

(b) ascertaining whether a person has complied with an undertaking or court order as to the continued use, or recommendation for use, of a term in contracts concluded with consumers.

(2) A qualifying body specified in Part One of Sched 1 may exercise the power conferred by this regulation for the purpose of:

(a) facilitating its consideration of a complaint that a contract term drawn up for general use is unfair; or

(b) ascertaining whether a person has complied with:

  (i)   an undertaking given to it or to the court following an application by that body; or

  (ii) a court order made on an application by that body,

as to the continued use, or recommendation for use, of a term in contracts concluded with consumers.

(3) The Director may require any person to supply to him, and a qualifying body specified in Part One of Sched 1 may require any person to supply to it:

(a) a copy of any document which that person has used or recommended for use, at the time the notice referred to in para (4) below is given, as a pre-formulated standard contract in dealings with consumers;

(b) information about the use, or recommendation for use, by that person of that document or any other such document in dealings with consumers.

(4) The power conferred by this regulation is to be exercised by a notice in writing which may:

(a) specify the way in which and the time within which it is to be complied with; and

(b) be varied or revoked by a subsequent notice.

(5) Nothing in this regulation compels a person to supply any document or information which he would be entitled to refuse to produce or give in civil proceedings before the court.

(6) If a person makes default in complying with a notice under this regulation, the court may, on the application of the Director or of the qualifying body, make such order as the court thinks fit for requiring the default to be made good, and any such order may provide that all the costs or expenses of and incidental to the application shall be borne by the person in default or by any officers of a company or other association who are responsible for its default.

Notification of undertakings and orders to Director

14   A qualifying body shall notify the Director:

(a) of any undertaking given to it by or on behalf of any person as to the continued use of a term which that body considers to be unfair in contracts concluded with consumers;

(b) of the outcome of any application made by it under reg 12, and of the terms of any undertaking given to, or order made by, the court;

(c) of the outcome of any application made by it to enforce a previous order of the court.

Publication, information and advice

15(1) The Director shall arrange for the publication in such form and manner as he considers appropriate, of:

(a) details of any undertaking or order notified to him under reg 14;

(b) details of any undertaking given to him by or on behalf of any person as to the continued use of a term which the Director considers to be unfair in contracts concluded with consumers;

(c) details of any application made by him under reg 12, and of the terms of any undertaking given to, or order made by, the court;

(d) details of any application made by the Director to enforce a previous order of the court.

(2) The Director shall inform any person on request whether a particular term to which these Regulations apply has been:

(a) the subject of an undertaking given to the Director or notified to him by a qualifying body; or

(b) the subject of an order of the court made upon application by him or notified to him by a qualifying body,

and shall give that person details of the undertaking or a copy of the order, as the case may be, together with a copy of any amendments which the person giving the undertaking has agreed to make to the term in question.

(3) The Director may arrange for the dissemination in such form and manner as he considers appropriate of such information and advice concerning the operation of these Regulations as may appear to him to be expedient to give to the public and to all persons likely to be affected by these Regulations.

SCHEDULE 1

Regulation 3

QUALIFYING BODIES

PART ONE

1   The Data Protection Registrar.

2   The Director General of Electricity Supply.

3   The Director General of Gas Supply.

4   The Director General of Electricity Supply for Northern Ireland.

5   The Director General of Gas for Northern Ireland.

6   The Director General of Telecommunications.

7   The Director General of Water Services.

8   The Rail Regulator.

9   Every weights and measures authority in Great Britain.

10   The Department of Economic Development in Northern Ireland.

PART TWO

11   Consumers' Association.

SCHEDULE 2

Regulation 5(5)

INDICATIVE AND NON-EXHAUSTIVE LIST OF TERMS WHICH MAY BE REGARDED AS UNFAIR

1   Terms which have the object or effect of:

(a) excluding or limiting the legal liability of a seller or supplier in the event of the death of a consumer or personal injury to the latter resulting from an act or omission of that seller or supplier;

(b) inappropriately excluding or limiting the legal rights of the consumer vis à vis the seller or supplier or another party in the event of total or partial non-performance or inadequate performance by the seller or supplier of any of the contractual obligations, including the option of offsetting a debt owed to the seller or supplier against any claim which the consumer may have against him;

(c) making an agreement binding on the consumer whereas provision of services by the seller or supplier is subject to a condition whose realisation depends on his own will alone;

(d) permitting the seller or supplier to retain sums paid by the consumer where the latter decides not to conclude or perform the contract, without providing for the consumer to receive compensation of an equivalent amount from the seller or supplier where the latter is the party cancelling the contract;

(e) requiring any consumer who fails to fulfil his obligation to pay a disproportionately high sum in compensation;

(f) authorising the seller or supplier to dissolve the contract on a discretionary basis where the same facility is not granted to the consumer, or permitting the seller or supplier to retain the sums paid for services not yet supplied by him where it is the seller or supplier himself who dissolves the contract;

(g) enabling the seller or supplier to terminate a contract of indeterminate duration without reasonable notice except where there are serious grounds for doing so;

(h) automatically extending a contract of fixed duration where the consumer does not indicate otherwise, when the deadline fixed for the consumer to express his desire not to extend the contract is unreasonably early;

(i) irrevocably binding the consumer to terms with which he had no real opportunity of becoming acquainted before the conclusion of the contract;

(j) enabling the seller or supplier to alter the terms of the contract unilaterally without a valid reason which is specified in the contract;

(k) enabling the seller or supplier to alter unilaterally without a valid reason any characteristics of the product or service to be provided;

(l) providing for the price of goods to be determined at the time of delivery or allowing a seller of goods or supplier of services to increase their price without in both cases giving the consumer the corresponding right to cancel the contract if the final price is too high in relation to the price agreed when the contract was concluded;

(m) giving the seller or supplier the right to determine whether the goods or services supplied are in conformity with the contract, or giving him the exclusive right to interpret any term of the contract;

(n) limiting the seller's or supplier's obligation to respect commitments undertaken by his agents or making his commitments subject to compliance with a particular formality;

(o) obliging the consumer to fulfil all his obligations where the seller or supplier does not perform his;

(p) giving the seller or supplier the possibility of transferring his rights and obligations under the contract, where this may serve to reduce the guarantees for the consumer, without the latter's agreement;

(q) excluding or hindering the consumer's right to take legal action or exercise any other legal remedy, particularly by requiring the consumer to take disputes exclusively to arbitration not covered by legal provisions, unduly restricting the evidence available to him or imposing on him a burden of proof which, according to the applicable law, should lie with another party to the contract.

2   Scope of paras 1(g), (j) and (l)

   (a)   Paragraph 1(g) is without hindrance to terms by which a supplier of financial services reserves the right to terminate unilaterally a contract of indeterminate duration without notice where there is a valid reason, provided that the supplier is required to inform the other contracting party or parties thereof immediately.

   (b)   Paragraph 1(j) is without hindrance to terms under which a supplier of financial services reserves the right to alter the rate of interest payable by the consumer or due to the latter, or the amount of other charges for financial services without notice where there is a valid reason, provided that the supplier is required to inform the other contracting party or parties thereof at the earliest opportunity and that the latter are free to dissolve the contract immediately.

         Paragraph 1(j) is also without hindrance to terms under which a seller or supplier reserves the right to alter unilaterally the conditions of a contract of indeterminate duration, provided that he is required to inform the consumer with reasonable notice and that the consumer is free to dissolve the contract.

   (c)   Paragraphs 1(g), (j) and (l) do not apply to: transactions in transferable securities, financial instruments and other products or services where the price is linked to fluctuations in a stock exchange quotation or index or a financial market rate that the seller or supplier does not control; contracts for the purchase or sale of foreign currency, traveller's cheques or international money orders denominated in foreign currency;

   (d)   Paragraph 1(l) is without hindrance to price indexation clauses, where lawful, provided that the method by which prices vary is explicitly described.

Director General of Fair Trading v First National Bank plc (1999) Ch

The defendant bank made loans at high rates of interest. The terms of the lending included a provision that interest should continue to run even after the bank obtained a judgment for the repayment of the loan. In practice, defaulting borrowers would agree to judgment for payment by instalments. The borrowers would pay the instalments and then be surprised to discover that they were not free of obligations to the bank. Indeed, the remaining interest would sometimes exceed the total amount of the instalments paid. Many borrowers complained to the Director

General of Fair Trading who brought proceedings under reg 8 of the Unfair Terms in Consumer Contracts Regulations 1994.

Held refusing the Director General's application for injunctions restraining the use of the term. (I) Although the rate of interest itself would be a 'core term' of which no assessment would be made under reg 3(2), the provision for interest to continue after judgment was not such a term because the borrower would not consider it to be one of the important terms of the agreement. (II) It was not inherently unfair for interest to continue to run in the event of default even after a judgment. A harsh effect may be produced by the rate of interest, but the rate itself was not reviewable because it was a 'core term'. (III) The requirement of good faith in reg 4(1) was 'not to be construed in the English law sense of absence of dishonesty but rather in the continental "Civil law" sense'. This type of unfairness takes two forms: (i) 'substantive unfairness, namely, the imposition of an onerous term out of proportion to a reasonable assessment of the obligations of the parties under the contract by the supplier on the consumer':

[ii] ... the second form of unfairness is procedural unfairness. This may occur where a consumer/borrower becomes unwittingly subject to an onerous term, which need not necessarily be substantively unfair, but which materially affects the balance of advantage of the consumer in entering into the contract. Academic commentators have referred to this unfairness as unfair surprise.

Per Evans-Lombe J:

It seems to me that a term not inherently unfair can still constitute a breach of the requirement of good faith if it unfairly deprives consumers of a benefit or advantage which they may reasonably expect to receive.

(IV) Although it would be better if the bank drew the attention of borrowers to the relevant clause before they entered into the agreement or before they agreed to any court order for payment by instalments, the clause itself did not give rise to either substantive or procedural unfairness.

13 Performance and Breach

13.1 Complete and substantial performance

13.1.1 Incomplete performance will give no right to payment in a lump sum contract

Cutter v Powell (1795) CKB

The defendant was the master of a ship at Jamaica who wished to hire one Cutter as second mate for a voyage to England. He gave Cutter a note saying:

> Ten days after the ship Governor Parry, myself master, arrives at Liverpool, I promise to pay to Mr T Cutter the sum of 30 guineas, provided he proceeds, continues and does his duty as second mate in the said ship from hence to the port of Liverpool.

The usual wages of a second mate were £4 a month and the voyage usually took about two months. Cutter went on board the ship on 31 July and sailed with her on 2 August. He did his duty as second mate until his death on 20 September. The ship arrived in London on 9 October. Cutter's administratrix now sought payment of a portion of the 30 guineas.

Held nothing could be recovered on Cutter's behalf. As a matter of construction, the contract was that Cutter would receive 30 guineas for completing his duty and nothing otherwise. Their lordships were influenced by the words of the contract and by the fact that the rate of pay was much higher than was normal suggesting that some risk was passed to Cutter.

Sumpter v Hedges (1898) CA

The plaintiff, a builder, contracted to build two houses and a stable on the defendant's land for a lump sum. When the buildings were still unfinished, the plaintiff informed the defendant that he had no money and would not continue with the work. The defendant completed the work himself.

Held the plaintiff could not recover anything for the incomplete work he had done. The plaintiff would have been able to claim for the work on a *quantum meruit* basis only if there had been a new contract to pay for the work done. The fact that the defendant had finished the building, taking advantage of the work done by the plaintiff, did not show such a new contract as the defendant had no other choice when the plaintiff abandoned the contract.

13.1.2 Substantial performance will give a right to payment under a lump sum contract

Hoenig v Isaacs (1952) CA

The defendant employed the plaintiff to decorate his flat and provide it with certain furniture. The contract was for:

> The foregoing, complete, for the sum of £750 net. Terms of payment are net cash, as the work proceeds; and balance on completion.

When the plaintiff said he had finished, £300 had been paid on account. The defendant paid a further £100 but refused to pay more, arguing that the workmanship was defective. It was found that the defects would cost less than £56 to remedy.

Held the plaintiff was entitled to the outstanding £350 less the cost of putting right the defects. (I) Only the breach of an important term, a condition precedent, gives the promisee a right to reject the performance of the promisor. The breach of a less important term, or warranty, only gives a right to damages. *Per* Denning LJ:

> When a contract provides for a specific sum to be paid on completion of specified work, the courts lean against a construction of the contract which would deprive the contractor of any payment at all simply because there are some defects or omissions. The promise to complete the work is, therefore, construed as a term of the contract, but not as a condition.

(II) Even if the plaintiff's breach in this case had been a breach of condition, the defendant had waived his right to reject the performance by moving into the flat and using the furniture.

Q Is the 'promise to complete the work' a warranty, or is it an innominate term?

Bolton v Mahadeva (1972) CA

The plaintiff agreed to perform some works in the defendant's house, including installing central heating. The price for installing the central heating was a lump sum of £560. The work was defective in that fumes were given out and the house was an average of 10% less warm than it should have been. It would have cost £174.50 to remedy the defects.

Held the plaintiff could not recover any payment for the installation of the central heating system. (I) *Per* Cairns LJ, with whom Buckley and Sachs LJJ agreed:

The main question in the case is whether the defects ... were of such a character and amount that the plaintiff could not be said to have substantially performed his contract ... In considering whether there was substantial performance, I am of opinion that it is relevant to take into account both the nature of the defects and the proportion between the cost of rectifying them and the contract price. It would be wrong to say that the contractor is only entitled to payment if the defects are so trifling as to be covered by the *de minimis* rule.

(II) Sachs LJ also noted that the plaintiff in this case refused the chance to remedy the defects himself so that his difficulty was entirely his own fault.

13.1.3 A tender of goods etc within the stipulated time may be substantial performance

Startup and Another v MacDonald (1843) EC

The parties agreed that the plaintiffs would sell to the defendant 10 tons of linseed oil to be delivered 'within the last 14 days of March 1838'. The plaintiffs delivered the oil to the defendant at his business address at 8.30 pm on 31 March, a Saturday. The defendant refused to accept the oil at that time and refused to pay for it. The jury found that the time was unreasonable and improper, but that there was time for the defendant to examine the oil before the period for delivery expired at midnight.

Held the defendant was wrong to reject the oil. The defendant had no obligation to be at his office at an unreasonable hour and the plaintiffs could not have tendered their performance of the contract if they had been unable to find him. But, since the plaintiffs did find the defendant in time, he could not refuse to accept the goods he had contracted for. *Per* Rolfe B, with whom Gurney B agreed:

Without acceptance on the part of him who is to receive, the act of him who is to deliver or to pay, can amount only to a tender. But, the law considers a party who has entered into a contract to deliver goods or pay money to another, as having, substantially, performed it, if he has tendered the goods or money to the party to whom the delivery or payment was to be made, provided only that the tender has been made under such circumstances that the party to whom it has been made, has had a reasonable opportunity of examining the goods, or the money, tendered, in order to ascertain that the thing tendered really was what it purported to be.

13.2 Anticipatory breach of contract

13.2.1 An anticipatory breach gives an immediate cause of action

Planché v Colburn and Another (1831) CCP

The plaintiff agreed with the defendants to write a book about costume and ancient armour for their series, The Juvenile Library, for which the defendants would pay £100. After the plaintiff had written some of the book, the defendants abandoned the series and said they would not publish the book.

Held after the defendants abandoned publication, the plaintiff was entitled to remuneration for the work he had done on a *quantum meruit* basis.

Q Was *quantum meruit* the correct measure of loss in this case?

Hochster v De La Tour (1853)

The parties agreed in April 1852 that the plaintiff would be employed by the defendant as a courier for three months from 1 June 1852 for £10 a month. On 11 May, the defendant wrote to the plaintiff withdrawing from the agreement. The plaintiff started the current action on 22 May. Later in May, the plaintiff obtained an equally good position as a courier to start in July.

Held the plaintiff could obtain damages from the defendant without waiting for the defendant to fail to employ the plaintiff on 1 June. The defendant's renunciation of the contract on 11 May would be treated as a breach of contract. The plaintiff was therefore entitled to minimise his loss by accepting another position without losing his right of action against the defendant.

13.2.2 A repudiation gives the promisee an election either to accept the repudiation or to continue with the contract

Frost v Knight (1872) EC

The defendant promised to marry the plaintiff on the death of the defendant's father. While his father was still alive, the defendant broke off the engagement and the plaintiff immediately brought this action for breach of promise of marriage.

Held the plaintiff could succeed in this action without having to wait for the defendant's father to die, applying the principle of *Hochster v De La Tour* (13.2.1). *Per* Cockburn CJ, with whom Keating and Lush JJ agreed:

> The law with reference to a contract to be performed at a future time, where the party bound to performance announces prior to the time his intention not to

perform it ..., may be thus stated. The promisee, if he pleases, may treat the notice of intention as inoperative, and await the time when the contract is to be executed, and then hold the other party responsible for all the consequences of non-performance: but in that case he keeps the contract alive for the benefit of the other party as well as his own; he remains subject to all his own obligations and liabilities under it, and enables the other party not only to complete the contract, if so advised, notwithstanding his previous repudiation of it, but also to take advantage of any supervening circumstance which would justify him in declining to complete it. On the other hand, the promisee may, if he thinks proper, treat the repudiation of the other party as a wrongful putting an end to the contract, and may at once bring his action as on a breach of it; and in such action he will be entitled to such damages as would have arisen from the non-performance of the contract at the appointed time, subject, however, to abatement in respect of any circumstances which may have afforded him the means of mitigating the loss.

White and Carter (Councils) Ltd v McGregor (1961) HL

The claimants supplied litter bins to local authorities. They were allowed by the authorities to attach advertisements to the bins, for which the claimants were paid by the advertisers. The defendant was in business as a garage and he advertised on the claimants' litter bins. In June 1957, the defendant's sales manager renewed the advertising contract for a further three years. That same day, the defendant found out and, not wishing to continue to advertise in this way, he wrote to the claimants cancelling the contract. The claimants refused to accept the cancellation and placed advertisements on bins as if the contract was still existing. They then sued for their fees.

Held the claimants were entitled to their fees. (I) The claimants had the right to elect to continue the contract, even though the benefit to them of doing so might be far less than the cost to the defendants. (II) However, *per* Lord Reid:

It may well be that, if it can be shown that a person has no legitimate interest, financial or otherwise, in performing the contract rather than claiming damages, he ought not to be allowed to saddle the other party with an additional burden with no benefit to himself.

Vitol SA Geneva v Norelf Ltd Bermuda: *The Santa Clara* (1996) HL

The buyers (Vitol) bought a cargo of propane from the sellers (Norelf). Following their agreement, the market for propane fell quickly. While the cargo was being loaded, the buyers repudiated the contract by a telex sent on 8 March 1991. On 9 March, the vessel sailed. On 11 March, the sellers became aware of the buyers' telex and from 12 March the sellers made attempts to sell the cargo elsewhere, which were successful on 15 March.

The sellers now claimed damages on the basis of the buyers' anticipatory repudiation of the contract. The buyers argued that the sellers had never accepted the buyers' repudiation which was accordingly of no effect. The question of law before the House of Lords was whether an aggrieved party can ever accept a repudiation of a contract merely by failing to perform.

Held the question of law would be answered in the affirmative. In some circumstances, including those in this case, a repudiatory breach could be accepted by the innocent party failing to perform the contract himself. *Per* Lord Steyn:

> An act of acceptance of a repudiation requires no particular form: a communication does not have to be couched in the language of acceptance. It is sufficient that the communication or conduct clearly and unequivocally conveys to the repudiating party that the aggrieved party is treating the contract as at an end. ... Sometimes in the practical world of businessmen, an omission to act may be as pregnant with meaning as a positive declaration. While the analogy of offer and acceptance is imperfect, it is not without significance that, while the general principle is that there can be no acceptance of an offer by silence, our law does in exceptional cases recognise acceptance of an offer by silence. Thus, in *Rust v Abbey Life Assurance Co Ltd* (1979), the Court of Appeal held that a failure by a proposed insured to reject a proffered insurance policy for seven months justified on its own an inference of acceptance ... Similarly, in the different field of repudiation, a failure to perform may sometimes be given a colour by special circumstances and may only be explicable to a reasonable person in the position of the repudiating party as an election to accept the repudiation.

13.2.3 The promisee must accept a repudiation if he has no legitimate interest in continuing with the contract

Clea Shipping Corp v Bulk Oil International Ltd: *The Alaskan Trader* (1983) QB

In December 1979, *The Alaskan Trader* was chartered for a period of 24 months. In October 1980, the vessel suffered a serious engine breakdown that would take several months to repair. The vessel would be off hire during the repairs. The charterers indicated that they would not continue with the charter after the repairs. The owners did not accept this and informed the charterers when the vessel was ready again in April 1981. The charterers still refused to use the ship but the owners kept her at anchor and fully crewed until the charter expired in December, when the vessel was scrapped.

Held the hire for the period from April to December 1981 did not have to be paid. *Per* Lloyd J, Lord Reid's speech in *White and Carter (Councils) Ltd v McGregor* (see at 13.2.2) contained two limitations to the principle that the promisee can elect to continue the contract. First, it only applies where the promisee is able to complete performance without the cooperation of the promisor. Secondly, the promisee could be denied his right to enforce the continuing contract if he had no legitimate interest in so doing. In this case, the owners had no legitimate interest in keeping the vessel fully crewed at anchor, so they could not recover the contractual hire for the period between April and December 1981.

13.2.4 If the promisee continues with the contract, the repudiator may take advantage of supervening circumstances

Avery v Bowden (1856)

By a charterparty, it was agreed that the plaintiff's ship, *The Lebanon*, would proceed from London to Odessa, where the defendant would, within 45 days, provide a cargo for *The Lebanon* to take to Hull. The charterparty excepted war and so on. *The Lebanon* reached Odessa on 11 March. According to the plaintiff, the defendant refused to load the cargo, but the plaintiff kept the ship at Odessa and demanded the cargo from the defendant. By 1 April, war between England and Russia had become known at Odessa, frustrating the contract. *The Lebanon* sailed out of Odessa without a cargo on 17 April. The plaintiff now sought damages for the defendant's refusal to load a cargo.

Held the plaintiff could not obtain any damages. (I) The plaintiff had failed to show that the defendant repudiated the contract before it was frustrated by the outbreak of war. (II) Even if there had been a repudiation, the plaintiff had lost any right of action in respect of it by continuing to insist on loading.

13.3 Notice to make time of the essence

British and Commonwealth Holdings plc v Quadrex Holdings Inc (1989) CA

The plaintiff company, B&C, made an agreement to sell two of its subsidiaries to the defendant company, Quadrex, as soon as reasonably practicable after certain clearances had been obtained. Delays occurred in completion because of Quadrex's difficulty in obtaining financing for the deal which was partly caused by the obstruction of the management of the subsidiaries, who were hoping to buy the subsidiaries themselves if the sale to Quadrex fell through. The various clearances were obtained by 16 December 1987. As Quadrex's problems continued, B&C gave them notice on 25 January 1988 that, if Quadrex did not complete by 28 February, B&C would treat the non-completion as a repudiation of the contract. Quadrex did fail to complete and the subsidiaries were sold to their own management teams for some £100m less than the contract price. B&C now claimed the £100m they had lost as damages from Quadrex. The appeal was from a summary judgment given against Quadrex.

Held although Quadrex would be given leave to defend the action on another ground, B&C's actions in making time of the essence were effective. *Per* Sir Nicolas Browne-Wilkinson VC, with whom Woolf and Staughton LJJ agreed, the question whether time is of the essence is to be asked not of a contract, but of each term:

> In equity, time is not normally of the essence of a contractual term ... However, in three types of cases, time is of the essence in equity: first, where the contract expressly so stipulates; secondly, where the circumstances of the case or the subject matter of the contract indicate that the time for completion is of the essence; thirdly, where a valid notice to complete has been given.

In this contract, time could not be of the essence without a notice to complete because the date for completion was not set by the contract. But, if that had not been the case, time would have been of the essence because of the volatility of the value of shares in the subsidiaries:

> In the ordinary case, three requirements have to be satisfied if time for completion is to be made of the essence by the service of a notice, viz (1) the giver of the notice (the innocent party) has to be ready, willing and able to complete; (2) the other party (the guilty party) has to have been guilty of unreasonable delay before a notice to complete can be served; and (3) the notice when served must limit a reasonable period within which completion is to take place.

As to requirement (2) that 'there has been undue or improper delay by the guilty party', his lordship said that:

> The law has been too long established in this sense to be overturned. But, the rule leads to manifest inconvenience and should not, in my judgment, be extended.

Behzadi v Shaftsbury Hotels Ltd (1990) CA

On 20 June 1988, the parties agreed the sale of two London hotels for £2.4m. They agreed that completion would take place on 31 August or, if later, within 28 days of the vendor notifying the purchaser that certain planning permissions had been received. If the permissions were not received by 31 October, the contract would become null and void. Under the National Conditions of Sale, incorporated in the contract, the vendor was to deliver documents proving his title to the land by 5 July. Because of delays at the Land Registry, the vendor could not produce the documents and did not reply to letters from the purchaser requesting them. On 23 August, the vendor told the purchaser of the problems. On 30 August, the purchaser gave the vendor a notice to make time of the essence that the vendor was required to produce the documents by 6 September. When the vendor could not comply, the purchaser withdrew from the transaction on 7 September. The planning permissions were received on 9 September.

Held the purchaser was wrong to withdraw and must compensate the vendor. Where the contract specified a particular date for completion, the innocent party could serve a notice making time of the essence at any time after that completion date had passed. Despite what Sir Nicolas Browne-Wilkinson VC said in *British and Commonwealth Holdings plc v Quadrex Holdings Inc* (above), there was no requirement that the delay should be unreasonable except where the contract did not specify the completion date. Therefore, the purchaser was entitled to serve a notice when she did as the date for providing the documents of title was given in the contract and had passed. However, the time she gave for compliance was not reasonable in all the circumstances, taking into account the fact that completion of the purchase was not yet due so that the purchaser would not have suffered any prejudice from a continued delay in producing the documents of title.

14 Remedies

14.1 Damages

14.1.1 Remoteness: the rule in *Hadley v Baxendale*

Hadley and Another v Baxendale and Others (1854) CE

The plaintiffs were millers at Gloucester. When their mill was stopped by the crank-shaft breaking, they had to return the shaft to its makers at Greenwich. The defendants (trading as Pickfords) were carriers who promised they could deliver the shaft to Greenwich in one day. The plaintiffs told the defendants that they were millers, but not that their mill was stopped without the shaft. The defendants delayed the delivery of the shaft by several days and the plaintiffs now claimed damages, including the profits they had lost by the delay.

Held the lost profits were not recoverable. *Per* Alderson B, giving the judgment of the court:

> Where two parties have made a contract which one of them has broken, the damages which the other party ought to receive in respect of such breach of contract should be such as may fairly and reasonably be considered either arising naturally, that is, according to the usual course of things, from such breach of contract itself, or such as may reasonably be supposed to have been in the contemplation of both parties, at the time they made the contract, as the probable result of the breach of it.

In this case, the defendants had no reason to think that the shaft was the only one that the plaintiffs had and that the plaintiffs had made no other provision for running the mill while it was away.

Victoria Laundry (Windsor) Ltd v Newman Industries Ltd (1949) CA

The plaintiffs were laundrymen and dyers who bought a boiler for use in their business from the defendants. The defendants knew that the boiler was wanted as soon as possible by the plaintiffs in their business. When the boiler was ready for delivery in early June, it was rejected by the plaintiffs because it was damaged. The defendants eventually agreed to make the necessary repairs. The plaintiffs took delivery of the boiler in November. The plaintiffs claimed damages including the profits they lost between June and November. They had lost normal business of £16 a week and some special dyeing contracts worth £262 a week. The trial judge rejected altogether the plaintiffs' claim for loss of profits.

Held the case should be remitted to the Official Referee for him to assess what general damages the plaintiffs had suffered. The principle of *Hadley and Another v Baxendale and Others* (14.1.1) was explained by Asquith LJ giving the judgment of the court. He said that a loss was not too remote if a reasonable man with the defendant's state of knowledge would have foreseen the loss as 'likely', 'a serious possibility', 'a real danger' or 'liable to result'. In this case, it should have been clear to the defendants that the likely result of a delay in their supplying the machine to the plaintiffs was a loss of business by the plaintiffs, but they had no reason to know of the special contracts, the loss of which was therefore too remote to be recovered.

Koufos v C Czarnikow Ltd: *The Heron II* (1967) HL

The Heron II was chartered to sail to Constanza to load a cargo of 3,000 tons of sugar and to carry it to Basrah or at the charterers' option to Jeddah. The charterers did not exercise their option to divert the ship to Jeddah, but the owners caused it to deviate from the route to Basrah so that it was delayed by nine days. As the owners knew, there was a sugar market at Basrah. What the owners did not know was that the charterers intended to sell the sugar there as soon as the ship arrived. In the event, the delay coincided with a significant fall in the price of sugar in the Basrah market. The charterers claimed the difference in price from the owners.

Held the price difference was recoverable as damages. Applying the test in *Hadley and Another v Baxendale and Others* (14.1.1), it must have been within the contemplation of the owners that the charterers would be planning to sell their sugar on arrival at Basrah. *Per* Lord Reid:

> The crucial question is whether, on the information available to the defendant when the contract was made, he should, or the reasonable man in his position would, have realised that such loss was sufficiently likely to result from the breach of contract to make it proper to hold that the loss flowed naturally from the breach or that loss of that kind should have been within his contemplation.

That does not require that it must have appeared to the defendant that the chance of the loss occurring should have been better than evens. The tort test of 'reasonable foreseeability' is wider than the contract test of 'contemplation'.

H Parsons (Livestock) Ltd v Uttley Ingham & Co Ltd (1977) CA

The plaintiffs were pig farmers. Their pigs were fed pig nuts from a large hopper. The plaintiffs ordered a suitable hopper from the defendants who delivered it and set it up. However, the delivery man forgot to open the ventilator, which remained unnoticed because it was 28 feet from the ground. As a result, the nuts became mouldy and the pigs became ill. An attack of E coli was triggered off by the mouldy nuts which killed 254 pigs.

Held the defendants were liable for the loss of the pigs. Even though it was very unlikely that such serious harm would be the result of the pigs eating mouldy nuts and an outbreak of E coli could not reasonably have been contemplated by the parties at the time of the contract, nonetheless, some physical injury to the pigs should have been contemplated as a serious possibility if the defendants forgot to open the ventilator. Since the *type* of damage was within the contemplation of the parties, the defendants were liable for the whole of it, even though the *amount* of damage was greater than the parties would have contemplated. Lord Denning MR suggested a distinction between damage to property and loss of profits caused by breach of contract, but this was rejected by Orr and Scarman LJJ. Lord Denning MR and Scarman LJ doubted whether there was much real distinction between the reasonable foreseeability test in tort and the reasonable contemplation test in contract.

14.1.2 Impossibility of accurate assessment is no bar to recovery

Chaplin v Hicks (1911) CA

The defendant invited photographs from those who wanted to enter a beauty contest. Six thousand people entered the contest, and 50 of them reached the final stage. Of those 50, 12 would win prizes. The plaintiff reached the final stage but, in breach of contract, the defendant did not give her a chance to compete.

Held the plaintiff could properly be awarded damages for her loss of chance, even though they were hard to assess. *Per* Fletcher Moulton LJ:

> Where by contract a man has a right to belong to a limited class of competitors, he is possessed of something of value and it is the duty of the jury to estimate the pecuniary value of that advantage if it is taken from him.

14.1.3 The distinction between an unenforceable penalty and liquidated damages

Dunlop Pneumatic Tyre Company Ltd v New Garage and Motor Company Ltd (1914) HL

The defendant company, New Garage, bought tyres, covers and tubes from the agent (A Pellant Ltd) of the plaintiff company, Dunlop. New Garage agreed not to sell the tyres etc in certain circumstances including selling them at a discount from Dunlop's list price. Clause 5 of the agreement, made in April 1911, said:

We agree to pay [Dunlop] the sum of £5 for each and every tyre, cover or tube sold or offered in breach of this agreement, as and by way of liquidated damages and not as a penalty.

When Dunlop discovered that New Garage had sold covers and tubes at a discount, Dunlop sought damages according to clause 5.

Held clause 5 was a liquidated damages clause which would be enforced. *Per* Lord Dunedin the principles on this matter are:

(1) Though the parties to a contract who use the words 'penalty' or 'liquidated damages' may *prima facie* be supposed to mean what they say, yet the expression used is not conclusive ... (2) The essence of a penalty is a payment of money stipulated as in terrorem of the offending party; the essence of liquidated damages is a genuine covenanted pre-estimate of damage ... (3) The question whether a sum stipulated is penalty or liquidated damages is a question of construction to be decided upon the terms and inherent circumstances of each particular contract, judged of as at the time of the making of the contract, not as at the time of the breach ... (4) To assist this task of construction various tests have been suggested, which if applicable to the case under consideration may prove helpful, or even conclusive. Such are: (a) It will be held to be a penalty if the sum stipulated for is extravagant and unconscionable in amount in comparison with the greatest loss that could conceivably be proved to have followed from the breach ... (c) There is a presumption (but no more) that it is a penalty when 'a single lump sum is made payable by way of compensation, on the occurrence of one or more or all of several events, some of which may occasion serious and others but trifling damage' ... (d) It is no obstacle to the sum stipulated being a genuine pre-estimate of damage, that the consequences of the breach are such as to make precise pre-estimation almost an impossibility. On the contrary, that is just the situation when it is probable that pre-estimated damage was the true bargain between the parties.

In this case, the damage caused to Dunlop by sales being made at a discount was that they would suffer indirect loss from the undermining of the ordered market they had created. Since there would be no direct loss, this case fell within test (d) in Lord Dunedin's principle (4) above. *Per* Lord Atkinson:

They had an obvious interest to prevent this undercutting, and on the evidence it would appear impossible to me to say that that interest was incommensurate with the sum agreed to be paid.

Per Lord Parmoor the sum of £5 per item 'cannot be said to be extravagant or extortionate, having regard to the nature of the contract'.

Note ───────────────────────────

In 1914, £5 was the equivalent of about £185 in 1999.

Bridge v Campbell Discount Co Ltd (1962) HL

The defendant entered into a hire purchase agreement with the plaintiffs for a used Bedford Dormobile car. The price was £482 10s to be paid by an initial rental of £105 followed by 36 monthly payments of £10 9s 2d. Clause 6 of the agreement was in these terms 'The hirer may at any time terminate this hiring by giving notice of termination in writing to the owners, and thereupon the provisions of clause 9 hereof shall apply'. Clause 9 said 'If this agreement or the hiring be terminated for any reason before the vehicle becomes ... the property of the hirer, then ... the hirer shall forthwith (a) ... deliver up the vehicle ... and (b) pay to the owners all arrears of hire ... and by way of agreed compensation for depreciation of the vehicle such further sum as may be necessary to make the rentals paid and payable hereunder equal to two thirds of the hire purchase price ...'. The defendant paid the initial rental and the first monthly instalment. He then wrote to the plaintiffs saying 'Owing to unforeseen personal circumstances, I am very sorry but I will not be able to pay any more payments on the Bedford Dormobile. Will you please let me know when and where I will have to return the car. I am very sorry regarding this but I have no alternative'. The plaintiffs now claimed £206 3s 4d to make up the amount paid to two thirds of the full price.

Held (I) The defendant breached the agreement and did not exercise his option under clause 6. This was clear from the apologetic nature of his letter to the plaintiffs. (II) The payment of two thirds of the price under clause 9(b) was not a genuine pre-estimation of the plaintiffs' loss, but a penalty that the court would not enforce. As time went on the depreciation of the car would increase, but the payment under clause 9(b) would decrease, showing that it was not a genuine estimate of depreciation. The purpose of clause 9(b) was to prevent the defendant from ending the agreement early. (III) If the defendant had exercised his option under clause 6 instead of breaching the contract, Viscount Simonds and Lord Morton of Henryton held that the payment under clause 9(b) would have been enforceable as the price of exercising the option, while Lord Denning and Lord Devlin held that it would have remained unenforceable as a penalty even then. Lord Radcliffe refrained from expressing a view on this point.

Q Can it be right that the defendant was better off by breaching the contract than he would have been if he had exercised the option in clause 6, as the view of Viscount Simonds and Lord Morton of Henryton seems to require?

Note ———————————————————————————

The damages were assessed in the county court at £30.

Interfoto Picture Library Ltd v Stiletto Visual Programmes Ltd (1987) CA

See 5.3.2.

Philips Hong Kong Ltd v Attorney General of Hong Kong (1993) PC

The Government of Hong Kong entered into a complex series of building contracts with the plaintiff company. The contracts contained clauses which set rates of liquidated damages for delays in completion of the building works. The company sought a declaration that the liquidated damages clauses were void as penalties. The company argued that in a number of hypothetical situations the sums payable under the liquidated damages clauses would have been out of proportion to the government's actual losses.

Held the liquidated damages clauses were valid and enforceable. Lord Woolf, giving the judgment of the Board, quoted at length from *Dunlop Pneumatic Tyre Company Ltd v New Garage and Motor Company Ltd* (14.1.3) and also gave the following guidance:

> Except possibly in the case of situations where one of the parties to the contract is able to dominate the other as to the choice of the terms of the contract, it will normally be insufficient to establish that a provision is objectionably penal to identify situations where the application of the provision could result in a larger sum being recovered by the injured party than his actual loss. Even in such situations, so long as the sum payable in the event of non-compliance with the contract is not extravagant, having regard to the range of losses that it could reasonably be anticipated, it would have to cover at the time the contract was made, it can still be a genuine pre-estimate of the loss that would be suffered and so a perfectly valid liquidated damages provision. The use in argument of unlikely illustrations should therefore not assist a party to defeat a provision as to liquidated damages. As the Law Commission stated in Working Paper No 61 (p 30):
>
> > The fact that, in certain circumstances, a party to a contract might derive a benefit in excess of his loss does not ... outweigh the very definite practical advantages of the present rule upholding a genuine estimate, formed at the time the contract was made of the probable loss.
>
> A difficulty can arise where the range of possible loss is broad. Where it should be obvious that, in relation to part of the range, the liquidated damages are totally out of proportion to certain of the losses which may be incurred, the failure to make special provision for those losses may result in the 'liquidated damages' not being recoverable. (See the decision of the Court of Appeal on very special facts in *Ariston SRL v Charly Records Ltd* (1990)) However, the court has to be careful not to set too stringent a standard and bear in mind that what the parties have agreed should normally be upheld. Any other approach will lead to undesirable uncertainty especially in commercial contracts.

14.1.4 Pre-contractual expenditure may be recovered

Anglia Television Ltd v Reed (1971) CA

The plaintiff company, Anglia, were minded to make a television play called *The Man in the Wood*. After Anglia had already incurred considerable expenditure on the production, they agreed with the defendant actor on 30 August 1968 that he would play the leading role. However, the actor had double booked himself and on 3 September he told Anglia that he could not come. Anglia could not find a replacement for the actor and so, on 9 September, they abandoned the production. Since it was impossible for Anglia to estimate their lost profit, they claimed instead for the expenditure wasted because of the cancellation.

Held a plaintiff can choose to sue for wasted expenditure instead of loss of profits, though he cannot claim both. *Per* Lord Denning MR, with whom Phillimore and Megaw LJJ agreed:

> If the plaintiff claims the wasted expenditure, he is not limited to the expenditure incurred *after* the contract was concluded. He can also claim the expenditure incurred *before* the contract, provided it was such as would reasonably be in the contemplation of the parties as likely to be wasted if the contract was broken.

14.1.5 Damages for mental distress and disappointment

Jarvis v Swans Tours Ltd (1972) CA

The plaintiff's main annual holiday was a two week skiing trip at Christmas. He booked the holiday with the defendants for a price of £63.45, but it failed to match its description in the brochure. The plaintiff was expecting to be one of a party of about 30 but was entirely alone for one of the two weeks. The entertainment, food and skiing were also not as they should have been.

Held the plaintiff was awarded damages of £125 to include an element for mental distress. *Per* Lord Denning MR:

> In a proper case, damages for mental distress can be recovered in contract, just as damages for shock can be recovered in tort. One such case is a contract for a holiday, or any other contract to provide entertainment and enjoyment.

Heywood v Wellers (a firm) (1975) CA

The plaintiff was being molested by a former boyfriend and went to the defendant firm of solicitors for advice. She saw only an unqualified clerk who handled her case without supervision from any partner of the firm. The clerk made many mistakes in the litigation including advising the plaintiff that the injunctions obtained to prevent the molestation could not be enforced. The clerk also advised the plaintiff that the cost of the whole process would be £25, but it ended up costing far more.

Held the plaintiff could recover not only the fees she had paid to the defendants but also an amount to compensate her for the mental distress caused by the molestation which should have been prevented if the defendants had carried out the contract properly. This kind of distress must have been in the contemplation of the parties at the time of the contract as being the foreseeable result of failure by the solicitors to perform their side of the contract. *Per* Bridge LJ:

> There is, I think, a clear distinction to be drawn between mental distress which is an incidental consequence to the client of the misconduct of litigation by his solicitor, on the one hand, and mental distress on the other hand which is the direct and inevitable consequence of the solicitor's negligent failure to obtain the very relief which it was the sole purpose of the litigation to secure. The first does not sound in damages; the second does.

Q Is the distinction drawn by Bridge LJ as clear as he supposes it to be?

Watts and Another v Morrow (1991) CA

The plaintiffs bought Nutford Farm House in Dorset as a second home to visit at weekends when they did not need to be in London where they had stressful jobs. In buying the house, they relied on a survey report carried out for them by the defendant. The report was done negligently and failed to reveal a number of defects which it should have revealed. The results were: (i) at the time the plaintiffs bought the house it was worth some £15,000 less than they paid for it; (ii) the plaintiffs spent some £33,961 on repairs to the house; (iii) for eight months the plaintiffs spent most weekends at a house which was having very substantial works carried out in it, causing them much distress and spoiling their relaxation. The defendant appealed against an award by the trial judge of damages amounting to the cost of repairs plus £4,000 for each of the two plaintiffs to compensate them for their distress and inconvenience.

Held (I) The plaintiffs were entitled to the £15,000 loss in value of the house, not to the cost of repairs. (II) The damages for distress and inconvenience would be reduced to £750 each. This was not a contract to provide 'peace of mind or freedom from distress'. *Per* Ralph Gibson LJ:

> The right course, in my view, is for this court, accepting and applying the principle that damages for mental distress resulting from the physical consequence of such a breach of contract should be modest, to accept the judge's finding that, during the weekends over a period of eight months, there was discomfort from the physical circumstances of living in the house caused by the presence of the plaintiffs during the carrying out of repairs in respect of unreported defects.

Q   Is there a clear distinction between distress which is the direct result of physical inconvenience and that which is not?

Alexander v Rolls Royce Motor Cars Ltd (1995) CA

The defendant agreed to repair the plaintiff's motor car, but breached the agreement. The plaintiff sought damages for his disappointment, loss of enjoyment or distress.

Held per Beldam LJ:

> ... the general rule was that damages for distress, inconvenience or loss of enjoyment were not recovered for breach of an ordinary commercial contract but only when the contract was one for the provision of pleasure, freedom from harassment or relaxation.

This contract was not in the special categories and was not akin to a contract for a holiday. Damages for loss of enjoyment and so on would not be awarded.

14.1.6 Restitutionary damages

Attorney General v Blake (1997) CA

Blake was a member of the Secret Intelligence Service from 1944 until 1961. He was a traitor who passed secret information to the Soviet Union. In 1966, he escaped from prison in England and fled to Moscow. In 1990, Blake's autobiography was published. The Attorney General brought an action claiming that the autobiography was published in breach of fiduciary duties owed by Blake to the Crown.

Held (I) The information contained in the autobiography was no longer confidential at the time of its publication. Blake did not owe to the Crown a fiduciary duty not to publish such information once it was already public. Therefore, the Attorney General's claim for breach of fiduciary duty did not succeed. (II) As a matter of public law, the court would grant an injunction at the suit of the Attorney General to prevent Blake from profiting from his crime, in this case, a breach of the Official Secrets Act 1989. An injunction was made restraining Blake from receiving any payment in connection with his autobiography. (III) When he joined the Service in 1944, Blake had signed an undertaking not to divulge any official information in book form even after his employment had ceased. The publication of the autobiography was thus a breach of contract. However, the Crown could not establish any loss resulting from this breach and accordingly did not make a claim for substantial compensatory damages. (IV) The Court of Appeal stated that it might have been willing to award restitutionary damages for this breach of contract, although the Attorney General had not made such a claim so the point had not been argued. *Per* Lord Woolf MR delivering the judgment of the court:

... we think that there are at least two situations in which justice requires the award of restitutionary damages where compensatory damages would be inadequate. The first may be described as the case of skimped performance. This is where the defendant fails to provide the full extent of the services which he has contracted to provide and for which he has charged the plaintiff. ... the second case is where the defendant has obtained his profit by doing the very thing which he contracted not to do.

14.2 Breach of condition

14.2.1 Anticipatory breach
See 12.2.

14.2.2 The election to affirm or rescind the contract is not made until the innocent party is aware of his right to elect

Peyman v Lanjani and Others (1984) CA

The first defendant, Mr Lanjani, wanted to buy the lease of a creperie in London from its then tenant. Because Mr Lanjani was scruffy and spoke no English it was arranged that a Mr Moustashari would impersonate Mr Lanjani to the landlord's agent in order that the landlord would consent to the assignment of the lease to Mr Lanjani. The impersonation was successful and Mr Lanjani bought the leasehold interest. The second defendant, Mr Rafique, a solicitor who acted for Mr Lanjani in the purchase, did not know of the impersonation.

The plaintiff, Mr Peyman, like Mr Lanjani, was an Iranian who spoke no English. Messrs Peyman and Lanjani agreed that Mr Peyman would buy the creperie from Mr Lanjani for £55,000 to be paid by Mr Peyman's house in Willesden and £23,000 'equalisation money'. It was arranged that Mr Rafique would act for both of them in the transaction. Contracts were exchanged on 2 February for completion on 2 April. Mr Rafique obtained false references for Mr Peyman to enable him to be accepted as the new tenant. On 9 February 1979, Mr Moustashari again impersonated Mr Lanjani to the landlord's agent to get permission for the assignment of the lease to Mr Peyman. Mr Peyman found out about the impersonation and asked his daughter (who spoke some English) to tell Mr Rafique. Mr Rafique brushed aside Mr Peyman's concerns. By 9 February, Mr Peyman wanted to withdraw from the deal due to various arguments with Mr Lanjani. Mr Lanjani was keen to return to Iran for political reasons and was also short of money. At a meeting on 22 February, Mr Rafique persuaded the reluctant Mr Peyman to continue with the deal and to sign five letters. These provided that Mr Peyman would pay £10,000 to Mr

Lanjani immediately and that Mr Peyman would run the creperie as Mr Lanjani's manager during the period up until completion. That evening, Mr Peyman went into occupation of the creperie and within a few days Mr Lanjani went to Iran.

On 23 March, Mr Peyman went to see another solicitor. The new solicitor advised Mr Peyman that Mr Lanjani's title to the lease was defective because of the impersonation used to obtain it, which rendered the assignment to Mr Lanjani liable to be avoided, and that Mr Peyman could therefore withdraw from the transaction. On 20 April, Mr Peyman left the creperie and returned the keys. The main question on the appeal was whether it was too late for Mr Peyman to withdraw from the transaction when he did.

Held it was not too late for Mr Peyman to withdraw. (I) Because of the defect in the title of the lease, Mr Peyman had a right at common law to elect whether to rescind the contract or to affirm it. An actual election to affirm which was communicated to Mr Lanjani would be enough to end Mr Peyman's right to rescind. (II) That election falls to be made when the innocent party (Mr Peyman) not only knows the facts which give him a right to rescind (which Mr Peyman knew on 9 February) but when he also knows that he has the legal right to do so. Therefore, Mr Peyman had not in fact made his election by anything which he did before he consulted the new solicitors. (III) Nonetheless, Mr Peyman would be held to have affirmed the contract, or to be estopped from denying he had affirmed it, if his actions had unequivocally conveyed an intention to affirm to Mr Lanjani who had suffered detriment in reliance upon that intention. (i) When Mr Peyman moved into the restaurant, he was doing so as Mr Lanjani's manager according to their agreement of 22 February. Therefore, it could not appear to Mr Lanjani that by moving in Mr Peyman was affirming the contract. So, Mr Peyman had not shown an intention to affirm. (ii) Mr Lanjani had been determined to go to Iran in any case and the receipt of £10,000 was not a detriment to Mr Lanjani. There was therefore no reason to hold that Mr Peyman was estopped from denying that he had affirmed the contract by taking over the restaurant and paying over £10,000.

14.3 Mitigation of loss

Payzu Ltd v Saunders (1919) CA

The parties agreed that the defendant would sell the plaintiffs 400 pieces of silk to be delivered as required and paid for on the 20th of the month following each month of delivery. The prices were fixed at the time of the contract. Some silk was delivered in November, for which the plaintiffs wrote a cheque on 21 December. However, the defendant did not receive the cheque and telephoned to inquire in early January. The plaintiffs sent a replacement cheque on 16 January and on the same day made a further order by telephone. However, the defendant had formed the mistaken opinion that the plaintiffs had financial problems and she wrote to them on 16 January refusing any further deliveries unless the plaintiffs paid cash. The plaintiffs would not accept this and sued the defendant for damages, claiming for a loss caused by a considerable increase in the market price of silk since the contract was made.

Held the plaintiffs could not recover the part of their claim which related to the rise in the price of silk. That loss was caused by their failure to accept the defendant's offer to supply for cash and not by the defendant's breach of contract. Their lordships cited *British Westinghouse Electric and Manufacturing Co v Underground Electric Railways Co of London* (1912) HL, in which Lord Haldane LC had laid down the principle of mitigation of damage when he said:

The fundamental basis is thus compensation for pecuniary loss naturally flowing from the breach; but this first principle is qualified by a second, which imposes upon a plaintiff the duty of taking all reasonable steps to mitigate the loss consequent on the breach, and debars him from claiming any part of the damage which is due to his neglect to take such steps.

Per Scrutton LJ:

In certain cases of personal service, it may be unreasonable to expect the plaintiff to consider an offer from the other party who has grossly injured him; but in commercial contracts it is generally reasonable to accept an offer from the party in default. However, it is always a question of fact.

Sotiros Shipping Inc and Aeco Maritime SA v Sameiet Solholt: *The Solholt* (1983) CA

In May 1979, the defendant sellers agreed to sell their vessel, *The Solholt*, to the plaintiff buyers for $5m, to be delivered by 31 August 1979. If delivery was late, the buyers had a right to cancel. In the event, the sellers did deliver a day or two late and the buyers exercised their cancellation right. The buyers refused to buy the vessel for $5m, although they did offer to do so for $4.75m, an offer which the sellers refused. The market value of the vessel at 31 August 1979 was $5.5m and the buyers now claimed damages of $0.5m, the 'profit' which they would have made on the value of the vessel if she had been delivered on time.

Held the buyers could not claim the $0.5m. *Per* Sir John Donaldson MR, giving the judgment of the court:

A plaintiff is under no duty to mitigate his loss, despite the habitual use by lawyers of the phrase 'duty to mitigate'. He is completely free to act as he judges to be in his best interests. On the other hand, a defendant is not liable for all loss suffered by the plaintiff in consequence of his so acting. A defendant is only liable for such part of the plaintiff's loss as is properly to be regarded as caused by the defendant's breach of duty.

The loss of $0.5m was initially caused by the sellers' breach but could have been avoided by reasonable action on the part of the buyers. The question whether the action required of the buyers to avoid a loss was reasonable was a question of fact in each case.

14.4   Enforcing contracts for personal service

Warner Brothers Pictures Inc v Nelson (1936) KB

The defendant was the actress, Bette Davis. She had a contract with the plaintiffs, who were film producers in America, by which she promised to perform as an actress solely for the plaintiffs and not to work for anyone else, as an actress or in any other occupation, without the plaintiffs' permission. The defendant broke her contract with the plaintiffs and entered into an acting agreement in England. The plaintiffs now sought an injunction to prevent the defendant from acting in any film or stage production for anyone other than the plaintiffs. The defendant did not give evidence herself or call any witnesses.

Held the injunction would be granted. An injunction should not be granted if it would amount to enforcing positive covenants of personal services, that is, the promises to work for the plaintiffs. It could be granted if it would leave the defendant with an alternative. In this case, the injunction would prevent the defendant from acting for persons other than the plaintiffs, but it would not prevent her from earning a living by any other means. The injunction would be limited to three years if the contract did not end sooner.

Page One Records Ltd and another v Britton and Others (trading as 'The Troggs') and Another (1967) Ch

The defendant pop group, The Troggs, made recording and management agreements with the plaintiffs under which they promised not to appoint anyone other than the plaintiffs as their manager nor to allow anyone else to publish music written by them for a period of five years. The agreements were similar to others in the music business. After about 14 months, The Troggs gave notice that they had terminated the agreements. The plaintiffs sought injunctions to prevent The Troggs from recording for, or under the management of, others.

Held the injunctions could not be granted. The obligations of the plaintiffs under the agreements were obligations of trust and confidence. They could not have been enforced by The Troggs if the plaintiffs had been in breach of them. *Per* Stamp J, the parties were tied together 'in a relationship of mutual confidence, mutual endeavour and reciprocal obligations'. He went on to state the general principle:

> ... where a contract of personal service contains negative covenants, the enforcement of which will amount either to a degree of specific performance of the positive covenants of the contract or to the giving of a decree under which the defendant must either remain idle or perform those positive covenants, the court will not enforce those negative covenants.

Warren v Mendy and Another (1989) CA

The plaintiff was the manager of the boxer, Nigel Benn, under an agreement which was supposed to last for three years. After five months, Benn became disillusioned with the plaintiff's management and made an arrangement with the defendant that the defendant would give Benn advice and so on. The plaintiff now sought injunctions against the defendant to prevent the defendant from inducing Benn to break the latter's contract with the plaintiff and to prevent the defendant from acting as Benn's manager or agent.

Held the injunctions would not be granted because to do so would have the effect of enforcing positive obligations in a contract requiring mutual trust and confidence. (I) The approach of Stamp J in *Page One Records Ltd and Another v Britton and Others (trading as 'the Troggs') and Another* (below) was in line with the earlier authorities. Referring to *Warner Brothers Pictures Inc v Nelson* (14.4), Nourse LJ, giving the judgment of the court, said:

> On a first consideration, that judge's view that Miss Bette Davis might employ herself both usefully and remuneratively in other spheres of activity for a period of up to three years appears to have been extraordinarily unrealistic ... But then, it is to be observed that Miss Davis did not give evidence, a feature of the case which made a great impression on the judge ... In the absence of evidence from her, the judge no doubt thought that it was not for the court to assume that she could not or would not employ herself both usefully and remuneratively in other spheres of activity. From what can be gathered from the report, it cannot be said with confidence that the injunction was wrongly granted.

(II) Nourse LJ said:

> This consideration of the authorities has led us to believe that the following general principles are applicable to the grant or refusal of an injunction to enforce performance of the servant's negative obligations in a contract for

personal services inseparable from the exercise of some special skill or talent ... In such a case, the court ought not to enforce the performance of the negative obligations if their enforcement will effectively compel the servant to perform his positive obligations under the contract. Compulsion is a question to be decided on the facts of each case, with a realistic regard for the probable reaction of an injunction on the psychological and material, and sometimes the physical, need of the servant to maintain the skill or talent. The longer the term for which an injunction is sought, the more readily will compulsion be inferred. Compulsion may be inferred where the injunction is sought not against the servant but against a third party, if either the third party is the only other available master or if it is likely that the master will seek relief against anyone who attempts to replace him. An injunction will less readily be granted where there are obligations of mutual trust and confidence, more especially where the servant's trust in the master may have been betrayed or his confidence in him has genuinely gone.

14.5   Enforcing positive covenants to trade

Co-Operative Insurance Society Ltd v Argyll Stores (Holdings) Ltd (1997) HL

In 1979, the defendants took a 35 year lease on a supermarket premises for use by the defendants as a 'Safeway' store. The supermarket was the largest shop in a shopping centre of about 25 stores. The lease included a positive covenant by the defendants to keep the premises open for retail trade during usual hours of business. In 1995, the defendants announced that they were to close this particular Safeway store. The plaintiff landlords sought an order for specific performance of the defendants' covenant to keep Safeway open.

Held specific performance would not be ordered. In all but exceptional cases, an injunction would not be granted requiring a defendant to carry on a loss making business.

15 Glossary

Adams v Lindsell	Wether fleeces by post
Aerial Advertising v Bachelors Peas	Remembrance Day flyover
Ailsa Craig Fishing v Malvern Fishing	Securicor loses fishing boat
Alan v El Nasr	Kenyan Shillings
Alderslade v Hendon Laundry	Handkerchiefs
Alexander v Rolls Royce	Enjoyment of Rolls Royce
Allcard v Skinner	Mother Superior
Alliance Bank v Broom	Consideration for charge
Allied Marine Transport v Vale do Rio Doce Navegacao	Silence
Amalgamated Investment & Property v Texas Commerce International Bank	Portsoken
Amalgamated Investment & Property v John Walker	Planning permission
Anderson v Daniel	Fertiliser
Andrews v Singer	New Singer cars
Anglia Television v Reed	Oliver Reed
Armhouse Lee v Chappell	Telephone sex
Archbolds v Spanglett	Whiskey
Associated Japanese Bank v Credit du Nord	Lease of non-existent machines
Atlas Express v Kafco	Woolworth's basketware
Attorney General v Blake	Spy memoirs
Attwood v Lamont	Kidderminster outfitter
Attwood v Small	Mines inspected
Avery v Bowden	Frustration at Odessa
Awilco v Fulvia SpA di Navigazione: *The Chikuma*	Payment not cash

Bainbridge v Firmstone	Weighing boilers
Balfour v Balfour	Husband in Ceylon
Bannerman v White	Sulphur in the beer
Barclays Bank v O'Brien	Undue influence of husband
Barclays Bank v Schwartz	Illiteracy no defence
Behzadi v Shaftsbury Hotels	Land Registry delays
Bell v Lever Brothers	Cocoa trading
Beswick v Beswick	Plaintiff administratrix
Bisset v Wilkinson	2,000 sheep
Blackpool and Fylde Aero Club v Blackpool BC	Tender on time
Bolton v Mahadeva	Central heating fumes
Boulton v Jones	Payment by set off mistake
Bournemouth and Boscombe Athletic Football Club v Manchester United Football Club	Reasonable opportunity to score goals
Bowerman v ABTA	ABTA bound by bond
Bridge v Campbell Discount	HP termination
Brinkibon Limited v Stahag Stahl	Telex to Vienna
British and Commonwealth v Quadrex	Time of the essence
British Crane Hire v Ipswich	Course of dealing
British Motor Trade v Salvadori	Interference with contractual rights
Brodie v Brodie	Conjugal rights
Brogden v Metropolitan Railway	Contract in the drawer
Bunge v Tradax Export	Later soya-bean meal
Butler Machine Tool v Ex-Cell-O	Whole correspondence
Byrne v Leon Van Tienhoven	Non-communication of withdrawal of offer
Callisher v Bishoffsheim	Claim against Honduras
Carlill v Carbolic Smoke Ball	Influenza cure
Casey's Patents, Stewart v Casey	Volatile liquids
Central London Property v High Trees	Rent remission
Centrovincial Estates v Merchant Investors Assurance	Rent agreed

Chapelton v Barry UDC	Deck chair
Chaplin v Hicks	Beauty contest
Chaplin v Leslie Frewin	*The Grass on My Father's Lawn*
Chappel v Nestlé	Chocolate wrappers for records
CIBC Mortgages v Pitt	Joint loan
Cie Commerciale Sucres et Denrees v Czarnikow: *The Naxos*	Late sugar
Circle Freight v Medeast Gulf Exports	IFF conditions
Clarke v The Earl of Dunraven and Mount: *The Satanita*	Yacht sunk
Clea Shipping v Bulk Oil: *The Alaskan Trader*	No legitimate interest
Clements v London and NW Railway	Minor porter
Collins v Godefroy	Attorney subpoenaed
Combe v Combe	Shield not sword
Commission for the New Towns v Cooper	Induced mistake
Condor v Barron Knights	Tired drummer
Cook v Wright	Whitechapel rates
Cooper v Phibbs	Salmon Fishery
Co-operative Insurance v Argyll Stores	Safeways loss making
Couchman v Hill	Heifer not unserved
Courtney and Fairbairn v Tolaini Brothers (Hotels)	Agreement to agree price
Couturier v Hastie	Damaged cargo of corn
Crabb v Arun DC	Right to access
Cricklewood Property v Leightons Investment	99 year lease not frustrated by war
CTN Cash and Carry v Gallaher	Ain't got no cigarettes
Cundy v Lindsay	250 dozen handkerchiefs
Currie v Misa	Consideration
Curtis v Chemical Cleaning	Stained wedding dress
Cutter v Powell	Dead second mate
D and C Builders v Rees	Builders held to ransom
Darlington v Wiltshier	No privity

Daulia v Four Millbank Nominees	Unilateral promise to exchange contracts
Davis Contractors v Fareham UDC	78 council houses
De La Bere v Pearson	Financial problem page
Derry v Peek	Tram prospectus
Dick Bentley v Harold Smith (Motors)	Mileage warranty
Dickinson v Abel	Farm commission
Dickinson v Dodds	Offer withdrawn
Dimmock v Hallett	Former Lady Day tenants
Director General of Fair Trading v First National Bank	Interesting
Dunbar Bank v Nadeem	Manifest advantage
Dunlop Pneumatic Tyre v New Garage	£5 per tyre
Dunlop Pneumatic Tyre v Selfridge	Due consideration
Eastham v Newcastle UFC	Retained players list
Edgington v Fitzmaurice	State of mind = state of digestion
Edmund Murray v BSP International	Drilling rig spec
Edwards v Skyways	*Ex gratia* payment to pilot
English Hop Growers v Dering	Hop market
Entores v Miles Far East	Sale by telex
Errington v Errington and Woods	The house will be yours
Esso Petroleum v Customs and Excise Commissioners	World Cup coins
Esso Petroleum v Mardon	200,000 gallons misrepresentation
Eyre v Measday	Sterilisation
Felthouse v Brindley	No acceptance by silence
Fibrosa Spolka Akcyjna v Fairbairn Lawson Combe Barbour	Return of money on frustration
Fisher v Bell	Flick knife
Flavell, in Re	Widow's annuity
Foakes v Beer	Lesser sum not consideration for greater
Foley v Classique Coaches	Petrol supply agreement enforceable
Frost v Knight	Broken engagement

Gallie v Lee: Saunders v Anglia BS	Nephew's fraud
Galloway v Galloway	First wife alive
Gibson v Manchester City Council	Council house sale
Glasbrook Brothers v Glamorgan CC	Policing miners strike
Goldsoll v Goldman	Imitation jewellery
Grainger v Gough	Champagne tax
Grist v Bailey	Protected tenant
Guthing v Lynn	Lucky horse
Hadley v Baxendale	Remoteness
Harling v Eddy	Tuberculous heifer
Harlingdon and Leinster v Christopher Hull Fine Art	Fake painting
Harris v Nickerson	Cancelled auction
Harris v Sheffield UFC	Policing football matches
Hart v O'Connor	Insane but legal
Hartley v Hymans	Waiver of delivery date
Hartley v Ponsonby	Dangerous voyage to Bombay
Hartog v Colin and Shields	Hare skins
Harvela Investments v Royal Trust	No referential bid
Harvey v Facey	Bumper Hall Pen
Heilbut, Symons v Buckleton	Rubber company
Henthorn v Fraser	Reasonable use of post
Herne Bay Steam Boat v Hutton	Coronation steam boat contract not frustrated
Heslop v Burns	*Ménage à trois*
Heywood v Wellers	Anti-molestation litigation
Hillas v Arcos	Fair specification
Hirachand Punamchand v Temple	Indian money lender
Hochster v De La Tour	Courier
Hoenig v Isaacs	Decorator's substantial performance
Hollier v Rambler Motors	Garage fire
Hong Kong Fir Shipping v Kawasaki Kisen Kaisha	Innominate term
Hopkins v Tanqueray	No warranty of California's legs
Horton v Horton (No 2)	Separation agreement

Household Fire and Carriage Accident
Insurance v Grant

Postal allotment

Howard Marine and Dredging
v Ogden

Deadweight misrepresentation

Hughes v Metropolitan Railway

Equitable waiver

Hutton v Warren

Seeds and labour

Hyde v Wrench

Counter offer

Ingram v Little

Three spinsters and a rogue

Interfoto Picture Library v Stiletto
Visual Programmes

Photographs retained

Jackson v Horizon Holidays

Damages for all the family

Jackson v The Union
Marine Insurance

Frustration at Caernarvon Bay

Jarvis v Swans Tours

The lone skier

Jones v Padavatton

A girl's best friend?

Jorden v Money

Promises, promises

Joscelyne v Nissen

Payment of household bills

KH Enterprise

Sub-bailment in carriage by sea

King's Norton Metal
v Erridge, Merrett

Sheffield Hallam

Kores Manufacturing v Kolok
Manufacturing

Tottenham typewriter products

Koufos v Czarnikow: *The Heron II*

Sugar market

Krell v Henry

Coronation frustration

L'Estrange v F Graucob

Signature

Lampleigh v Brathwait

Murderer's pardon

Laurizen v Wijsmuller: *The Super
Servant Two*

Rig transporter

Leaf v International Galleries

Constable

Les Affréteurs Réunis v Leopold
Walford

Trust of broker's commission

Leslie v Shiell

Minor fraud

Lewis v Averay

Robin Hood rogue

Linden Gardens Trust
  v Lenesta Sludge Disposals   Assignment
Liverpool CC v Irwin   City flats
Lloyds Bank v Waterhouse   Farm guarantee
London and Northern Bank, in Re,
  ex p Jones   Town postman
London Holeproof Hosiery v Padmore Factory fire
Lord Strathcona Steamship
  v Dominion Coal   Steamship charters
Luxor v Cooper   Estate agent's commission

Magee v Pennine Insurance   Car insurance payment
Malins v Freeman   Bid for wrong lot
Manchester Diocesan Council for
  Education v Commercial
  and General Investments   Old school tender
Marcan Shipping v Polish Steamship:
  The Manifest Lipkowy   Broker's risk
Maredelanto Compania Naviera
  v Bergbau-Handel:
  The Mihalis Angelos   Expected ready
Miles v New Zealand Alford Estate Dividend guarantee
Mitchell (George) v Finney Lock Seeds White cabbage failure
Mohamed v Alaga   Share of legal aid fees
The Moorcock   Grounded
Morgan v Manser   Charlie Chester
Morris v Martin   Stolen stole
Motor Oil Hellas v Shipping Corp of
  India: *The Kanchenjunga*   Waiver and estoppel

Nash v Inman   Waistcoats
National Carriers v Panalpina   Road closed
National Westminster Bank
  v Morgan   No manifest disadvantage
Naughton v O'Callaghan   Fondu
New Zealand Shipping v AM
  Satterthwaite: *The Eurymedon* Drill damaged
Nicolene v Simmonds   No usual form

Nordenfelt v The Maxim Nordenfelt Guns and Ammunition	Reasonable restraint
Norfolk County Council v Dencor Properties	Lease re-negotiation
North Ocean Shipping v Hyundai Construction: *The Atlantic Baron*	Shipbuilder's price increase
Norweb v Dixon	Electricty non-contract
Ocean Tramp Tankers v *The Eugenia*	Shut in Suez
Olley v Marlborough Court	Hotel room key
Oscar Chess v Williams	Old Morris
Page One Records v Britton	The Troggs
Pao On v Lau Yiu Long	Share loss guarantee
Paradine v Jane	Rent payable
Parker v Clark	House share
Parker v The South Eastern Railway	Left luggage ticket
Parsons (Livestock) v Uttley Ingham	Mouldy pig nuts
Partridge v Crittenden	Partridge sells Bramblefinches
Payne v Cave	Bid withdrawn
Payzu v Saunders	Silk for cash
Peyman v Lanjani	Creperie lease
Pharmaceutical Society of Great Britain v Boots Cash Chemists	Where is a supermarket sale?
Philips Hong Kong v AG of Hong Kong	Building penalty
Phillips v Brooks	'I'll just take the ring'
Photo Production v Securicor Transport	Guard starts fire
Pinnel's Case	A lesser sum
Planche v Colburn	Armour book
R and B Customs Brokers v United Dominions Trust	Company car
R v Clarke	Suspect's reward
Raffles v Wichelhaus	Peerless mistake
Ramsgate Victoria Hotel v Montefiore	Share application lapsed
Redgrave v Hurd	Partnership with house

Smith v Land and House Property	Tenant not desirable
Société Italo-Belge pour le Commerce et l'Industrie v Palm and Vegetable Oils (Malaysia): *The Post Chaser*	Palm oil string
Solle v Butcher	Controlled rent mistake
Sotiros Shipping and Aeco Maritime v Sameiet Solholt: *The Solholt*	Cancellation by buyers
Spencer v Harding	Tender
Startup v MacDonald	Saturday night delivery
Steinberg v Scala	Tulip
Stevenson, Jacques v McLean	Mere query
Stewart Gill v Horatio Myer	No set-off unreasonable
Stilk v Myrick	Seamen stay aboard
Sudbrook Trading v Eggleton	Valuers' appointment
Suisse Atlantique Société d'Armement Maritime v Rotterdamsche Kolen Centrale	No fundamental breach
Sumpter v Hedges	No part payment for late mate
Tailor v Bhail	Headmaster's fraud
Tamplin v James	Unreasonable mistake
Tamplin Steamship v Anglo-Mexican Petroleum Products	WW 1 Time Charter
Taylor v Caldwell	Music hall burnt down
Thomas v Thomas	Widow's promise to pay
Thompson v London Midland and Scottish Railway	Reasonable to injure illiterate
Thornton v Shoe Lane Parking	Red hand
Tinn v Hoffman	Cross-offers
Tinsley v Milligan	Social Security fraud
Tool Metal Manufacturing v Tungsten Electric	Reasonable notice to resume rights
Trentham v Archital Luxfer	Building contract found in performance
Tsakiroglou v Noblee Thorl	Back door route
Tulk v Moxhay	Leicester Square
Tweddle v Atkinson	Privity

Index